Contents

★ ★ ★

G·A·M·E
CHANGER$

HOW **DARK MONEY** AND **SUPER PACS** ARE TRANSFORMING U.S. CAMPAIGNS

HENRIK M. SCHATZINGER
RIPON COLLEGE

STEVEN E. MARTIN
RIPON COLLEGE

ROWMAN & LITTLEFIELD
Lanham • Boulder • New York • London

Executive Editor: Traci Crowell
Assistant Editor: Deni Remsberg
Higher Education Channel Manager: Jonathan Raeder
Interior Designer: Rosanne Schloss

Credits and acknowledgments for material borrowed from other sources, and reproduced with permission, appear on the appropriate pages within the text.

Published by Rowman & Littlefield
An imprint of The Rowman & Littlefield Publishing Group, Inc.
4501 Forbes Boulevard, Suite 200, Lanham, Maryland 20706
www.rowman.com

6 Tinworth Street, London SE11 5AL, United Kingdom

British Library Cataloguing in Publication Information Available

Library of Congress Cataloging-in-Publication Data
Names: Schatzinger, Henrik M., 1978– author. | Martin, Steven E., 1974– author.
Title: Game changers : how dark money and super PACs are transforming
   U.S. campaigns / Henrik M. Schatzinger, Steven E. Martin.
Description: Lanham : Rowman & Littlefield, [2020] | Includes bibliographical
   references and index.
Identifiers: LCCN 2019047113 (print) | LCCN 2019047114 (ebook) |
   ISBN 9781538136171 (cloth) | ISBN 9781538136188 (paperback) |
   ISBN 9781538136195 (epub)
Subjects: LCSH: Campaign funds—United States. | Political action committees—
   United States. | Political campaigns—United States. | United States—Politics and
   government—2009-2017. | United States—Politics and government—2017-
Classification: LCC JK1991 .S33 2020 (print) | LCC JK1991 (ebook) |
   DDC 324.7/80973—dc23
LC record available at https://lccn.loc.gov/2019047113
LC ebook record available at https://lccn.loc.gov/2019047114

Brief Contents

★ ★ ★

Figures and Tables

★ ★ ★

FIGURES

TABLES

Preface

★ ★ ★

WHEN THE U.S. SUPREME COURT decided *Citizens United v. FEC* in 2010, it created a public outcry. The highest court in the land had ruled that corporations, unions, and certain nonprofits could use funds from their treasury to independently support candidates or attack political opponents, without any financial limitations. Thereafter, other court decisions held that this right would also apply to individuals who—without being subject to contribution limits—want to support so-called Super political action committees (PACs) that will then use the money for political messages explicitly recommending the election or defeat of political candidates. Immediately following these decisions, citizens and journalists alike expressed concerns that billionaires and corporations would be able to buy future election outcomes and strongly influence, if not determine, subsequent public policy, thereby undermining American democracy.

Two years later, a comprehensive national survey about Americans' opinions on *Citizens United* conducted on behalf of the Brennan Center for Justice at the New York University School of Law revealed that the public's negative reactions to the Court's decision had not changed. Sixty-nine percent of respondents agreed that "new rules that let corporations, unions and people give unlimited money to Super PACs will lead to corruption." Seventy-four percent of self-identified Republicans and 73 percent of self-identified Democrats agreed with this statement. Only one in five Americans agreed that, under the current rules, average Americans would have the same access to candidates as big donors. Two-thirds said that they would trust government less because of the influence of big donors and outside groups.

Moreover, one in four Americans said they would be less likely to vote because of the disproportionate influence megadonors have over elected officials, a major setback for those who want to see greater political participation.

Since then, poll after poll has shown similar results. If anything, Americans' desire to do something about the power of megadonors, Super PACs and nondisclosing nonprofit groups, so-called dark money organizations, has grown even further. For example, in 2018, a study by the University of Maryland and nonpartisan research group Voice of the People found that three-fourths of survey respondents—including 66 percent of Republicans and 85 percent of Democrats—backed a constitutional amendment that would overturn *Citizens United*. Eighty-eight percent of respondents said they wanted to see political action that would reduce the influence large campaign donors wield over politicians.

Yet, despite citizens' great concern over the impact of *Citizens United* on the political system, academic research has not fully acknowledged the scope and magnitude of the Supreme Court's monumental decision. The existing academic research is primarily written for other academics and is focused on rather specific issues. Therefore, our goal in this book is to provide a broadly accessible overview of the changes *Citizens United* brought to political campaigns and political representation, based on both rigorous academic research and many real-word examples and journalistic accounts of ongoing trends. Our discussions surrounding campaign finance are grounded in academic concepts and often involve complex legal issues, but the book is set up to be engaging for both students and civically engaged citizens who want to learn more about outside groups and their impact on campaigns and public policy.

We argue that Super PACs and dark money groups qualify as *game changers* of political campaigns not only because of what these groups can do independently from candidates and their increasing ability to match or even exceed candidates' financial resources but also because their actions influence the political incentives and strategies of candidates and political parties. We also point to evidence that those changes go beyond campaigns—they affect how legislators represent their constituents, how donors put pressure on lawmakers to adopt certain legislation after outside groups supported them, how the regulatory environment can benefit donors as a result of actions taken by federal agencies to repeal or dismantle existing laws, and how extreme positions by politicians can be incentivized and progress stalled when megadonors and outside groups reward political ideologues.

Our hope is that this text inspires readers to draw their own conclusions about the effects the Court's decision has had and continues to have on the inner workings of American democracy. Some may even feel moved to take action that will empower ordinary citizens who want to have more of a voice in the democratic process. Given the high stakes associated with elections and the political changes they can bring due to the highly polarized political environment in which we live, we believe this book will add value not only to courses focusing on campaigns, elections, interest groups, and political communication but also to other courses, such as introductory American government.

Chapter 1 summarizes five key consequences for how campaigns operate in the post–*Citizens United* era, affecting the following parts of campaigns: campaign finance, campaign communication, political parties, anonymous influence via dark money, and representation. Chapter 2 explores the legal framework of campaign finance with an emphasis on the competing constitutional tensions that affect campaign finance laws. Chapter 3 offers an overview of who the donors and recipients of outside money are, what purposes Super PAC and dark money expenditures serve, and what the donors are getting in return for their investment.

Chapter 4 examines a host of new trends for presidential campaigns stemming from the *Citizens United* decision, ranging from officially delaying announcements to run for president to more consequential dilemmas wherein outside groups can help candidates during the primaries but also wound the party's eventual nominee. Chapter 5 identifies new trends for congressional campaigns, with a focus on what types of races outside money is spent, the organizational characteristics of Super PACs and their effects, and the rise of party leadership Super PACs.

Chapter 6 delves more deeply into the primary category of most outside spending, advertising, to consider how the *Citizens United* ruling has altered the political advertising world. Chapter 7 offers an array of potential reform ideas broken down into six categories: increasing hard money limits, public election funding, Super PAC insurance, legislative recusal, enhanced disclosure, and Federal Election Commission reform.

We would like to acknowledge the support of Ripon College's administration, staff, and students. We are sincerely thankful for the help from our student assistants Abby Korb, Palasha Tuladhar, Ali Hamza, and Hannah Boyum. We would like to thank Rowman & Littlefield's wonderful staff, in particular Executive Editor Traci Crowell, who offered outstanding guidance and encouragement throughout the process, and Assistant Editor Deni Remsberg, who also offered excellent support. Karen Trost was also instrumental in guiding the book early in its development.

We would also like to thank Michael J. Malbin and Heath Brown, both distinguished scholars, for their helpful feedback, as well as an anonymous reviewer.

I, Henrik Schatzinger, would like to thank my wife, Jolene, for her support, understanding, and encouragement throughout the process of writing this book. Also, I would like to thank my colleague and friend, Aaron Dusso (Indiana University–Purdue University Indianapolis), for his assistance. I also want to thank my graduate school mentors, Paul-Henri Gurian and the late Allan J. Cigler, who continue to inspire me in my scholarship, teaching, and life.

I, Steve Martin, would like to thank my colleagues Marty Farrell (Ripon College) and Jeremy D. Johnson (University of the Pacific) for helpful feedback along the way. My longtime mentor, dearest friend, and departmental colleague, Jody Roy (Ripon College), deserves special gratitude for her decades of encouragement and always-sage advice. Lastly, I thank my wife, Michelle, for her support and understanding of my long hours spent in my office completing this book.

About the Authors

★　★　★

HENRIK M. SCHATZINGER is Associate Professor and Chair of Politics and Government at Ripon College, where he teaches and conducts research on interest groups and money in politics. He is also Codirector of the Center for Politics and the People at Ripon College, which hosts numerous events to promote constructive political discourse.

STEVEN E. MARTIN is Professor of Communication and Chair of the department at Ripon College. He is the author of various articles and book chapters analyzing the rhetorical strategies of politicians and social movement leaders. He teaches courses on political campaign communication, the First Amendment, media and society, and rhetorical criticism.

1

Super PACs and Dark Money as Game Changers

★ ★ ★

GROUPS ARE CHANGING THE LANDSCAPE of political campaigns in America. Traditionally, people think of campaigns as two candidates (and their staff) running against each other for elected office, trying to persuade citizens to vote for them. Although political groups have always been present in campaigns, they have aggressively stepped up their efforts in terms of funding and their scope of activities in recent years. In this book, we argue that the changes and consequences of the increased campaign activity by so-called **outside groups**—all organizations that engage in **outside spending**, political expenditures made by groups or individuals independently of, and not coordinated with, candidates' committees—run so deep that these groups qualify as "game changers." This is because of not only what they can do independently from candidates and their march toward resource parity but also the significant effect of their actions on the political incentives, strategies, and actions of both candidates and political parties.

Based on what scholars and journalists have found thus far, we also examine how the changes to the campaign environment affect U.S. citizens in fundamental ways. Some questions we explore include the following: Do outside groups help inform voters, or do they cause misinformation and political cynicism? More broadly, do outside groups enhance or hurt American democracy? Who is gaining power in the United States as a result of how campaigns are conducted today? What is happening to representation; to whom are politicians listening? Similarly, whose voices do voters hear in campaigns? Finally, do

1

the changes in how campaigns are conducted affect subsequent policy making? As you will see, the answers often are not easy, but we believe that they certainly are worth exploring.

Much like significant rule changes alter the strategies of sports teams, changes to political campaign rules have significantly altered how political groups are able to "play the game" of winning an election. The most important rule changes were put into place in 2010, when the U.S. Supreme Court decided two important cases: *Citizens United v. Federal Election Commission* and *SpeechNow v. Federal Election Commission*, which allowed certain groups to accept unlimited contributions from corporations, unions, and other organizations (see chapter 2 for a detailed discussion of these cases).

Since 2010, outside groups including **political action committees** (PACs; committees formed by corporations and labor unions to contribute funds to candidates [or officeholders] or political parties) have spent more than $4 billion on federal elections alone. This excludes traditional party committees affiliated with the Democratic or Republican Parties.[1] Even more interesting is how and to what effect the money is spent. For example, in the past few years, outside groups have started to expand their range of activities far beyond TV ads; what implications does this have for candidates, political parties, and citizens?

The rule changes made by the U.S. Supreme Court do not explain the changing nature of campaigns completely. In some ways, those decisions just accelerated ongoing trends. Several significant developments in American politics are fueling changes in political campaigns. One is strong competition for control of the government where smaller changes in political support can mean the gain or loss of considerable party power. The book *Insecure Majorities* captures the phenomenon of party competition well.[2] Another development is the intense political polarization not only among political elites but also within the American public. As both parties often offer substantially different solutions to public policy issues, the stakes associated with changes in government control are high.[3] Put differently, when both parties "have a shot" at governing at the federal level and the dislike among elites and voters for the "other side" is high—a phenomenon known as **negative partisanship**[4]—it is no wonder that campaigns are changing and getting more intense.

In academia, there has been little acknowledgment of the game-changing aspect that political groups have brought to political campaigns. Aside from analyzing electoral rules and processes, and the choices of citizens, most existing textbooks and courses focus primarily on candidates and their campaigns—their decisions and strategies and their interactions with voters, the media, and their own political party. The focal point is often on what opportunities and changes the media environment and technology represent for candidates, not political groups.

The "game" metaphor is not intended to make light of the significance of campaigns and the political process but to demonstrate the important effects of the rules and laws guiding them. Take, for example, the introduction of the three-point shot in basketball. That change altered the game in significant ways, including which types of athletes could succeed and who became less desirable. Politics 101 tells us that rules matter in explaining political structures and outcomes, and we believe that we are in the process of entering a new campaign era as a result of rule changes and political trends. In this new era, which we call the **triumvirate campaign era**, three actors—candidates, parties, and outside groups—all play crucial roles in the conduct of campaigns, sometimes in concert and sometimes in conflict. With each new election cycle, outside groups are becoming increasingly more significant in this triumvirate relationship, a trend that, absent any major new laws in the near future, is unlikely to change.

This chapter outlines the major changes that outside groups have brought to campaigns for candidates and parties and highlights their changes in operations. We start by defining some terms. Then we examine the interactions between the Trump campaign and pro-Trump groups in the spring and summer of 2019. Finally, we discuss five key consequences for how campaigns operate in the post–*Citizens United* era, ranging from implications for campaign finance, campaign communication, and political parties to anonymous influence via dark money and effects on representation.

UNDERSTANDING DIFFERENCES AMONG GROUPS

Before delving more deeply into the specifics of outside groups, this section provides some definitions of the various actors involved, their limitations, and how they are permitted to operate in the larger campaign context. Corporations and labor unions must form separate PACs if they want to contribute funds to candidates (or officeholders) or political parties. There are legal limits on donation size. PACs can give $5,000 to a candidate committee per election (primary elections, general elections, and special elections are considered separate elections). PACs can also give up to $5,000 to any other PAC and

$15,000 to any national party committee annually. On the flip side, PACs may receive up to $5,000 from an individual, PAC, or party committee per calendar year.

Super PACs, officially known as *independent-expenditure only committees*, are PACs that cannot make direct (cash) contributions to candidates or political parties and receive contributions from sources including individuals, corporations, unions, and other groups. Super PACs can raise and spend unlimited amounts of money—the direct result of *Citizens United* and *SpeechNow* cases, which represents *the* major rule change since 2010—and they are not associated with a specific political party or organization. Super PACs are required to disclose their donors. Note, however, that Super PACs can accept unlimited contributions from political nonprofits and "shell" corporations that may not have disclosed their donors, which means that Super PACs can be opaque rather than transparent about funding sources. **Single-candidate Super PACs** focus almost exclusively on one candidate and their political opponent. **Multi-candidate Super PACs** receive contributions from at least fifty-one individuals and contribute to at least five federal candidates.[5]

527 organizations are tax-exempt groups that must register with the Internal Revenue Service (IRS) and are required to disclose their donors. There are no contribution limits and no restrictions on who may contribute. Technically, almost all political committees are 527 groups, including Super PACs. 527s played an import role in the 2004 presidential election. That year, the Swift Boat Veterans for Truth frequently aired TV ads questioning John Kerry's military service during the Vietnam War, arguing that he was unfit to be president. That publicity campaign is widely recognized as a significant reason for his election loss.[6]

501(c) organizations are tax-exempt nonprofit organizations named after section 501(c) of the IRS tax code. Because 501(c)s do *not* have to disclose their donors and can exert influence anonymously, they are frequently referred to as **dark money groups.** The fastest-growing and most politically active 501(c) organizations are **501(c)(4) organizations,** which are legally required to operate for the promotion of social welfare. According to the IRS, 501(c)(4) groups "must operate primarily to further the common good and general welfare of the people of the community (such as by bringing about civic betterment and social improvements)."[7] 501(c)(4) organizations may engage in some political activity, but it cannot become their primary purpose. Examples include the National Rifle Association and the Sierra Club. Labor and agricultural groups have 501(c)(5) status, while **501(c)(6) organizations** include business leagues, chambers of commerce, real estate boards, and boards of trade. Just like 501(c)(4) groups, both 501(c)(5) and 501(c)(6) organizations can engage in political campaign activities and lobbying.

Hybrid PACs (also known as *Carey committees*) are political action committees that are not affiliated with a candidate and can operate both as a traditional PAC and as a Super PAC. In other words, hybrid PACs are not only allowed to contribute directly to a candidate's committee but also can make independent expenditures. Hybrid PACs must register with the Federal Election Commission (FEC) and maintain two separate bank accounts, one for the candidate's committee and one for independent expenditures. All receipts and expenditures must be reported to the FEC regularly.

Individuals, groups, corporations, labor organizations, and various types of political committees may support or oppose candidates by making independent expenditures. According to the FEC, **independent expenditures** are expenditures "for a communication, such as a website, newspaper, TV or direct mail advertisement that expressly advocates the election or defeat of a clearly identified candidate; and [that] is not made in consultation or cooperation with, or at the request or suggestion of a candidate, candidate's committee, party committee or their agents."[8] Independent expenditures are not classified as contributions and are therefore not subject to limits.[9] Independent expenditures by Super PACs, 527s, and 501(c)s alone should be referred to as **nonparty outside spending.**

Most political action committees are considered **connected PACs,** meaning that a business or other organization (labor union, trade group, health organization) "uses its treasury funds to establish, administer or solicit contributions to a separate segregated fund."[10] For example, the Boeing corporation cannot make direct contributions to candidates, so it has formed The Boeing Company Political Action Committee, which is directly connected to Boeing. **Nonconnected PACs** are not connected to a corporation, labor organization, party, or candidate committee.

Members of Congress often establish leadership PACs to support candidates for various federal and nonfederal offices. A **leadership PAC** is a political committee that is maintained or controlled by a candidate or officeholder but is not an authorized committee or committee affiliate. Separate from political party committees (described next), leadership PACs can accept money from other PACs and up to

$5,000 from individuals even after they max out campaign donations but cannot use the funds to support the campaign. A leadership PAC makes independent expenditures; if those expenditures are not coordinated with the other candidate, this type of spending can be unlimited. Consequently, members of Congress sometimes use the funds for expensive meals, hotels, private jets, and tickets to professional sports games.[11]

Political party committees are the official bodies of party organizations that raise and spend funds for political campaigning. In addition to national party committees, such as the Democratic National Committee (DNC) and Republican National Committee (RNC), there are state, district, and local party committees. Contribution limits for political parties are higher than those for individual candidates and/or PACs. For the 2020 election cycle, individuals can give up to $35,500 per year to the national party committee; $10,000 combined to state, district, and local party committees; and up to $2,800 for each federal candidate.[12]

TRUMP VERSUS PRO-TRUMP GROUPS

In May 2019, President Trump's reelection campaign began feuding with several pro-Trump groups trying to get the president reelected in 2020. One of these groups, the Keeping America Great Super PAC, is led by Trump's former 2016 campaign staffer Corey Stewart. To help the president win the election, Stewart's focus is on raising money from big-dollar donors,[13] which is certainly not unusual. So how did the dispute escalate, and what caused it?

At first glance, Stewart's efforts sound like something the Trump campaign would welcome. An unpaid supporter is spending his own time and energy, including hiring staff and performing fundraising tasks, trying to get President Trump reelected. However, the official Trump campaign does not want Stewart's help. The Trump campaign went so far as to file a **notice of disavowal** with the FEC;[14] these are sometimes filed as a response to media requests about whether a candidate agrees or disagrees with the message of any given independent political effort. Candidates can file notices of disavowal so they cannot be accused of coordination with independent spenders, which is illegal under federal campaign finance law.

The official answer to the question of why the Trump campaign denounced a like-minded organization is easy to figure out because the Trump campaign sent a letter to donors at the same time as the notice of disavowal, criticizing "any organization that deceptively uses the President's name, likeness, trademarks, or branding and confuses voters."[15] In other words, Trump's campaign is concerned that voters and donors will confuse some organizations as official Trump campaign organizations when, in fact, they are legally required to be independent. The Trump campaign has only approved a single Super PAC, the America First Action PAC.[16] One of America First Action's goals is to spend up to $300 million by Election Day 2020 in the six swing states that proved crucial in 2016: Florida, Georgia, Michigan, North Carolina, Ohio, and Pennsylvania.[17]

When asked about Trump's combative tone and actions toward Keeping America Great, Stewart points to a different motivation. "They're very controlling. They want to control everything," Stewart told ABC News.[18] In other words, according to Stewart, the Trump campaign itself wants to set specific goals and to decide on messaging and strategy. A few weeks after the quarrel started, Keeping America Great decided to shift its focus to helping down-ballot Republicans. It also removed Trump's name from its social media accounts. Other Super PACs, such as Great America, which was indirectly criticized in the Trump campaign's letter to donors, have decided to stay the course and to run digital and TV ads promoting President Trump. "The art of the Super PAC is to act independently," said Eric Beach, a political consultant affiliated with Great America.[19]

In the meantime, the Trump campaign experienced conflict with yet another pro-Trump political group, the Presidential Coalition, a 527 organization run by Trump's former deputy campaign manager and early political adviser David Bossie. The Trump campaign was angered for several reasons. Trump himself felt that the group's efforts might be tricking people, including elderly, into believing that they would be directly supporting Trump's reelection campaign.[20] This concern was substantiated by a report produced by the Campaign Legal Center (CLC) in collaboration with *Axios*, which found that "according to Facebook's political ad archive, most of Presidential Coalition's Facebook ads are overwhelmingly targeted to, and viewed by, Facebook users 65 and older."[21]

There was also the issue of competing for dollars from donors. A senior Trump administration official explained that "every dollar groups like Bossie's and similar groups raise is a dollar the campaign does not."[22] Finally, according to the CLC report, only 3 percent of the $15.4 million the Presidential Coalition spent in 2017 and 2018 went to candidates, political committees, and a small number of state-level candidate ads. Most went to fundraising and donor list cultivation, direct mail, book purchases, telemarketing, payments to other groups, and salaries. According to the Trump senior official, the president felt that in this case someone closely connected to the president was "profiting off of him."[23]

These concerns are not unfounded. According to the CLC report, the Presidential Coalition spent at least $445,972 on book purchases in 2017 and 2018. One of the books was written by David Bossie himself. A direct-mail solicitation claimed: "Join the Presidential Coalition today with your membership gift of $45 or more and you'll receive a special brand-new hardcover copy of my new book, TRUMP'S ENEMIES."[24] When asked, Bossie explained that only a small amount was spent on *Trump's Enemies* and that the majority of the money went toward copies of *Trump's America*, authored by former House Speaker Newt Gingrich. However, the conclusion in the executive summary of the eighteen-page CLC report is sobering and blunt: "There is a cottage industry of groups targeting vulnerable communities with self-serving borderline scams. What sets the Presidential Coalition apart is that it is explicitly—and successfully—capitalizing on Bossie's connection with the President of the United States."[25]

These testy reactions from the president and his campaign toward supportive groups provide some insight into how campaigns are changing. More important than the issue of capitalizing on connections is that the reactions conflict between candidates and groups, including competition for campaign funds and the tension between independence and control. All candidates like to be, as much as possible, in charge of their own "destiny": the election outcome. Today, doing so is constrained not only by strong party identification and surrounding circumstances, such as a booming or faltering economy, but also by some loss of control over strategy and messaging as a result of outside group activities. The next sections discuss the specific changes that are taking place.

HOW ARE CAMPAIGNS CHANGING?

Outside groups cause multiple changes in campaigns. The changing nature of group activity and intensity in political campaigns affect:

- Overall campaign funding and the identity of donors
- Signaling between candidates and groups, coordination among groups, and candidate-voter communication

- The role of political parties
- The ability to influence the political system anonymously (dark money)
- Representation and power in our constitutional republic

Of course, these changes affect some candidates more than others. The biggest changes have occurred in presidential campaigns, followed by competitive congressional campaigns, particularly for Senate seats. Primary elections have become more and more consequential,[26] and this is where the impact of outside groups has been steadily increasing. This is because of a decrease in competitiveness for congressional general elections, stemming from factors including gerrymandering, the incumbency advantage, and geographic and ideological voter sorting.[27] Also, political parties are generally staying out of primary contests in their own party, opening the door for outside group influence. The key changes to campaigns can be explained by examining the changes to campaign funding that resulted from the 2010 U.S. Supreme Court decisions.

Campaign Finance

How does America First Action's goal of raising and spending up to $300 million by Election Day 2020 compare to the overall spending goal for the Trump campaign? "I definitely think we're looking at a billion-dollar operation, minimum," Trump's campaign manager Brad Parscale said during a TV interview with Eric Bolling in April 2019.[28] Put differently, the Trump campaign hopes that a single Super PAC will raise and spend about 30 percent of its reelection campaign operations, assuming that it considers the Super PAC's expenditures as part of "its" campaign. This does not include all the other outside groups (other Super PACs, regular PACs, hybrid PACs, 527 organizations, and 501[c]s). At the beginning of the presidential campaign in 2012, influential Republican donor Barry Wynn from South Carolina, who served as finance chair and co-chair of several statewide campaigns, said on Fox Business: "I think the decision by the Supreme Court two years ago was certainly a game changer. It really changes the entire way we finance the presidential campaigns." Wynn's analysis has proved to be accurate.

Should outside groups continue to increase their spending, the combined independent spending by all groups could make up 50 percent or more of all presidential campaign expenses for the 2020 presidential campaign cycle and beyond. The trend toward more equal spending between candidate committees and outside groups is part of the basis for the triumvirate campaign era. In 2016, spending by Hillary Clinton's outside groups made up 36.5 percent ($206,122,160) of her total spending ($563,756,928), while expenses by Trump's outside groups composed almost 31 percent ($103,265,530) of his own campaign spending ($333,127,164).[29] The impact of the Court's decision becomes even clearer if we compare those numbers to the pre–*Citizens United* era; in 2008, independent expenditures made up only 12 percent of President Obama's and 6.7 percent of John McCain's overall campaign spending.

Overall outside spending for both congressional and presidential races has been increasing consistently over the past two decades. In 2000, outside spending was a mere 1 percent of all spending in congressional and presidential campaigns; in 2008, it was 6.4 percent; in 2012, 16.5 percent; in 2016, 22.7 percent; and in 2018, 19.1 percent (see figure 1.1). There is no doubt that the 2010 Supreme Court decisions increased overall campaign spending in federal campaigns. In the November 2010 election, federal campaign spending jumped more than $1 billion, and it has not decreased since. Increases in outside spending for U.S. Senate races are similarly dramatic. In 2012, 22 percent of the expenditures came from outside groups, but by 2016 that share had gone up to 47 percent. That does not tell the whole story, however. Competitive U.S. Senate races are unsurprisingly the most expensive. The share of outside spending for the ten

Figure 1.1 Outside Spending as a Percentage of Total Federal Election Spending (excluding party committees)

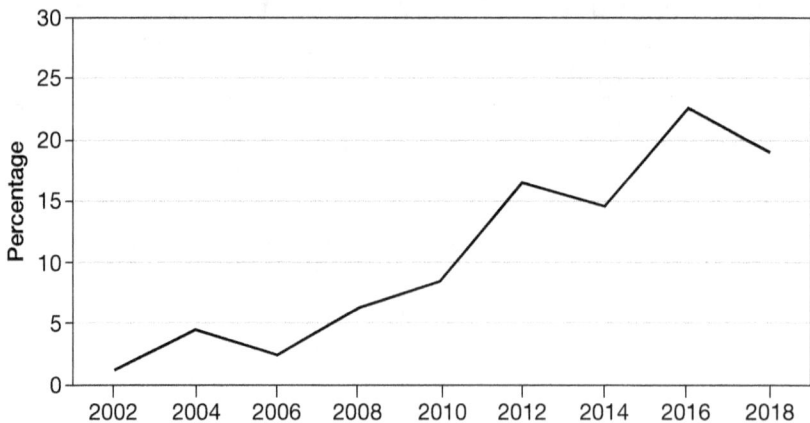

most expensive U.S. races went from 6 percent in 2000 to 62 percent in 2016.[30] Talk about a game changer! In 2018, total spending on congressional races jumped by about $1.6 billion compared to 2016, from $4.1 billion to $5.7 billion.[31]

Beyond the overall rise in independent expenditures in federal elections compared to candidates since 2010, we see another change, but not the one many predicted. When *Citizens United* was decided, some in the public expressed great concern about a substantial increase in independent expenditures by corporations, essentially allowing them to buy elections and policy outcomes. This is not what has happened. Although corporate involvement in electoral politics has not changed dramatically, concentrated involvement by ultra-wealthy individuals has become a feature of national elections. Between 2010 and October 2018, a mere eleven individuals spent $1 billion on U.S. elections via Super PACs, according to an analysis by the *Washington Post*.[32] In other words, roughly one-quarter of all independent spending in federal campaigns came from fewer than a dozen individuals.

Although party committees receive a large percentage of their contributions from small donations ($200 or less), most of the larger Super PACs get almost no money from such sources. One study found that for the Senate Majority PAC, the largest Super PAC in 2014, the average *contribution* of $170,525 was more than three times the national average household *income* that year. That same year, the average contribution for Ending Spending, the second-highest-spending Super PAC, was more than half a million dollars, more than nine times the median American household income.[33] Individuals giving more than $100,000 usually make up over 90 percent of all Super PAC donors (figure 1.2). So the biggest Super PACs are simply not that interested in soliciting contributions from small donors—they can raise their money from a relatively small number of wealthy individuals. Chapter 3 explores megadonors in more detail, including their affiliations and their causes.

What are the political affiliations of these megadonors? Between 2010 and 2018, five of the eleven megadonors supported Republican candidates, and the other six donated to Democrats. The top three were Sheldon and Miriam Adelson ($287.5 million), Tom Steyer ($213.8 million), and Michael Bloomberg ($123.4 million). Most Americans will likely be unfamiliar with any of the other seven top donors except George Soros, a Hungarian American investor and philanthropist, known for his support of Democratic Super PACs. The next four names on the list—Fred Eychaner, Donald Sussman,

Figure 1.2 Megadonors Dominate Giving to Presidential Super PACs, 2012 and 2016

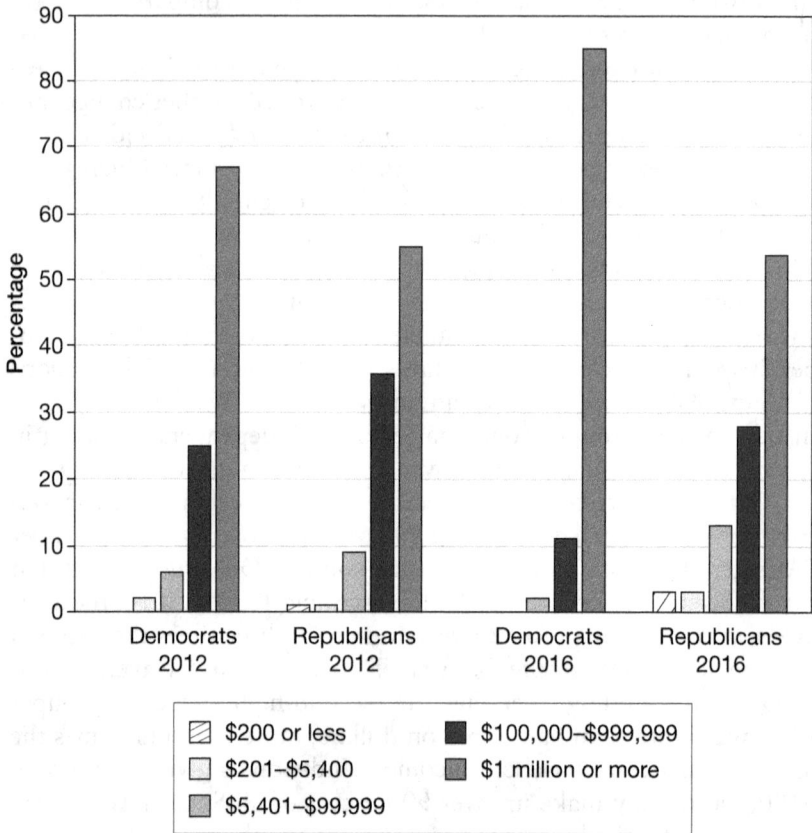

Richard Uihlein, and James and Marilyn Simmons—gave a combined total of more than $250 million to political candidates.[34] In other words, staying out of the public spotlight is possible even for donors who have given $60 or $70 million to political campaigns in less than a decade.

Although the gloomy predictions about a corporate take-over of elections and legislation did not transpire, note that many megadonors are corporate owners. An early analysis of the financial market's reaction to the *Citizens United* decision was skeptical of a change in political involvement by for-profit corporations. The empirical study showed that the share prices of large firms with considerable political engagement were not significantly affected by *Citizens*

United, consequently, investors did not believe that the Court's decision would have an effect on corporate America policy outcomes.[35] Another study pointed out that most publicly traded corporations are pragmatic and access-oriented and would have more to lose than gain from attacking candidates or incumbents. Switching contributions from Super PACs to dark money groups would reduce the risk of disclosure but not necessarily increase motivation.[36]

So instead of corporations flooding newly formed outside organizations with cash to "buy" elections and policy outcomes, the biggest change caused by *Citizens United* and *SpeechNow* was significant increases in independent expenditures by ultra-wealthy individuals. This has led some critics, among them Matthew Dowd, a former George W. Bush strategist, to decry the practice of "kissing the ring of Sheldon Adelson"[37] and to call the 2016 GOP primaries the "Sheldon Adelson Primary."[38] We have never had elections in which a single couple, the Adelsons, injected close to $300 million into political campaigns and in which other individual donors contributed tens of millions of dollars. For more on how their money is spent, see chapter 4.[39]

Candidate-Group Signaling, Group-Group Coordination, and Candidate-Voter Communication

Particularly in presidential and congressional races, *Citizens United* and *SpeechNow* have significantly impacted candidate-group signaling, group-group coordination, and candidate-voter communication. Because there is little empirical research that examines these changes, we rely on journalistic accounts and comments from candidates and campaign officials for support.

Candidate-Group Signaling

Current rules undoubtedly impact *candidate-group signaling*, how candidates directly and indirectly communicate with various groups and how they push the boundaries of legality. According to FEC guidelines, candidates cannot legally cooperate or coordinate their activities with Super PACs. Thinking back to the conflicts between the Trump campaign and its Super PACs, we can understand that candidates may have to spend a significant amount of time dealing with various political groups during a campaign, both friendly and antagonistic. The Trump campaign would certainly prefer to spend its energy on its own campaign strategy without the need to deal with what they consider rogue groups. Campaigns must decide which groups to approve or disavow, how to give groups unambiguous signals without violating federal laws, and how to respond to media requests for responses to actions or statements by sympathetic or hostile outside groups.

The triumvirate campaign era is characterized by complex legal rules guiding communication among candidates, political parties, and outside groups. The idea that candidates cannot have any interaction with Super PACs is a myth, perpetuated by false reporting in the media. What Super PACs cannot do is coordinate their *expenditures* with candidates. Federal candidates are not allowed explicitly to ask a donor to give more than $5,000 to a Super PAC but can meet privately with a single wealthy donor and one Super PAC operative to discuss fundraising.[40] For fundraising events, FEC guidelines only require a written invitation, a disclaimer or a formal program indicating that a candidate is appearing as a "special guest" at an event and will not solicit large contributions.[41]

Candidates and sympathetic groups can do a lot without running afoul of FEC guidelines, and they are. In addition to appearing at Super PAC fundraisers, they can have the same lawyers as sympathetic Super PACs, which can be and are run by close friends or even family members. What is confusing for the public is that Super PACs are considered outside groups but are often run by political insiders (political friends or former campaign aides). For example, the America First Action Super PAC is run by close Trump allies, including Linda McMahon, Trump's former Small Business Administration chief.[42] In 2012, when presidential nominee Mitt Romney was asked about his candidate-specific Super PAC Restore Our Future, which was running several million dollars' worth of ads, he nonchalantly replied, "of course it's former staff of mine" who run it.[43]

Candidates and outside groups have found many other ways to help one another without violating coordination laws. Legally, no coordination can take place before a candidate announces his or her candidacy for public office,[44] but Super PACs sometimes organize town-hall meetings, announce candidate endorsements, host conference calls with the media, and prepare ads before a campaign is officially announced. One Super PAC, Correct the Record (CTR), went beyond these activities in 2016. CTR said that it would coordinate with the Clinton campaigns via *unpaid* communication through Facebook and Twitter accounts, without actual independent expenditures (posting free online content does not qualify as an independent expenditure). The FEC eventually allowed CTR and the Clinton campaign to coordinate.[45]

Candidates even provide outside groups with *b-roll footage* on YouTube and other websites, showing candidates on the campaign trail giving speeches at events, showing enthusiastic crowds, shaking hands with voters, and visiting corporations. Outside groups can use the footage for ads, creating a consistent message along with a well-produced visual appeal. For example, in 2019, State Senator Dan Bishop from North Carolina, running for the Ninth Congressional District against Democrat Dan McCready, uploaded a ten-minute silent video showing him in conversation with people on sidewalks and at a sandwich shop.[46] More recently, some candidates have shied away from making campaign footage available for everyone because political opponents may use such footage to their advantage. In 2014, Senate Majority Leader Mitch McConnell was ridiculed on social media and in late-night comedy shows after posting b-roll footage of himself on YouTube.[47] The hashtag #McConnelling became a Twitter meme.[48]

Candidates have also found other ways to support Super PACs. For example, in 2015 former Hewlett Packard CEO Carly Fiorina retweeted a Super PAC ad.[49] Senator Pat Toomey, a Republican from Pennsylvania, went further by giving $50,000 to Prosperity for Pennsylvania, one of his own Super PACs, to aid his reelection bid.[50] Many other leadership PACs have contributed to party-specific Super PACs. In 2014, leadership PACs contributed more than $1 million to the Senate Majority PAC (for Democrats), Mississippi Conservatives (for Republicans), and other Super PACs.[51]

No presidential candidate has pushed the boundaries of candidate-group interaction further than Carly Fiorina in 2015. Fiorina's Super PAC, CARLY for America, was better funded than her own campaign, so the campaign found ways to be helpful to the Super PAC. Fiorina made her campaign schedule public, allowing CARLY for America to send staff in advance to help organize and run many events.[52]

> At a typical Fiorina campaign stop, a CARLY for America staffer was stationed at a table outside of the event space to sign up attendees for the Super PAC's email list. Another staffer handed out CARLY for America stickers to attendees as they arrived. When Fiorina and her staff entered the event, they were usually met by a room covered in red "CARLY" signs and tables covered in pro-Fiorina literature, all produced by CARLY for America.[53]

When asked about the staffing of candidate events, Leslie Shedd, CARLY for America's spokeswoman, told *The Atlantic*, "What you're seeing now is the modern campaign. This is how campaigns are evolving and moving, and I think that we just kind of latched onto that." Shedd went on to say, "For a candidate like Carly Fiorina, who is a political outsider, who does not have the political base that a lot of these other kind[s] of career politicians in the race have had, what we decided as an outside group that the best thing that we could help to provide is ground-game support."[54]

Group-Group Coordination
The past ten years have seen new forms of *group-group coordination*, coordination among groups that allow groups to synchronize and amplify their messages. According to *The New York Times*, outside groups used to be the "guerrilla warriors of presidential elections, tossing explosive advertisements into the middle of a campaign like hand grenades, with little regard for the strategy of the candidate they support."[55] Those days are gone. Today, group activities are carefully targeted, timed, tested, and worked out in tandem with those of other groups. Increased efforts to coordinate tasks and messages is true for both groups with the same status (such as Super PACs) and those with different legal statuses. An example illustrates what groups can do to be more effective.

The New York Times reported that in 2012, Republican nominee Mitt Romney focused on a narrative that portrayed President Obama as a failed president. Outside groups followed suit, amplifying this message. Crossroads Grassroots Policy Strategies (Crossroads GPS), a major Super PAC founded by Republican strategist Karl Rove, aired ads arguing that his job record showed that Obama had "failed" as a president. Restore Our Future, another pro-Romney Super PAC, made the case for failure because of the allegedly ineffective stimulus program by the Obama administration after the Great Recession.[56] In other words, outside groups found a way to stay "on message." In addition, outside groups coordinated advertising purchases to allow for an uninterrupted presence on the air "while plugging many of the holes in Mr. Romney's ad schedule."[57]

How were they able to accomplish this? According to the *Times*, Super PACs "operate largely from the same playbook, sharing polling data and focus group research to develop many of the same lines of attack."[58] Although outside groups do not necessarily work with the same producers or studios, they have become more careful about consistency with the candidates' campaign themes. According to Steven J. Law, president of Crossroads GPS and its sister Super PAC, American

Crossroads, "outside groups have to view themselves in a supportive and amplifying role, not as some rogue enterprise trying to score their own points. In the past, groups would go off on their own and come up with what they thought was a great idea. And they could potentially do significant harm. . . . There's a great deal of sharing."[59]

Coordination among groups goes back to 2010 and has "evolved and gotten tighter," says Steven J. Law, president of Crossroads GPS.[60] Organizations must file documents with the Federal Communications Commission website indicating when and on what stations their ads will run. In 2014, when Republican Representative Cory Gardner of Colorado announced he would run for the U.S. Senate, supportive groups such as American for Prosperity, Freedom Partners, the U.S. Chamber for Commerce, American Crossroads, and Crossroads GPS all coordinated their ad buys. That way, the Gardner campaign also knew when to air its ads.[61] "You're seeing all of the other groups start to layer in," Carl Forti, political director for American Crossroads and Crossroads GPS, told *Bloomberg Businessweek*. "That's a coordinated effort."[62]

The second type of group-group coordination shows how groups with different legal statuses can work together. Super PACs legally can have supportive nonprofit, that is, dark money, sister companies. American Bridge 21st Century is a liberal Super PAC well known for its opposition research targeting Republican candidates in efforts to weaken them. Former American Bridge president Brad Woodhouse, who has also served as communications director for the DNC, says the following about American Bridge's opposition research: "the parties don't do it; the campaigns don't invest in it. There's no one that [*sic*] has the ability to pull this type of stuff—video, news archives, our own video archives—as quickly and as cleanly to use in a rapid-response fashion as we do."[63]

To do its work, American Bridge 21st Century counts on donations from its sister nonprofit organization, American Bridge 21st Century Foundation. Between 2017 and 2018 alone, the Foundation gave $7.23 million.[64] The donors to the Foundation, who support the Super PAC, are anonymous. Dark money groups can financially support Super PACs and may even share the same physical address.[65]

Candidate-Voter Communication

Third, candidates often are in a situation where they feel the need to respond to voters regarding claims and actions of outside group activity. The rise of outside groups has impacted *candidate-voter communication* in many ways. One way is by delaying announcements of presidential candidacies. The unofficial reason is simple: without declaring themselves presidential candidates, aspirants can set up their campaigns, request large donations from individuals and organizations for future campaigns, and coordinate their activities with whomever they wish. The stated reasons differ. For example, in 2015, when asked about this, Chris Christie told CBS News that he had to check with his heart if he wanted to run. John Dickerson of CBS's *Face the Nation* then asked, "Last time you checked your heart, what did it say?" "Oh, I don't check it on a regular basis, John. It's linear," Christie responded.[66] Marco Rubio had a different response: "I have to decide through careful prayer where's the best place for me to serve this country," he said in February 2015.[67]

A more common way to affect candidate-voter communication is candidates' perceived need to respond to negative information shared by outside groups. Negative information comes in different forms: via ads, flyers, brochures, or some attack on social media. The responses also have different forms: statements on social media or YouTube, clarifications in interviews, or creating ads to counter accusations. This is even true for municipal races. For example, when Brandon Martin, candidate for Superior Court judge in Kern County, California, felt attacked by a Super PAC in 2018, he used those attacks to create his own statements and videos and shared them on YouTube with potential voters. In one video, Martin stated how stunned he was that a Super PAC decided to smear him: "OK, let me just pause right there . . . Yes, in my small local judge's race, there is a Super PAC from Los Angeles smearing me. And yes, the claim in the newspaper isn't even remotely true."[68] So Super PACs affect not only presidential candidates but also those running for all kinds of offices across the country.

EFFECTS ON POLITICAL PARTIES

Because outside groups can raise and spend unlimited money since *Citizens United*, we need to ask several questions: How are political parties responding to this new environment? Is there now competition between campaign activities of parties and outside groups? Have parties lost influence in campaigns or developed new ways to stay relevant? Have both parties been equally affected by the rise of outside groups? We only provide initial answers to these questions here but discuss them in more depth in chapters 4 and 5.

One of the difficulties in answering these questions stems from the definition of political parties. Some scholars view them as "coalition managers" who aggregate various interests,[69] including those of various political groups. Others speak of them as being part of broader, extended party networks (EPNs) or "partisan webs" that include outside groups.[70] In other words, EPN theorists argue that outside groups are part of political party networks,[71] some going so far as to claim that party organizations "guide or even 'orchestrate'" outside group activities.[72] Debate among scholars is ongoing as to how much, if any, separation there really is between political parties and outside groups, many of which are run by political insiders with deep ties to political party leadership.

One key challenge for political parties in campaigns today is that the *Citizens United* and *SpeechNow* decisions allowed for unlimited independent expenditures by various organizations that cannot be coordinated with political parties. FEC rules specifically state that the independent expenditures for communication cannot be made "in consultation or cooperation with, or at the request or suggestion of a candidate, candidate's committee, a party committee or their agents."[73] However, after an initial slump in fundraising, by modifying their strategies and after creating Super PACs affiliated with their own party leadership, parties have found ways to stay highly relevant in campaigns. In fact, political parties have not only managed to stay relevant but are now thriving, primarily because of their own Super PACs. The Democratic Party's leadership created the House Majority PAC and Senate Majority PAC. Republicans leaders formed the Congressional Leadership Fund (CLF) and Senate Leadership Fund (SLF).

How successful have the parties' Super PACs been in raising money for independent expenditures? The CLF raised only $11.3 million in the 2011–12 election cycle, almost half of which came from Miriam and Sheldon Adelson.[74] However, for the presidential election year 2016, the CLF was able to increase its commitments significantly by spending a little over $50 million. During the most recent midterm elections in 2018, CLF spent $158.7 million on Republican candidates. In other words, the extended party network is now fighting fire with fire when it comes to competing with other Super PACs. The SLF took longer to get off the ground. Formed in 2015, it has close ties to American Crossroads, a Super PAC affiliated with Republican consultant and policy advisor Karl Rove. The SLF spent $114.2 million in the 2016 elections and was able to increase its spending for the 2018 midterm elections to $127.3 million, despite 2018 not being a presidential election year.[75]

Unofficial Democratic Party Super PACs have also shown tremendous growth in recent years. The House Majority PAC spent $35.7 million in 2012, $55.7 million in 2016, and $95.6 million in 2018. The Senate Majority PAC went from spending $42.1 million in 2012, to $91.2 million in 2016, to $165.6 million in the 2018 election cycle.[76] What does all of this tell us? Although it took political parties a couple of years to reverse their fortune, they have come back with their own Super PACs run by—or at least affiliated with—each party's leadership. In fact, the four largest Super PACs in 2017–18 were the four party leadership Super PACs, not the Super PACs outside the inner-party network that receive the most media attention (figure 1.3).

That today's biggest Super PACs are quasi-party committees not only because of their connections to the leadership of both major parties but also because these Super PACs are vote maximizers, just like parties, is noteworthy; they focus on winning majorities, not pushing the most extreme candidates or single issues. At the same time, political parties have retained their national committees (the RNC and the DNC), and their official national campaign committees, one

Figure 1.3   Party Leadership Super PAC Independent Expenditures since January 2011

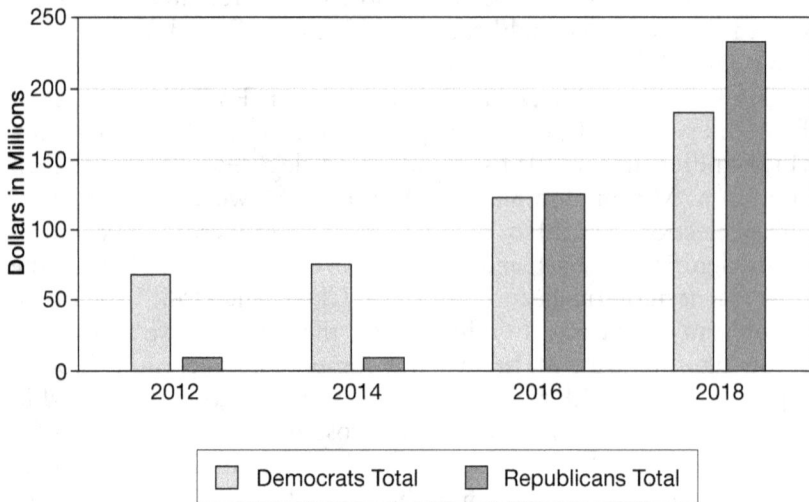

for the House of Representatives and one for the U.S. Senate. Combined, those committees have raised $682 million for Republicans and $621 million for Democrats.[77] So with the creation of unofficial party Super PACs, fundraising for both parties has reached new heights, allowing the Republican Party to raise $998 million in the 2018 election cycle and the Democratic Party to raise $882 million.

DARK MONEY GROUPS AND ANONYMITY

The *Citizens United* and *SpeechNow* decisions have triggered a rise in political spending by nonprofit 501(c) organizations or dark money groups that are not required to disclose their donors to the FEC. During the 2018 election cycle, the largest dark money groups were Majority Forward (a liberal organization that spent $45.8 million), the U.S. Chamber of Commerce (a conservative organization that spent $10.9 million), and Americans for Prosperity (a conservative organization that spent $8.9 million).[78] Between 2010 and 2018, spending by such organizations totaled more than $1 billion. When we add another billion dollars spent by hybrid PACs that keep some donors hidden or are funded by dark money sources, then "spending by groups that do not fully disclose donors has exceeded $2 billion since the 2006 election cycle."[79]

How does this compare to the pre–*Citizens United* era? In the 2006 election cycle, nondisclosing groups spent only $5.17 million. The trend toward nondisclosure began during the 2008 election cycle, with a little over $102 million in dark money spending.[80] Some argue that the trend toward anonymous giving to political campaigns was temporary and is currently subsiding. For instance, this November 9, 2018, headline from the Institute for Free Speech (IFS) reads: "Money Doesn't Buy Elections, *'Dark Money' Keeps Falling*, and Other Lessons from the 2018 Midterms." The article claims that dark money spending was down by about $40 million to $139.2 million in the 2018 election cycle compared to the 2014 midterm election.[81] A cursory analysis would conclude that the IFS is correct: dark money spending did, in fact, decrease by that amount in 2017–18. There is a catch, however.

The nearly $140 million spent by dark money groups in 2017–18 only accounts for the money that the groups themselves *directly* spent. During the 2018 election cycle, dark money groups also gave over $176 million to Super PACs and other outside spending organizations.[82] In other words, more recently, dark money groups have started to give the majority of their funds to other organizations. Combined, direct and indirect dark money spending continues to increase.

This fact identifies a broader trend in campaign finance. It has gotten ever more complex, and it has become increasingly confusing and difficult for citizens and experts alike to identify the individuals and organizations engaged in campaign politics, understand what they do, and determine their effects. The problem is that even for experts, following the money trail can be *impossible* because of the lack of required disclosures. People may be comforted to hear that Super PACs must disclose their donors, but in fact some of those funds come from 501(c) organizations with anonymous donors. However, a recently published database allows us to shed some light on dark money group donors and their motivations. For more, see chapter 3.

You might say, "Some organizations are not disclosing their donors. Big deal. So what; why should I care?" That is a good question. There are many reasons to care. First, the spending of these groups, which reflects the power they hold, is incredibly concentrated. For the bigger part of the post–*Citizens United* era, a small number of groups—only 15 out of 1.56 *million* nonprofit organizations in the United States[83]—accounted for 75 percent of all dark money expenditures.[84] Second, TV and online ads sponsored by undisclosed groups make up a substantial proportion of political ads in congressional races.[85] Third, experiments show that when viewers are aware that the donors behind an ad are undisclosed, they are more supportive of the candidates being attacked.[86] This is known as a *backlash effect*. Fourth, there are more deceptive claims in ads sponsored by groups that do not disclose their donors.[87] Finally, research has shown that ads sponsored by dark money groups are more effective and successful than candidate-sponsored ads.[88] The trends in and effects of political advertising are explored more completely in chapter 6.

To keep their status as a social welfare organization, 501(c) organizations must spend less than 50 percent of their budget on political activities. However, one study takes into account additional spending on deregulated speech. Such speech, known as **issue advocacy**, is a public position on a particular cause or policy without a call to action to elect a candidate for public office or on specific legislation (lobbying).[89] This is different from the regulated speech of **express advocacy**, which covers "communications that expressly advocate the election or defeat of a clearly identified candidate."[90] According to the Supreme Court, "expressly advocate" encompasses only words such as " 'vote for,' 'elect,' 'support,' 'vote against,' 'defeat,' and 'reject.' "[91] This is known as the *magic words test*.

So when we use a broader definition that includes express and issue advocacy, policy research, turnout mobilization, and spending on local or state politics, authors of a study estimated that the total revenue dedicated to political activity by nonprofits was $760 million in 2011.[92] So 501(c) organizations, which are not required to disclose their donors, spend a substantial amount of money on influencing politics and policy but leave the public "in the dark" about their sources.

One irony here is that the justices argued in favor of disclosure and transparency when deciding *Citizens United*. In 2010, Justice Kennedy said, "Disclaimer and disclosure requirements may burden the ability to speak, but they 'impose no ceiling on campaign-related activities,' or 'prevent anyone from speaking.' . . . Transparency enables the electorate to make informed decisions and give proper weight to different speakers and messages."[93] Although the transparency that Justice Kennedy envisioned did not materialize, anonymity in political giving is not necessarily bad. We look at the arguments for and against anonymous political giving in chapter 2.

REPRESENTATION AND POLITICAL INFLUENCE

The changes that brought about the triumvirate campaign era have implications for representation and political power and may affect some public policy decisions. When asked, politically informed people are most concerned about the influence of independent expenditures. The way people view independent expenditures predicts negative views of representation and Congress at large.[94] In other words, there is some evidence of **spillover effects**, the effect of perceptions of campaign funding on the view of Congress as a national institution. Outside groups contribute negatively to how people view the nation's main legislative body and the democratic process it represents.

In terms of representation, some are concerned about politicians' reliance on a few wealthy individuals for the funding of their campaigns. This donor class[95] lives in only a handful of congressional districts, and their ideological leanings are often distinct from the parties' electoral bases. The worry is that megadonors will drive the national policy agenda in ways that are inconsistent with what the majority of U.S. citizens want.[96] One survey in November 2018 found that only 51 percent of Americans said they "have faith" in American democracy. Two years earlier, that number stood at 60 percent.[97] Dissatisfaction with representation is likely a contributing factor.

What does this mean in practice? The answer is that the billionaires in the Twelfth Congressional District in California, represented by Nancy Pelosi (D), can have more of their interests represented in advertising and other campaign activities in districts other than their own. We chose the Twelfth District in California, which represents San Francisco, for this example because it has the highest number of billionaires per capita, with one for every 11,612 residents.[98] The overwhelming majority of citizens who live in a district with some of the lowest median household incomes, such as the Fifteenth Congressional District in New York, will not have the same opportunities to have their voices heard. New York's Fifteenth District has a median household income of only $28,042,[99] less than half of the U.S. median household income ($61,372 in 2017).[100] During the 2018 election cycle, fewer than half of 1 percent of Americans (0.48 percent, to be exact) made 71 percent of all individual contributions to federal candidates, political action committees, political parties, and outside groups, a new record since the *Citizens United* ruling.[101]

Other studies confirm a disconnect between the policy preferences of voters and the megadonors.[102] What makes this divergence even more problematic is the political polarization described briefly at the beginning of the chapter. For example, one study examined government shutdowns in California. It turns out that these extreme situations—which are becoming increasingly frequent—are a boon for legislators who hold extreme positions. Put simply, politicians with extreme opinions, particularly Republicans, raise a lot of money for their reelection campaigns during times of crises. Campaigns are expensive, and "raking in" a lot of cash incentivizes politicians to prolong conflicts without compromising.[103] This disturbing conclusion was confirmed in another study, in which dependency on outside contributions decreased congressional members' responsiveness to their districts and increased the probability of ideologically extreme positions.[104] These findings do not bode well for the impact of money on politicians' primary job: representing their constituents.

Some express fear that politicians will listen to the megadonors rather than their own constituents. There is some evidence that Democratic representatives are more likely to engage in *populist* representation, where individuals with the lowest incomes see the best alignment between their positions and those taken by their representatives, while districts with Republican legislators are more likely to see *oligarchic* representation, with much more representation by wealthy individuals.[105]

In December 2017, the Tax Cuts and Jobs Act was signed into law by President Donald Trump. Before the "Trump tax cuts" became law, Republican politicians were candid about the pressure they experienced from megadonors. For example, New York representative Chris Collins told people what he had heard from his financial backers about tax reform: "My donors are basically saying, 'Get it done or don't ever call me again.'"[106] Prior to the passage of the law, an NBC News reporter asked South Carolina senator Lindsey Graham what the consequences would be if Republicans failed to pass tax reform, and Graham said that "financial contributions will stop" for the Republican Party.[107]

Outside groups were also weighing in before the bill became law. A representative from a Super PAC funded by the Koch brothers, the second-wealthiest family in the world behind the Waltons of Walmart, warned that "there are going to be consequences" in case of a failure to cut taxes for businesses.[108] How would tax reform affect the Koch brothers? The organization Americans for Tax Fairness calculated how much Charles Koch, David Koch, and/or Koch Industries would save in taxes if the GOP tax reform became law. According to the organization's estimates, the savings for the Kochs would be between $1 billion and $1.4 billion in income taxes each year if the bill passed. Each year! As we know, the bill became law.

These statements from legislators and outside groups are not intended to pass judgment on megadonors. However, as chapter 3 shows, the peer-reviewed research is unambiguous: the U.S. Supreme Court's 2010 decisions have impacted how members of Congress represent their constituencies. We cannot conclude that legislators have fundamentally changed their way of thinking about how and who to represent since *Citizens United*, but we are seeing increased attention toward an influential donor class and changing incentives for legislators to act in certain ways.

CONCLUSION

In this chapter, we have made the case for how the changing nature of political campaigns has resulted in a triumvirate campaign era. The changes that outside groups have brought to campaigns in America affect not only individuals who run for office but also those candidates who win their races and how they approach the representation of their respective constituencies. The actions of outside groups affect how candidates communicate with citizens. Candidates often feel like they must respond to the usually negative messages outside groups broadcast, putting candidates on the defensive and less in a position to control the "game." Some advertising blitzes come so close to Election Day that candidates have no time to respond.

The ability of outside groups to raise and spend unlimited money has had profound effects not only on how campaigns are financed but also on how candidates cooperate with supportive groups and how groups coordinate their efforts with other like-minded organizations. Outside groups play by the rules given to them and are doing so with increasing intensity, sophistication, and effectiveness.

The way outside groups receive funds is also becoming more sophisticated and difficult to trace. These days, more Super PACs—which have to disclose their donors—are receiving funds from 501(c) organizations who do *not*. Citizens are becoming increasingly uncertain about who is behind the messages they see in flyers, pamphlets, and TV advertisements. Last, but certainly not least, outside groups affect political parties. Campaign finance rules with hard money (i.e., cash) limits initially put political parties at a disadvantage. However, parties have been adapting, have created their own party leadership Super PACs, and have built alliances with other Super PACs, 501(c) organizations, and 527 organizations.

KEY TERMS

DISCUSSION QUESTIONS

1. How is the triumvirate campaign era different from candidate-centered campaigns?
2. Thinking of the stories about Trump versus pro-Trump groups already transpiring in anticipation of the 2020 election, do you think (more) candidates should be concerned about the groups affiliated with them? Why?
3. Has the rise of Super PACs and dark money contributed to political polarization in the United States?
4. Should we be concerned about the increasingly significant role of the so-called megadonor in the political campaign process? Why or why not?
5. Do you believe the *Citizens United* and *SpeechNow* decisions have affected how legislators represent their constituencies? Explain your answer.
6. After reading this chapter, do you believe outside groups are "game changers" for political campaigns? Explain your answer.

ADDITIONAL READING

Bartels, Larry M. *Unequal Democracy: The Political Economy of the New Gilded Age.* 2nd ed. New York: Russell Sage Foundation, 2018.

Beckel, Michael. "Dark Money Illuminated." Issue One. September 2018. https://www.issueone.org/dark-money.

Donovan, Todd, and Shaun Bowler. "To Know It Is to Loath It: Perceptions of Campaign Finance and Attitudes About Congress." *American Politics Research* 47, no. 5 (2019): 951–69.

Gilens, Martin. *Affluence and Influence: Economic Inequality and Political Power in America.* Princeton, NJ: Princeton University Press, 2012.

Manento, Cory. "Party Crashers: Interest Groups as a Latent Threat to Party Networks in Congressional Primaries." *Party Politics* (March 2019). doi: 10.1177/1354068819834528.

2

The First Amendment and Legal Issues

★ ★ ★

IN 1912, THE CITIZENS OF MONTANA passed a law that prohibited corporations from donating to candidates or spending money to influence state elections. The law was written because the owners of the copper mining companies in the state were known for using their wealth to influence legislators. In particular, W. A. Clark, a wealthy copper mine and railroad owner, was known for giving hundreds of thousands of dollars to elected officials.[1] At that time, state legislators, not the citizens of the states, chose U.S. senators,[2] which made it easier for Clark to have influence at the federal level, including "suggesting" which senators should represent Montana. As it turns out, the person Clark most wanted to be elected to the Senate was himself.

Clark's ploy worked. On December 4, 1889, the Montana state legislature elected him to the U.S. Senate. Almost immediately, his opponent, also a wealthy copper mine owner, accused him of securing the election through corrupt means. A full investigation by the Senate's Committee on Privileges and Elections found that Clark had engaged in a lengthy list of corrupt practices, ranging in value from several hundred dollars to $100,000.[3] He paid legislators' mortgages, bought them new properties, paid their debts, or had friends hand them envelopes filled with cash with his initials on them. The Committee that investigated Clark unanimously voted to have him removed from office, and when it became clear that the entire Senate would vote similarly, he resigned.[4]

Yet that did not end his time in the Senate. Clark resigned (technically), but he had another scheme up his sleeve. His resignation left a vacancy that the governor of Montana was obligated to fill. On the same day Clark knew he would resign, he tricked the governor into leaving Montana on a business trip, which put the lieutenant governor temporarily in power. The lieutenant governor, unsurprisingly another politician beholden to Clark, appointed him back into the U.S. Senate. Upon learning of this deception, the governor of Montana, three days later, appointed Martin Maginnis to fill the position, and Clark could not serve his term.

Like a cat with many lives, Clark's time in office would not die. In 1901, the newly elected Montana state legislature, most of whom were indebted to him in one way or another, elected Clark to the U.S. Senate. His main opponent, Marcus Daly, another mining mogul, had died a few months earlier, so, this time, no one challenged the legitimacy of Clark's election. He served his six-year term in the U.S. Senate and, in 1907, returned to his businesses.[5]

Much has changed since then—wealthy individuals such as Clark generally avoid illegal methods of corruption such as handing bags of cash to elected officials—but Montana citizens are proud of their long-standing, bipartisan tradition of fair and transparent elections. So when the Supreme Court ruled in *Citizens United* that corporations, labor unions, and other associations could spend unlimited independent expenditures, Montana prepared to defend its campaign finance laws. Shortly after *Citizens United* was decided, a nonprofit group, the Western (now "American") Tradition Partnership, sued the state of Montana for what it argued was an unconstitutional ban on corporate spending in state elections. Montana's Supreme Court disagreed, ruling 5–2 that the 1912 law could still be enforced to keep corporate spending out of Montana politics because of its history of corruption.[6] On appeal, the Supreme Court ruled in a 5–4 decision that Montana's 1912 law was unconstitutional, upholding the *Citizens United* ruling.[7] The dissenting justices, however, reiterated their disagreement with the Court's previous conclusion from *Citizens United* that "independent expenditures, including those made by corporations, do not give rise to corruption or the appearance of corruption."[8]

Prior to *Citizens United*, Montana was not the only state that had such prohibitions on election financing; twenty-three others had similar campaign financing and election laws. Ten states banned both corporate and labor union contributions, nine banned only corporate money, and one banned only union contributions.[9] Following *American Tradition Partnership v. Bullock* (2011), there was no doubt that states were now compelled to allow spending in campaigns according to the Supreme Court's decision. As a result, most of those laws have now been amended or repealed to comply with the federal ruling.[10] Unsurprisingly, most of those states have seen an increase in campaign spending, partly because of new Super PACs (super political action committees) and a rise in undisclosed campaign expenditures.

***

This chapter explores the transformation of laws and court rulings related to federal elections. Because election and campaign financing laws are almost always challenged on free speech grounds, we first consider several ways of understanding the significance of the First Amendment. Second, we provide brief snapshots of the key legislation and legal challenges that have affected campaign finance law. Finally, we discuss four key areas of tension where First Amendment interpretation and application have collided with some of the expectations of living in a free and representative democracy.

Before delving into specific court cases and rulings, an understanding of the various interpretations of the First Amendment and its legal underpinnings is critical to understanding the evolving landscape of the role of Super PACs and dark money in politics. How the Supreme Court has interpreted and applied the First Amendment has depended upon its composition, so the following is offered as an overview of the range of possible interpretations. Readers can decide for themselves which perspectives are most valid or most important, but the takeaway is that there are multiple approaches to understanding the First Amendment, and each school of thought has different implications.

UNDERSTANDING THE FIRST AMENDMENT: THEORETICAL APPROACHES

The text of the First Amendment reads as follows: "Congress shall make no law respecting an establishment of religion, or prohibiting the free exercise thereof; or abridging the freedom of speech, or of the press; or the right of the people peaceably to assemble, and to petition the Government for a redress of grievances." The interpretation of the First Amendment is far more complicated than it may initially appear. To whom does it apply? Under what circumstances? Are there any limits? What counts as "speech"? These questions are just a few that must be considered if we are to untangle the rights of groups in the electoral process. Before answering those questions, however, we should consider the history and theory of the First Amendment.

First Amendment Theory

First Amendment scholars generally agree that there are two main approaches—utilitarian and intrinsic—to interpreting and understanding the significance of the First Amendment. A utilitarian approach means there is an ultimate societal benefit or outcome, such as the discovery of truth or the process of deliberation to reach a sound policy decision, whereas an intrinsic approach views free speech as an "end in itself, stressing the value of a free expression to the speaker."[11] Under the utilitarian category, both the marketplace of ideas model and the self-governance model are defined. The liberty model is considered as an example of the intrinsic purpose of the First Amendment.

The Marketplace of Ideas Model

The metaphorical **marketplace of ideas model** asserts that there needs to be a free and open exchange of speech to enable the public to hear all the available ideas. This concept, which is based largely upon the writings of John Milton and John Stuart Mill, was born as a popular way of viewing the First Amendment in Justice Holmes's dissenting opinion in *Abrams v. United States,* a case in 1919 that upheld the Espionage Act, making dissent about World War I a crime. Holmes wrote, against the majority decision, that the "best test of truth is the power of the thought to get itself accepted in the competition of the market."[12] Open debate and exchange must be protected, he argued, for it is the only way we can discern the truth. After Holmes first used the marketplace of ideas metaphor, many Supreme Court justices have followed suit. In fact, the *marketplace of ideas* analogy is the "generally accepted judicial choice among First Amendment theories."[13]

The Supreme Court has said that the competition of ideas is at the core of the electoral process and the First Amendment.[14] In fact, the Court has argued that the primary purpose of the First Amendment is to protect an uninhibited "marketplace" where differing ideas can clash,[15] that the widest dissemination of ideas is essential to the welfare of the public,[16] and that a free marketplace is a principal protector of the republican form of government.[17] For those reasons, the government is not allowed to engage in **viewpoint discrimination**.[18] When the government engages in viewpoint discrimination, it restricts or limits a particular opinion or perspective, a practice that would run counter to the marketplace of ideas model.

Despite its favored status in the courts, critics argue that the marketplace of ideas is a romantic myth. They contend that it is based on flawed assumptions, especially in a mass-mediated era.[19] According to critics, the first faulty assumption is that everyone has access to this marketplace. Power, influence, and wealth can make some ideas "louder" than others, critics point out, and many citizens have little or no access to the nation's marketplace of ideas. When those with wealth and influence prefer certain ideas, others can be diminished effectively or silenced altogether. For example, political advertising expenditures in the 2018 midterm elections exceeded $5 billion.[20] Critics argue that when the total pool of money in any given election cycle is that substantial, the voices and perspectives of those with little or no wealth are unlikely to be heard.[21]

Some contend that social media solves the problem of gaining access to the marketplace because nearly anyone can have a voice on the various social media platforms,[22] but such an argument also rests on the assumption that ideas are able to be distributed widely on social media without wealth and influence. In most cases, however, money (or fame of some kind) is still needed to spread ideas beyond one's circle of a few hundred "friends" or followers on social media platforms.

Second, this model assumes that the truth will be among the ideas exchanged in the marketplace. Either by accident or by design, there is no guarantee that any of the ideas in the marketplace are factual or worthy. In some cases, we need to be mindful of the first argument that critics make: those with power and those who can afford access to the mechanisms of distribution control the contents of the marketplace of ideas.[23]

Finally, the model assumes that humans are rational and that the best ideas will prevail because we have both the ability and the desire to discern fact from fiction, sound arguments from fallacies, and verifiable evidence from speculation or fabrication. But humans often fail at those tasks, as evidenced in part by the "backfire effect" wherein people become more convinced of their original belief in the face of evidence that proves them wrong.[24]

The Self-Governance Model

This **self-governance model** asserts that freedom of expression is an essential value to self-government in a democratic society. It is utilitarian because the goal relates to the policies, rules, and laws of the nation via our elected, representative government. Deliberation is a central and necessary function of a citizenry, and therefore speech that is a part of that process is more strongly protected.[25]

Under this model, most adherents contend that government has at least some power to limit speech and expression that does not serve the purpose of self-governance. Other forms of expression may not be deemed worthy of protection, so a potential disadvantage of this model is that it might result in privileging certain forms of speech that directly support the goals of running a democracy while limiting or even censoring other forms of expression, especially if an argument can be made that certain speech hinders our ability to self-govern.

Likewise, speech that criticizes the actions of the government must be protected. An important role of speech in a democracy is to hold government accountable. The suppression of criticism is a trait of other forms of government (authoritarian, totalitarian, etc.), not a democracy. Justice Brennan wrote that the "freedom to discuss public affairs and public officials is unquestionably . . . the kind of speech the First Amendment was *primarily designed* [emphasis added] to keep within the area of free discussion."[26] Later, Chief Justice Rehnquist argued that the free flow of ideas is important not because it will lead to the discovery of any objective truth but because it is essential to a system of self-governance.[27]

Critics of this model point out that there is potential danger in thinking of free speech only in terms of "political speech." For example, the government could be granted sweeping powers to regulate speech and expression that do not directly relate to deliberation about governmental matters.[28] If judges interpret the model too literally, the courts might rule that only a narrow slice of speech and expression is granted protection under the law. Where might artistic expression, such as music and art, fall under this model? What about novels, films, and theatrical productions? On the one hand, many artists and writers are commenting on political matters; on the other hand, one can imagine an argument against these forms of expression as being unnecessary, or even as an obstacle, to self-governance.[29]

The Liberty Model
Law professor C. Edwin Baker articulated the **liberty model** as an alternative to the "marketplace of ideas" model because, he argued, "speech or other self-expressive conduct is protected not as a means to achieve a collective good but because of its value to the individual."[30] The model is intrinsic because there are no necessary goals

aside from individual autonomy and self-fulfillment. All expression is protected because all individuals have an inherent right to form and express opinions. Those opinions could be used to deliberate policy or to criticize the government's decisions but are not necessarily required to serve such purposes or any purpose at all for that matter.

This model can result in conflicting implications. If the First Amendment exists primarily to protect our personal autonomy, then the government would have virtually no authority to limit any form of speech or other expressions. Conversely, if the rationale of the First Amendment rests on individual liberty, then speech and other expressions covered under the First Amendment deserve no special protection beyond what any other freedom would have. Under such a model, to use a stark example, one's right to create and distribute pornographic material is no different in the eyes of the law than would be a campaign advertisement.

These theories of First Amendment interpretation have often been among the reasons for differing Court rulings. In some cases, these interpretative frameworks have been invoked explicitly in oral arguments, majority opinions, and dissenting opinions. We have offered them here not only to assist in understanding some of the legal rulings as they relate to campaign finance but also to serve as a framework for the reader's consideration and as a possible starting point for discussion about both campaign finance laws and legal rulings. From what perspective was the majority justifying its ruling? Did the dissenting judges seem to favor a different outcome, in part, because they approached the significance of the First Amendment from a different "model"? Following some brief snapshots of significant campaign finance legislation and court cases, the next section brings us more specifically into the applications of First Amendment law as it affects political campaigns and the electoral process.

SIGNIFICANT LEGISLATION AND COURT CASES

Prior to the 1970s, there was little regulation on campaigns. The following is a brief timeline of some important campaign finance reforms up to the passage of the Federal Election Campaign Act in 1971:

> **1757:** After George Washington buys $195 worth of punch and hard cider for friends in connection with an election, the Virginia legislature passes a law prohibiting candidates, or persons on their behalf, from giving voters "money, meat, drink,

entertainment or provision . . . any present, gift, reward or entertainment, etc. in order to be elected."

1883: The Pendleton Civil Service Reform Act makes it illegal for government officials to solicit contributions from any civil service workers or award these positions on anything but merit. Prior to this act, many people who worked in government positions were expected to make contributions in order to keep their jobs.

1907: The **Tillman Act** makes contributions to federal candidates by corporations and national banks illegal. Because of enforcement issues, the act was largely ineffective.

1910: The Federal Corrupt Practices Act requires House candidates to disclose their finances. One year later, U.S. Senate and primary candidates are required to disclose their finances, and expenditure limits are set for all congressional candidates.

1921: In *Newberry v. United States*, the Supreme Court rules the Federal Corrupt Practices Act unconstitutional because the Constitution does not grant Congress the authority to regulate political parties or federal primary elections.

1925: Congress amends the Federal Corrupt Practices Act to include a ban on any corporate contribution to a federal campaign, requiring financial disclosure reports to be made quarterly. Any contribution over $100 now must be reported, and the Senate campaign spending limit is raised to $25,000.

1939: The **Hatch Act** bans most federal employees from contributing to candidates in national elections and from participating in political activities or campaigns.

1943: The **Smith-Connally Act** prohibits unions from contributing to federal candidates. Prior to this law, unions had been using dues for political donations. The first PAC is established by the Congress of Industrial Organizations.

1947: The **Taft-Hartley Act** bans corporations and unions from making independent expenditures in federal political campaigns. If candidates promise not to use their primary money during the general election campaign or collect private donations, they can campaign with publicly funded dollars.

1967: Although legally required for nearly fifty years, Congress finally begins to collect campaign finance reports.[31]

The Federal Election Campaign Act

In 1971, the **Federal Election Campaign Act** (FECA) was signed into law. The primary focus of the original act was to increase transparency by monitoring campaign financing; the act required that every candidate or committee involved in federal campaigns submit quarterly reports of all contributions and expenditures of $100 or more. FECA was amended several times, most prominently after the Watergate scandal.

In 1974, the act was amended to include contribution limits, spending limits, and voluntary public financing for presidential candidates. The Federal Election Commission (FEC) was established as the administrative and oversight committee of federal election law. FECA prohibited individuals or groups from spending anything beyond $1,000 that advocated for or against a candidate. It also limited donations by a political committee to $5,000 to any single candidate. A total expenditure cap at the federal level of $25,000 by an individual donor was also put in place.

Buckley v. Valeo (1976)

In **Buckley v. Valeo** (1976), the U.S. Supreme Court upheld the limits on contributions to candidates, the reporting and disclosure rules, and the system of voluntary public financing for presidential campaigns. However, the Court also ruled that caps on campaign spending, limits on independent expenditures, and limits on how much candidates could contribute to their own campaigns were in violation of the First Amendment. The Court's rationale was that nearly every method of communication in the modern world requires some kind of relationship to money. Individuals and groups, including the candidates themselves, could now spend as much as they wanted so long as the content of the message was a form of issue advocacy that would not expressly advocate the election or defeat of a federal candidate (*express advocacy*). The Court reasoned that issue advocacy was political speech that would not raise concerns about corrupting the political process. By making a distinction between express and issue advocacy, restrictions on unions and corporations could remain in place. For speech to qualify as issue advocacy, the Court ruled that it could not violate the magic words test. The **magic words test** lists eight words or phrases that qualify as "express advocacy" and therefore could be regulated. The "magic words" listed in *Buckley* are "vote for," "elect," "support," "cast your ballot for," "[candidate name] for Congress," "vote against," "defeat," or "reject."

The *Buckley* ruling, then, led to an increased use of **soft money**, or unregulated donations given to the political parties for general purposes. But the parties found ways to use the money for election purposes; they funneled money into 527 committees, which would create "issue ads" that avoided the use of the "magic words" but were still rather obvious campaign ads.[32] These ads became known as *sham ads*.

The reasoning behind these decisions is significant because it has shaped the way the courts have ruled on campaign financing issues. Anything short of corruption "or the appearance" of corruption has often been ruled constitutional, and it was on these grounds that the Court upheld the contribution limits. Ever since *Buckley*, the legal arguments and decisions, if not the popular discussions, have centered on the meaning of "corruption," with arguments in favor of equality often losing by narrow margins in the Court.

Colorado Republican Federal Campaign Committee v. FEC (1996)

In **Colorado Republican Federal Campaign Committee v. FEC**, the Supreme Court overturned part of FECA prohibiting independent expenditures made by parties without coordination with candidates as a violation of the First Amendment.

The Bipartisan Campaign Reform Act

In 2002, Congress passed the **Bipartisan Campaign Reform Act** (BCRA), often referred to as the McCain-Feingold Act after its two chief proponents, Republican Senator John McCain (AZ) and Democratic Senator Russ Feingold (WI). The primary goal of the legislation was to rein in the use of soft money that the *Buckley* ruling had created. BCRA attempted to accomplish its goal in two main ways.

First, BCRA kept campaign contribution limits. The limits applied to individuals, political party committees, and PACs and determined how much donors could give to candidates, parties, and PACs. The act also raised many of those **hard money** limits because the original amounts were in 1970s dollars and were not tied to inflation. Money directly contributed to candidates, parties, and PACs is known as hard money. At the same time, McCain-Feingold banned national parties from raising and spending soft money. It also prohibited state and local party committees from spending soft money for federal election activities.

Second, BCRA attempted to eliminate sham ads by expanding the "magic word" test of *Buckley v. Valeo*—because avoiding those exact words and phrases was easy enough while still clearly advocating for or against a particular candidate—with an additional *blackout period* during which outside groups could not even mention or show a visual image of a candidate thirty days before a primary or sixty days before a general election, a restriction that would be tested in the next court case.

FEC v. Wisconsin Right to Life, Inc. (2007)

Wisconsin Right to Life (WRTL), a 501(c)(3) group against abortion and euthanasia, proposed to run three advertisements, two radio, and one TV, during the 2004 blackout periods prohibited by BCRA. The following describes one version of the proposed ads:

* * *

[The scene is a wedding.]

> PASTOR: And who gives this woman to be married to this man?

> BRIDE'S FATHER: Well, as the father of the bride, I certainly could. But instead, I'd like to share a few tips on how to properly install drywall. Now you put the drywall up . . .

> VOICE-OVER: Sometimes it's just not fair to delay an important decision. But in Washington, it's happening. A group of Senators is using the filibuster delay tactic to block federal judicial nominees from a simple "yes" or "no" vote. So qualified candidates don't get a chance to serve. It's politics at work, causing gridlock and backing up some of our courts to a state of emergency. Contact Senators Feingold and Kohl and tell them to oppose the filibuster.

> Paid for by Wisconsin Right to Life, which is responsible for the content of this advertising and not authorized by any candidate or candidates [*sic*] committee.[33]

* * *

Senator Feingold was up for reelection that year, but Senator Kohl was not, a detail that helped WRTL win its case because it could argue that if the ads were about voting for or against a specific candidate, then why mention Senator Kohl at all? In a split 5–4 decision, the Supreme Court ruled in favor of WRTL, arguing that the ads were true issue ads, not express advocacy ads or sham issue ads. The majority on the Court applied the **"reasonable person"** standard to the case, stating that if an ad reasonably could be interpreted as being about anything other than advocacy for or against a candidate, then it was protected under the First Amendment.

This ruling effectively allowed for all independent groups to make and produce advertisements at any time during an election so long as it could be interpreted as anything other than express advocacy of voting for or against a particular candidate. As chapter 6 explores, this ruling is why so many outside group ads following this ruling were (and many still are) phrased such as "Tell Senator X that you support issue Y" as opposed to "vote against Senator X on November 12."

Citizens United v. FEC (2010)

In **Citizens United v. FEC**, the Supreme Court ruled that limits on independent expenditures by corporations, unions, and other associations within sixty days of a general election or thirty days of a primary election, known as an **electioneering communication**, violate the First Amendment's protections of freedom of speech. Citizens United was a nonprofit organization that produced a ninety-minute film called *Hillary: The Movie*. The film was unfavorable in its portrayal of Hillary Clinton. The film concluded with this message: "These are things worth remembering before you go in potentially to vote for Hillary Clinton."[34] Citizens United wanted to show the film in theaters and other special screenings, but it also wanted to run advertisements to get people to see the movie. Furthermore, Citizens United wanted to give Comcast (a cable TV provider) $1.2 million to make it available free of cost on a video-on-demand channel. It wanted to do this within the blackout period defined in BCRA of thirty days before the Democratic nomination (a primary election) of its presidential candidate. The FEC treated the documentary as an argument against Clinton's election and therefore considered the documentary electioneering communication. Thus, Citizens United would have been breaking the law, according to the FEC.

The Supreme Court saw it differently. In a 5–4 decision, the majority ruled in Citizens United's favor, allowing for unrestricted independent expenditures. The decision also effectively overturned and rendered ineffective the regulations on soft money BCRA had established. Additionally, since 501(c)(4) social welfare organizations, such as Citizens United, are not required to disclose their donors, the decision opened the door for nonprofits to raise and spend more money without disclosing the sources of the funding.

SpeechNow v. FEC (2010)

In *SpeechNow v. FEC*, a nonprofit 527 organization challenged the FEC's contribution limits to PACs. The U.S. Court of Appeals for the District of Columbia ruled that contribution limits from individuals are unconstitutional. It also ruled that organizations created to accept contributions and make independent expenditures must register as a political committee. The Supreme Court confirmed the decision but did not hear the full case. This case resulted in what are now called Super PACs, political action committees with no restrictions on how much money they can accept to fund efforts (often advertisements of some kind) in support of or opposition to federal candidates. In conjunction with *Citizens United*, the case suggested that unions and corporations could make unlimited contributions to PACs that only make independent expenditures.

McCutcheon v. FEC (2014)

In *McCutcheon v. FEC*, Shaun McCutcheon, the CEO of an engineering firm that specialized in mining, sued the FEC, claiming that **aggregate contribution limits,** or the total amount allowed to be donated toward elections in a two-year cycle, were a violation of his First Amendment rights. The Supreme Court agreed (5–4), striking down aggregate limits. Prior to *McCutcheon*, an individual could donate a maximum of $123,200 to federal candidates, national party committees, and other committees such as PACs in a two-year cycle.[35] Following this ruling, a single person can now donate the maximum amount to every candidate up for federal election and give $5,000 to as many PACs as he or she wants. The FEC calculated that an individual could now donate $3,628,000 to federal candidates, a national party committee, and other committees, assuming the person supported only one political party.[36]

LEGAL ISSUES RELATED TO POLITICAL CAMPAIGNS: FOUR TENSIONS

Political campaigns, at their core, are about getting a message to citizens that a candidate hopes will garner votes. But is that process, from start to finish, the same as granting individual citizens the right to exercise their First Amendment rights? Perhaps within some schools of thought (the "marketplace of ideas") it is, but it also may be at odds with aspects of the self-governance model. Legislators and the courts also have struggled with this question, especially in the past century: to whom does the First Amendment apply, when, and under what circumstances? We know that the First Amendment is not absolute; there have always been exceptions to when, how, and to what extent it applies. These exceptions are commonly referred to as **time, place, and manner restrictions** and are controversial as well. Most people are familiar with the falsely-shouting-fire-in-a-crowded-theater example, which was not based on any actual event despite popular misbelief.[37] Rather, the theater-fire example was a hypothetical scenario Justice Oliver Wendell Holmes used to suggest that the First Amendment is not absolute.[38]

Of course, many other restrictions to free speech have arisen as the result of valid but competing interests. This is often known as **balancing**.[39] How can the courts balance the rights of individuals against a legitimate government function, such as protecting the integrity and legitimacy of the electoral process? How should we balance free speech rights against other civil liberties, such as the right to privacy and the right to avoid being falsely accused? We compromise (i.e., try to "balance" the rights); that is why there are libel and slander laws, which are certainly restrictions on free speech but arguably for good reasons.

Likewise, there are many competing and legitimate interests in political campaigns. There are two broad ways to think about campaign finance laws. The first argument is about liberty. This position holds that laws and regulations limiting donations and expenditures are stifling citizens' abilities to participate in the political process. The second is an argument about equality: that laws and regulations are justified in the context of elections because they are trying to put citizens on relatively equal footing. Advocates of this position argue that everyone should have a chance to be heard and not be drowned out by those with vast resources. Although the Court in *Buckley* rejected this argument, claiming that to "restrict the speech of some elements of our society in order to enhance the relative voice of others is wholly foreign to the First Amendment,"[40] critics argue that an egalitarian goal is not necessarily at odds with those who advocate the liberty perspective. Rather than being thought of as mutually exclusive, the egalitarian and libertarian viewpoints exist on a continuum.[41] This balancing act has resulted in four main tensions that can be expressed as questions:

- Should First Amendment rights apply equally to individuals *and* corporations, and, if so, are all corporations the same?
- Should the First Amendment apply to the spending of money in the same way it does to the content of expression?

- Where should the line be drawn on defining and classifying corruption (or even "the appearance of corruption," as the courts have often argued)?
- Should we favor privacy rights or disclosure laws so the public can know who is funding campaigns?

These are written as "should" questions because these issues are not, and possibly never will be, completely settled. Future legislation and court rulings can change any or all the current laws, but these questions are likely to remain pertinent. Campaign and election laws can be understood as the result of tensions that are constantly in flux. As we know, a court ruling the day after this book is released could significantly impact political campaigning but understanding these competing ideas will always have relevance.

To What Extent Should "Corporations" Have First Amendment Rights?

Opponents of the *Citizens United* ruling frequently argue that corporations are not people. There is no shortage of witty slogans that express this view: "I Refuse to Believe Corporations Are People Until Texas Executes One" and "If Corporations are People, Why Don't They Go to Jail When They Break the Law?" come to mind. Unfortunately, these positions tend to oversimplify the long history of how and why corporations sometimes are granted civil liberties and sometimes are denied them. Some of the tension surrounding the question of corporations' rights resides in the imprecise uses of the word "corporation."

When people say, "corporations are not people," they tend to have in mind the image of a large, for-profit, multinational corporation, such as Walmart or Exxon Mobil. Yet a "corporation" is a legal entity that can refer to a wide range of different types of associations of people for an even wider range of purposes. Colleges and universities, for example, are a type of (usually) nonprofit corporation. Most churches and charities are nonprofit corporations. In chapter 1, we defined 501(c)(4)s organizations, which are not allowed to spend more than half of their budget on political activities. Churches, charities, and educational institutions, however, are all tax exempt 501(c)(3)s and therefore are prohibited from political involvement and allowed only "insubstantial" lobbying efforts. To remain tax exempt, 501(c)(3)s must stay true to their stated missions of advancing religion, performing an educational function, or conducting charitable work.[42]

All corporations are not the same, and legislators and judges also have struggled to develop consistent and meaningful distinctions, particularly when the question is whether corporations can participate in the election process. Most major Supreme Court rulings about campaign finance since the Watergate era have been split decisions (5–4 in one direction or the other), which further demonstrates the perseverance of questions about whether, when, and how corporations enjoy constitutional rights.

One might be tempted to divide corporations into two categories—"for profit" and "nonprofit"—and then the concern of corporate influence in elections would be lessened if not resolved. The Supreme Court has even ruled similarly in the past in another case about campaign finance. In *Federal Election Commission v. Massachusetts Citizens for Life* (MCFL; 1986), the Court ruled that parts of FECA 1974 were unconstitutional. MCFL spent approximately $10,000 on flyers urging people to vote for pro-life candidates, which also arguably crossed into "express advocacy" speech, but that is not our immediate concern. A significant argument in the majority's opinion was that MCFL did not have shareholders and was not formed as a *business* corporation or labor union.[43] In other words, the Supreme Court narrowly ruled (another 5–4 decision) that the existing campaign laws were unconstitutional as they applied to a certain type of corporation (defined largely by what it was *not*: nonbusiness, nonlabor union, nonstock, and it did not accept donations from for-profit businesses) because they put substantial burdens on MCFL's First Amendment Rights. Presumably, given the Court's reasoning, had Pepsi or Nike been a defendant in the case, the ruling would have been the opposite.

So now we had a way to determine whether independent expenditures and advocacy were allowed, right? Not really. The ruling did not resolve the matter. The First Amendment explicitly protects the freedom of the press, and the press (i.e., the news media) are, for the most part, for-profit corporations (businesses, with shareholders). In fact, many media outlets are owned by some of the largest corporations in the world. General Electric owns NBC, Disney owns ABC and all the former Fox TV networks except Fox News, and so on. Some advocates of limiting corporate influence in U.S. elections argue for a news media exemption, particularly if journalism is the primary function of a business.[44] The rationale for the press exemption is that the First Amendment enumerates a free press as a right; this is often referred to as the **Free Press Clause**. Justice Potter Stewart argued that the press should be considered independently from other corporations insofar as the First Amendment is concerned because the "publishing business is . . . the only organized private business that is given explicit constitutional protection."[45] Likewise, in his *Citizens United* dissent (in part), Justice Stevens also argued that "one type of corporation, those that are part of the press, might be able to claim special First Amendment status."[46]

Opponents of the press exemption offer two main objections. The first is that there is no constitutional justification to privilege the rights of some members of society (the press) over other individuals. In *First National Bank of Boston v Bellotti*, for example, the majority argued that the press "does not have a monopoly on the First Amendment or the ability to enlighten."[47] The second is a definitional objection. There is, according to critics, "no coherent way to distinguish the institutional press from others who disseminate information and opinion to the public through communications media."[48]

Whether news media corporations constitute meaningfully distinct entities is a difficult question, which is why legal scholar Richard Hasen points out that "most reformers simply ignore or gloss over it."[49] For now, news media corporations highlight the difficulty we have discussed in limiting some but not all corporate speech and some but not all types of corporations. Some argue that a press exemption is not only possible but also legally warranted,[50] but for now the Supreme Court has prohibited the government from limiting for-profit corporations' independent expenditures.

Free "speech" is one issue, and perhaps corporations, no matter their classification, should be allowed free expression of ideas, but usually the expression of "speech" is not what bothers people. Instead, big money seems to be the determining factor in most people's objections to corporate (and the megadonors') involvement U.S. elections.[51] Thus, the push and pull of the "Is money really speech?" question is considered next.

(When) Should Money Be Protected as Speech?

Just like many slogans argue that corporations are not people, opponents also contend that money is not speech. Technically, of course, money is not speech. The phrase sounds self-evident, but the reality is more complicated. Restricting the use of money in certain situations would almost certainly be recognized as the same as prohibiting the right itself. What if Congress passed a law against buying paper or printer toner cartridges? Technically, the law does not restrict "speech," but it sure would make it harder—and illegal, most importantly—to create and print flyers or to circulate petitions. In that case, surely such a law would trigger a legitimate First Amendment challenge. At the same time, is spending $100 on a few hundred flyers the same as a billionaire spending hundreds of millions of dollars on TV advertisements in efforts to affect the outcomes of elections across the country?

There are several ways to define money in political campaigns. Imagine that you have $100 and want to support a candidate. There are several options for spending that money. You could simply write a check and send it to the candidate's official campaign. Or you could give $50 to the candidate (online or in-person), which is known as a *direct contribution*, and spend $50 on an advertisement that says, "Vote for Pedro," which would be considered an independent expenditure. Perhaps you make flyers to hand out in front of the local library, or maybe you put $50 toward Facebook ads. Maybe you think flyers are the most effective at getting votes, so you spend all $100 on the flyers.

Our first distinction to consider, then, is the difference between direct contributions and independent expenditures. This distinction is important because the laws and the courts have ruled differently depending under which category the money falls. In *Buckley v. Valeo* (1976), the Court ruled that limits on election *spending* were a violation of the First Amendment. The Court's rationale was that nearly every method of communication in the modern world requires a relationship to money. TV, radio, and print advertisements all have costs. Direct mail, pamphlets, and other printed forms of communication cost money. Today we would certainly add that digital advertising is not free. Even organizing rallies and campaign events comes with substantial costs. In short, the Court reasoned that disseminating any given message is (almost) never free. The reality is that money is often needed to express political speech to a larger group of people.

Yet there are methods to regulate the ways in which money can be spent in the context of elections. As a result of the Watergate scandal, FECA limited political contributions by an individual or a group to $1,000 and put other hard money contribution limits in place. The government's justification for these limitations was to prevent corruption in the political process. Still, limits are in place on how much can be contributed *directly* to candidates, PACs, and parties. An individual U.S. citizen or permanent resident (for the 2019–20 election cycle) can give $2,800 to a candidate committee, $5,000 to a PAC, and $35,000 to a national party committee (per election; primaries and general elections count as two separate elections).[52]

Second, recall that First Amendment law often invoked time, place, and manner restrictions. This is another way that money does not equal speech in all cases. The ruling in *Buckley*, for example, upheld the *limits* of direct donations, but individuals and groups, including the candidates themselves, could then spend as much as they wanted so long as the content of the message did not violate the magic word test. To regulate electioneering communications that were masquerading as issue ads (sham ads), BCRA of 2002 implemented time periods during which express advocacy ads could not be aired by outside groups. Individuals and groups were restricted from running any advertisements that even mentioned a candidate thirty days prior to a primary contest and sixty days prior to a general election.

The role of money in campaigns is nearly impossible to discuss in isolation from other, related issues. The next two sections, therefore, consider the tensions that arise when excessive money in campaigns from a wealthy few is, or is at least perceived to be, incompatible with representative democracy.

Where Should We Draw the Lines of Responsiveness and Corruption?

In the *Federalist Papers 57*, Madison responded to an antifederalist's argument that the House of Representatives would "be taken from that class of citizens which will have the least sympathy with the mass of the people, and be most likely to aim at an ambitious sacrifice of the many to the aggrandizement of the few." Put simply, our representatives would not actually *represent* most of us. Madison put forth a rebuttal, in which he claimed that members of the House would need to be responsive to all the people they represent because there would be frequent elections (two-year terms in the House) that would create "a habitual recollection of their dependence on the people."[53]

The antifederalist "Brutus" (a pseudonym) wrote that being held accountable through frequent elections was not enough. He wrote that representatives needed to be "a true likeness of the people." He doubted that anyone other than the wealthy ever would be elected and that "the great body of the yeoman [farmers] of the country," or anyone whom today we might refer to as a blue-collar worker, "cannot expect any of their order in this assembly." He argued that "wealth always creates influence" and that the wealthy "will always favour each other." He therefore warned that the House would "not only be an imperfect representation" but also that there would "be no security . . . against bribery, and corruption."[54] As a result, the government would not "possess the confidence of the people," and the "execution of laws in a free government rests on this confidence."[55] Of concern before the Constitution was even adopted was that U.S. citizens needed to have confidence that their elected officials would be responsive to their entire constituency, not just the wealthy few. Corruption, or the appearance of corruption, is a sure way to decay and destroy that confidence, something that Supreme Court justices also have reasoned frequently.

Fittingly, many of the legal decisions relevant to campaign finance since FECA make the case that preventing corruption is, when balanced against other factors, a **compelling state interest** that justifies restrictions and spending limits. This means that certain campaign finance restrictions will have to withstand **strict scrutiny** in the courts. Strict scrutiny means the government must not only have a compelling state interest in justifying a law but that the law must also be narrowly defined. What has changed, however, are the ways in which the courts have defined "corruption." In general, the definition of "corruption" has narrowed significantly over time. Early on, and in some rulings, the courts demonstrated concern for a wide range of potential negative effects that fell under the umbrella of corruption, which included everything from decreased responsiveness to constituents, to elected officials feeling obligated via a sense of gratitude towards more generous donors, to the more obvious **quid pro quo forms of corruption.** Quid pro quo corruption means that a politician is doing favors in direct exchange for a campaign contribution.

In *Buckley*, the Court offered a rather broad conception of corruption and even added that campaign contribution limitations were justified because they also affected the public's perception of the electoral process. The majority wrote, "Of almost equal concern as the danger of actual *quid pro quo* arrangements is the impact of the *appearance of corruption* stemming from public awareness of the opportunities for abuse inherent in a regime of large individual financial contributions" [emphasis added].[56] Even as recently as 2003, in *McConnell v. FEC*, the Court reiterated that "improper influence" extends beyond obvious corruption, such as bribery, and includes "the broader threat from politicians too compliant with the wishes of large contributors" and of "undue influence on an officeholder's judgment."[57] This decision is significant because even though the courts struck down limits on independent expenditures in 2010, they still recognized that citizens' confidence in elected government (by preventing even the possible perception that corruption exists) was a compelling enough interest for regulating spending in political campaigns.

Compare the statement in *McConnell* with what the majority wrote in the *McCutcheon* ruling: "the Government's interest in preventing the appearance of corruption . . . is confined to the appearance of *quid pro quo* corruption." Therefore, the Court continued, "the Government may not seek to limit the appearance of mere influence or access."[58] By 2014, then, the Supreme Court had narrowed corruption, essentially, to bribery. Anything short of quid pro quo corruption was no longer a legitimate legal justification for most campaign finance laws.

At the core of these decisions has been the issue of "responsiveness" to elected officials' constituents, but, like "corruption," responsiveness has been interpreted inconsistently as well. Critics of rulings such as *Citizens United* and *SpeechNow* argue that candidates, if elected, will, at a minimum, keep the interests of their biggest donors in mind so that they can continue to get large donations for future campaigns. Their argument is that small donations are becoming less significant to overall campaign fund raising in the era of unlimited independent expenditures, and, whether intentionally or not, candidates will favor the interests of big donors and be less concerned and responsive to the smaller donors (and those who do not or cannot donate at all.)[59]

In *McCutcheon*, the Court reasoned that aggregate limits "seriously [restrict] participation in the democratic process."[60] Yet critics make the case that unlimited funding actually runs counter to the idea of representative democracy.[61] An individual only has two U.S. senators and one member of the House representing them at the federal level.[62] The *McCutcheon* ruling, according to critics, makes it hard to believe that the Supreme Court truly has the interests only of *constituents* in mind.[63] Now that individuals no longer have a biennial aggregate contribution limit, they can donate to every candidate in every state, every leadership PAC, and every state and national party committee, provided they have enough resources to do so. This means that the wealthy can affect elections across the nation, which distorts responsiveness. Politicians at the federal level are supposed to represent their own constituents, but the removal of aggregate limits further threatens the likelihood that they will care about less wealthy residents in their home districts or states.

Do Voters Have a Right to Know Who Is Funding Campaign-Related Speech?

Several months after the *Citizens United* ruling, the DISCLOSE Act was introduced into the 111th Congress on April 29, 2010. The acronym "DISCLOSE" stands for "Democracy Is Strengthened by Casting Light on Spending in Elections." The main provisions of the bill would have required all 501(c) organizations to disclose the identities of any donors who contributed more than $1,000 during the year. There was also a "Stand by Your Ad" provision similar to that in BCRA, which would have required prominent individuals, such as CEOs and top donors of 501(c) organizations, to appear in advertisements to endorse the message. Also of concern was foreign money; the bill would have forbidden corporations with more than 20 percent foreign ownership from making independent expenditures in U.S. elections.[64] The bill passed in the House by a 219–206 vote two months after it was introduced but was killed in the Senate.[65] The bill has been reintroduced in either the House or the Senate nine times and has always been defeated on procedural grounds in the Senate.[66]

The primary rationale behind disclosure requirements in campaigns and elections has been **informational interest**.[67] Informational interest means that the public gains valuable knowledge when it knows about the sources of campaign funding. In *Buckley*, for example, the Court argued that the content of disclosure "allows voters to place each candidate in the political spectrum more precisely than is often possible solely on the basis of party labels and campaign speeches."[68] More specifically, advocates of transparency argue in favor of three functions: (1) to increase knowledge of who is speaking, (2) as a method of evaluating arguments more effectively, and (3) as a way to avoid voter confusion.[69] Current disclosure laws allow donors to remain hidden, making it difficult for voters to access truthful and useful information about the sources of speech.

Opponents of disclosure worry about new laws for several reasons: (1) individuals who donate money to nonprofits have a right to their privacy, (2) disclosure laws are a burden to free speech, and (3) the evidence does not demonstrate that disclosure laws result in a more informed electorate.

One argument against disclosure laws, particularly those individuals who donate to 501(c) organizations, is based on privacy. Part of this concern is based on the idea of balancing privacy rights against the public's right to transparent campaigns and elections. Additionally, these critics argue, individuals may be reluctant to donate to certain organizations for fear of retaliation. There is, then, a potential **chilling effect**, meaning that such regulation potentially dampens free speech by creating a reluctance to be willing to speak out, an argument the courts have used as a rationale against free speech regulation.[70]

Second, opponents argue that disclosure laws are unnecessarily burdensome because of the difficulties in navigating the laws.[71] Finally, critics of disclosure laws argue that the evidence in favor of the informational interest claim is weak.[72]

For now, the courts have upheld most disclosure laws,[73] and disclosure requirements appear to be "the lone area of campaign finance regulation that even the Roberts Court appears to support."[74] Justice Kennedy, in the *Citizens United*'s majority opinion, wrote that "a campaign finance system that pairs corporate independent expenditures with effective disclosure has not existed before today."[75] However, the effective disclosure of independent expenditures that Kennedy predicted has not come to fruition. In fact, given the rise in dark money in recent years, effective disclosure has decreased. As chapter 1 demonstrated, there are many loopholes around disclosure laws, and that is why dark money, despite the Court's apparent support for transparency and disclosure, has continued to rise. There is also no guarantee that disclosure laws will continue to hold up in the courts.

CONCLUSION

In this chapter, we explored several models of understanding and interpreting the significance of the First Amendment in the United States. The marketplace of ideas model, the self-governance model, and the liberty model were defined. Criticisms of each model also were considered. The different implications of these interpretations can affect both legislative and legal outcomes as they relate to campaign finance.

In the next section, we offered a brief outline to provide a historical picture of campaign finance laws, as well as the most significant legal challenges to those laws. We noted, as a result of a series of legal cases, that corruption has become narrowly defined as quid pro quo corruption and that the courts have not viewed donations and expenditures as having a corrupting influence in campaigns and elections.

After explaining those laws and court cases, we moved into a much more detailed consideration of the most important tensions between maintaining the integrity of a representative democracy while also attempting to remain true to the First Amendment. Shown throughout were the difficult but crucial balancing acts between sometimes conflicting goals. Four main questions were considered to tease out the implications of those tensions. Should corporations (and, if so, which types of corporations) be granted many of the same civil liberties as individual citizens? Does money equal speech, and if so under what circumstances and conditions? Where should the line be drawn on what counts as corruption versus legitimate attempts to influence candidates and elections? Finally, are disclosure and transparency laws justifiable in the context of political campaigns, or should privacy rights take precedence? This section considered the main legal issues as questions that reveal a spectrum of possibilities because, as history has shown, the pendulum can swing to the other side of any given issue quickly. Knowing the current laws is important, but equally important is understanding their underlying tensions. When democratic goals are contested, awareness of historical and political contexts is especially crucial.

KEY TERMS

aggregate contribution
   limits   40
balancing   41
Buckley v. Valeo   36
chilling effect   49
Citizens United v. FEC   39
*Colorado Republican Federal
   Campaign Committee v.
   FEC*   37
compelling state interest   47
electioneering
   communication   39
*FEC v. Wisconsin Right to
   Life, Inc.*   38
Federal Election Campaign
   Act   36
Free Press Clause   43
hard money   37
Hatch Act   35

informational interest   49
liberty model   33
magic words test   36
marketplace of ideas model   31
McCutcheon v. FEC   40
quid pro quo corruption   47
"reasonable person"
   standard   38
self-governance model   32
Smith-Connally Act   35
soft money   37
SpeechNow v. FEC   40
strict scrutiny   47
Taft-Hartley Act   35
Tillman Act   35
time, place, and manner
   restrictions   41
viewpoint discrimination   31

DISCUSSION QUESTIONS

1. What are the pros and cons of each of the models (marketplace of ideas, self-governance, liberty) of First Amendment interpretation?
2. Do you believe that groups (corporations, both for profit and non-profit, unions, etc.) should have the same First Amendment rights as individuals? Justify your answer.

3. How would you define "corruption"? Why do you agree or disagree with the current legal status on what qualifies as corruption? Explain your reasoning.
4. How should we balance free speech rights against individuals' other civil liberties, such as the right to privacy and the right to avoid being falsely accused?
5. Do you think politicians are more responsive to donors than their other constituents? What implications, if any, do you think this has in our political system?
6. Should the voting public have a right to know who is funding political activities and advertisements, or do you think the Supreme Court is correct when it argues that disclosure creates a "chilling effect" on free speech? Explain your reasoning.

ADDITIONAL READING

Dawood, Yasmin. "Classifying Corruption." *Duke Journal of Constitutional Law & Public Policy* 9, no. 4 (2014): 103–33.

Hasen, Richard. *Plutocrats United: Campaign Money, the Supreme Court, and the Distortion of American Elections*. New Haven, CT: Yale University Press, 2016.

Hellman, Deborah. "Liberty, Equality, Bribery, and Self-Government: Reframing the Campaign Finance Debate." In *Democracy by the People: Reforming Campaign Finance in America*, edited by Eugene D. Mazo and Timothy H. Kuhner, 58–73. Cambridge: Cambridge University Press, 2018.

Post, Robert C. *Citizens Divided: Campaign Finance Reform and the Constitution*. Cambridge, MA: Harvard University Press, 2014.

Smith, Bradley A. *Unfree Speech: The Folly of Campaign Finance Reform*. Princeton, NJ: Princeton University Press, 2003.

3

Donors, Expenditures, and Representation

★ ★ ★

THIS CHAPTER OFFERS AN OVERVIEW of the individual donors who support outside groups, how outside groups spend the money they receive, and what effects outside spending has in terms of representation and public policy. Whereas Super PACs principally have to disclose their donors, dark money groups—by definition—do not have to, seemingly making it a futile exercise to speculate about who may be behind the donations. However, in 2018, the watchdog organization Issue One created a public database that tracked dark money donors and recipients between 2010 and 2016, and another organization, Pro Publica, added additional data for 2016 through 2018. The Issue One database was made possible by voluntary disclosures of contributions by individuals and organizations to dark money groups. The sources for the database are many but include tax forms, Federal Election Commission (FEC) filings, corporate filings, press releases, and lobbying reports.

In terms of outside group spending, several questions arise regarding these expenditures: Is nearly all the money spent on advertising? What other activities are being funded by outside money? For dark money groups, we present original research to address these questions. Because political activity cannot be the primary purpose for nonprofit 501(c) groups, how do organizations that want to maximize their political involvement set up legal structures that allow them to stay within the limits of the law?

The last part of the chapter examines the normative concerns associated with the influx of outside spending. From the perspective of democratic governance, should the American people be worried about the effects of Super PAC and dark money spending? Is there concrete evidence that ordinary people's voices are being drowned out by outside groups? Are political decision makers in the post–*Citizens United* era more inclined to make public policy that pleases those who fund their campaigns? These questions are paramount for those striving to live in a republic where supreme power is held by the people.

DONORS

In the first chapter, we introduced the fact that outside groups receive strong financial support from megadonors. Who exactly are these individuals, what are their backgrounds, and what motivates them? Also, how concentrated is political giving? To answer these questions, *The New York Times* featured a series of articles that analyzed the political donors who contributed during the early phases of the 2016 presidential campaign. Almost half of all the **seed money**—the initial funds required to set up a political campaign—raised for Democratic and Republican candidates in the first half of 2015, $178 million, came from just 158 families, out of 125 million American households.[1] The vast majority of that money went to Super political action committees (PACs).[2] Most of these families are clustered around just nine cities, often live in the same neighborhood, and many are neighbors. More than fifty members of these families have made the Forbes 400 list of the country's top billionaires. When asked about this concentration of ultra-wealthy donors, Michael J. Malbin, executive director of the Campaign Finance Institute, said, "The question is whether we are in a new Gilded Age or well beyond it—to a Platinum Age."[3]

Megadonors share more characteristics than just wealth and geographic concentration. Megadonors are overwhelmingly white, older, and male in a country that, demographically, is rapidly changing. Beyond that, almost 42 percent (64 individuals and families) of the 153 biggest donors in 2015 were associated with just one industry: financial services. Many individuals who have managed other people's wealth have become owners of significant capital themselves. The financial managers who have become megadonors often formed their own hedge funds or started private equity and venture capital firms. The other most popular industries from which megadonors come are the following: energy and natural resources (17 individuals), real estate and construction (15), media and entertainment (12), health (10), technology (10), and transportation (9).[4]

The high concentration of donors with backgrounds related to finance, energy, and real estate suggests that many of them are focused on changes to the regulatory environment in which they operate. The fossil fuel industry, for example, has seen major regulatory **rollback**— actions to repeal or dismantle existing laws or regulations—in the past few years. Until the end of August 2019, the Trump administration had completed forty-nine rollbacks affecting the sector, while thirty-five were still in progress with an aggressive schedule to complete the process by the end of 2019. The Trump administration considered the rollback necessary to relieve fossil fuel companies from allegedly onerous rules that held companies back.[5]

Millions of dollars in contributions to outside groups by an individual is not much when the payoff for one's company is in the billions. Put differently, an average citizen can go to a roulette wheel in a casino and has almost a 50 percent chance to double his or her money (let us not forget the 0 plus the 00 in American roulette). A megadonor, on the other hand, may spend $5 million in hopes of seeing relief in regulatory burden worth somewhere between $2.5 to $10 billion. In other words, a megadonor could see a presidential election as a contest where the odds of winning are almost 50/50 for either side, but the payoff could be 1,000 or 2,000 times the original investment in terms of additional profits for one's company when the preferred candidate wins and relevant policy changes take place.

Another characteristic shared among the overwhelming number of megadonors is their desire to stay out of the spotlight: the group strives to protect its anonymity. *The New York Times* describes what most megadonors do to draw as little attention as possible:

> Very few of those contacted were willing to speak about their contributions or their political views. Many donations were made from business addresses or post office boxes, or wound through limited liability corporations or trusts, exploiting the new avenues opened up by *Citizens United*, which gave corporate entities far more leeway to spend money on behalf of candidates. Some contributors, for reasons of privacy or tax planning, are not listed as the owners of the homes where they live, further obscuring the family and social ties that bind them.[6]

Consequently, information about the specific motivations of megadonors is difficult to obtain. However, casino mogul Sheldon Adelson shared his primary motivations in a rare interview with *Politico* during Obama's presidency. First, Adelson said he is worried that liberal administrations and majorities will vilify him and damage his business. According to Adelson, there were accusations against his businesses that leaked from government employees under Obama. Second, he also wants to have political allies who agree with him on issues that he cares deeply about, such as the security and prosperity of Israel and the opposition to unions. Third, Adelson was offended when President Obama said that financiers receiving bailouts after the financial crisis of 2008 should not "go take a trip to Las Vegas . . . on the taxpayers' dime" because he believed Obama's statement hurt his casino businesses. Fourth, the coordination among outside groups makes his financial contributions more effective. Last, Adelson, son of a Boston cab driver and a seamstress, wants to empower small businesses, and he believes that giving to conservative groups and candidates is the best way to accomplish that.[7]

Peer-reviewed research has analyzed the ideological positions of the neighborhoods in which megadonors reside. One study found that on many political issues, megadonor neighborhoods "can be characterized as cosmopolitan and libertarian, rather than populist or moralistic."[8] The authors speculate that large donors may steer the national political agenda in unrepresentative directions.[9] Another study examined the percentage of contributions that went to extreme as opposed to more moderate candidates in Republican presidential primaries both before and after *Citizens United*. The author found that extreme candidates have benefited from their position taking and received additional contributions post–*Citizens United*.[10] Other research finds evidence that Republican candidates have benefited more from outside spending than have Democrats, leading to more conservative state legislatures.[11]

Yet another study—briefly mentioned in chapter 1—confirmed that extremism pays off for lawmakers. The study tracked the financial contributions California state legislators received during its many budget shutdowns. The results showed that elites increased their contributions to extremist legislators during times of crisis. This can be interpreted as an incentive for those legislators to extend political conflict and to delay or even refuse any compromise, a dangerous tactic not only for a state that requires a supermajority to pass the state budget but also for one that can stall many other decisions.[12]

Super PAC Donors

Between 2010 and 2018, the most noteworthy trend among known megadonors to Super PACs specifically has been the increasing importance of the donors at the apex of the pyramid, meaning the top five to top ten donors in each election. As stated in the first chapter, just eleven donors contributed more than $1 billion to Super PACs between 2010 and 2018. This means that this small group has contributed more than 20 percent of the $4.5 billion collected by Super PACs during that timeframe.[13]

The 2012 election cycle was the first full cycle in which Super PACs operated. The top one hundred individual donors represented 0.5 percent of all individual donors to Super PACs during that time but raised 67 percent of all Super PAC funds. Six years later, during the 2018 election cycle, the top one hundred individual donors shrank as a share of all individual donors to 0.08 percent but made up more than three-fourths (77.7 percent) of the money collected by Super PACs. Between 2010 and 2018, the top one hundred individual donors gave $2.15 billion to Super PACs, and some voluntarily disclosed dark money groups, roughly half of all individual contributions to these outside groups. That number breaks down almost perfectly between contributions given to Republicans (51.3 percent) and Democrats (48.7 percent).[14] Unsurprisingly, nearly all these larger donors contribute 100 percent of their money to Super PACs affiliated with only one political party. Among those individual donors who gave several million dollars per election cycle to outside groups, bipartisan support is almost nonexistent.[15] When David Donnelly, national campaigns director for the advocacy group Public Campaign Action Fund, was asked about Super PAC donors, he said this about the top one hundred contributors: "When you think about the amazing impact that this small number of people have on deciding the election, on the information that people will have on who to vote for, it's mind-boggling."[16]

Super PAC Recipients

In the first few years after *Citizens United*, Republican Super PACs dominated outside spending. However, in the 2013–14 election cycle, Democratic Super PAC spending caught up and, in fact, slightly exceeded (53.1 percent) spending by Republican Super PACs. Since then, the pendulum has swung back to Republicans but not dramatically, whereby conservative Super PACs have made up about 55 percent of overall Super PAC spending. In all but one election cycle (2012) until the end of 2016, between 77 and 82 percent of the donors behind the independent expenditures of Super PACs were fully disclosed, which means that, on average, roughly 20 percent of Super PAC funds comes from dark money groups and undisclosed, individual donors supporting these groups. In 2017–18, full disclosure of donors to Super PACs dropped significantly to only 51.9 percent, with almost half of all funds seeing only partial disclosure and, in some cases, no disclosure at all.[17]

Overall, outside spending confirms this trend toward partial disclosure. Figure 3.1 shows that in the last full election cycle prior to *Citizens United* (2007–08), only 3.1 percent of outside spending was partially disclosed, roughly one-third was undisclosed (30.1 percent), and approximately two-thirds (64.5 percent) was fully disclosed. For the most recent full election cycle (2017–18), outside spending disclosure breaks down this way: half of the money (49.9 percent) can be traced back to specific donors, 13.7 percent were not disclosed, and 36.3 percent of the spending came from a combination of disclosed and undisclosed donors. This confirms the recent trend among outside groups to partially disclose donors. In essence, more undisclosed funds from nonprofits, some other Super PACs, and **limited liability companies** (LLCs)—a corporate structure whereby the owners are not personally liable for the company's debts or liabilities—are being funneled to Super PACs who by law are required to disclose their donors.

The LLCs are often formed in Delaware and Wyoming where no individuals need to be associated with an LLC, which makes them popular for anonymous giving. At this point, one could argue that

Figure 3.1 Fluctuation of Outside Spending Disclosure since 2008 (including Super PACs)

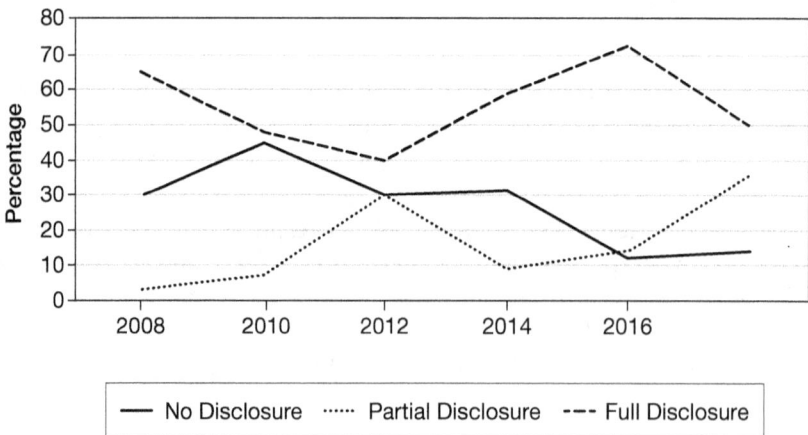

Super PACs enjoy a misleading degree of legitimacy and transparency at a time when the proportion of secret donations to them is increasing.[18]

The largest Super PACs of the post–*Citizens United* era can be categorized into two groups: those associated with the leadership of political parties (for a detailed analysis, see chapter 5) and single-candidate Super PACs, particularly for presidential and some U.S. Senate candidates. In 2016, the three largest single-candidate Super PACs were all supporting presidential candidates: Priorities USA Action (pro–Hillary Clinton; $133.4 million in independent expenditures), Right to Rise USA (pro–Jeb Bush; $86.6 million), and Conservative Solutions PAC (pro–Marco Rubio; $55.4 million). In the presidential race four years earlier, the largest Super PAC to date spent $142 million in independent expenditures in support of Mitt Romney, followed by the pro-Obama Priorities USA Action Super PAC, which spent $65.1 million. The largest Super PACs focused on U.S. Senate races between 2010 and 2018 were the New Republican PAC (supported Rick Scott, R-FL), Granite State Solutions (opposed Maggie Hassan, D-NH), and Put Alaska First (supported Mark Begich, D-AK).[19]

Dark Money Donors

The Washington, D.C.–based watchdog group Issue One describes itself as a leader of a cross-partisan movement wanting to reduce the influence of money in politics and to initiate reforms through increased transparency and accountability.[20] Issue One's research team has expanded the research done by other organizations such as the Center for Responsive Politics, the Center for Public Integrity, and the Center for Political Accountability to better understand who the donors are behind dark money organizations. To do so, Issue One analyzed many public records, such as tax forms, corporate filings, and lobbying reports, and some more obscure documents that are publicly available. That way, the organization identified close to four hundred unique donors who gave more than $400 million to dark money groups between 2010 and 2016.[21]

Here are some of the main findings from Issue One's report "Dark Money Illuminated":

- The Dow Chemical Company has contributed $13.5 million to the largest dark money organization in the United States, the U.S. Chamber of Commerce. Other significant Chamber of Commerce contributors are the health insurance company

Aetna Inc. ($5.3 million) and the energy company Chevron ($4.5 million).

- Firearm manufacturer Sturm, Ruger, & Co. has contributed $1.2 million to the National Rifle Association.
- The American Federation of Government Employees, the United Association of Journeymen and Apprentices of the Plumbing and Pipe Fitting Industry, and the American Federation of State, County and Municipal Employees have been significant union donors for the VoteVets Action Fund, a progressive 501(c)(4) organization. The VoteVets Action Fund is also an example of an organization that some voters may confuse as a conservative organization because of its pro-military focus, something that can be part of some organizations' strategy (see chapter 6).
- More than twenty-five trade associations, including the American Petroleum Institute, the Motion Picture Association of America, and Pharmaceutical Research and Manufacturers of America (PhRMA), have contributed to some of the largest dark money groups. PhRMA has contributed $12 million to the conservative American Action Network (AAN), making it the AAN's top donor.
- The Susan Thompson Buffett Foundation, primarily funded by investor Warren Buffett, has contributed $26 million to the Planned Parenthood Action Fund.[22]

A closer look at Issue One's database of dark money donors reveals that most large undisclosed donors to nonprofits are other 501(c) dark money groups themselves, not corporations or individuals. This still begs the question: who is funding these dark money groups? In the end, the money to fund these organizations must come from individuals or corporations, but we often do not know who they are. Instead, dark money groups sometimes send funds to like-minded nondisclosing groups, creating a maze of transactions that obscure the transparency of political giving.

There are other reasons for financial nonprofit-to-nonprofit transactions: when dark money groups make expenditures in the form of grants, then these grants are considered part of an organization's primary purpose budget. Substantial grantmaking can help politically active nonprofits reduce their **political spending**—nonprofit expenditures for express advocacy need to be kept under 50 percent total group expenditures—and thus comply with federal law. At the same time, grant recipients can then spend a portion of the donor's gift on political advocacy, and the recipient's budget increases, allowing it to disburse more money on political activity.[23]

Dark Money Recipients

Issue One has identified the fifteen largest dark money groups based on overall political spending by nonprofit organizations. Between 2010 and 2016, these fifteen organizations spent more than $600 million of the dark money out of $800 million in undisclosed expenditures. Put differently, the top fifteen dark money groups make up three-fourths of dark money spending, which speaks to a high concentration of political activity among very few nonprofits in the United States. The following nonprofits make up the top fifteen dark money groups between 2010 and 2016, from largest to smallest organization: U.S. Chamber of Commerce ($130 million for political activity), Crossroads Grassroots Policy Strategies (Crossroads GPS, $110 million), Americans for Prosperity [AFP], $59 million), National Rifle Association ($58 million), American Future Fund ($51 million), American Action Network ($44 million), League of Conservation Voters ($34 million), National Association of Realtors ($31 million), Americans for Job Security ($25 million), 45Committee ($21 million), Americans for Tax Reform ($20 million), Patriot Majority USA ($18 million), 60 Plus Association ($13 million), VoteVets Action Fund ($11 million), and Planned Parenthood Action Fund ($11 million).[24]

Because most citizens are unlikely to associate any individuals or political leanings with many of the organizations in this list, here are a few basic facts about some of the largest, but less well-known, nonprofits:

- Crossroads GPS was a conservative organization associated with political strategist Karl Rove; it is now defunct.
- AFP was set up by industrialists Charles and David Koch and originally helped organize the fiscally conservative Tea Party movement.
- The American Future Fund is associated with individuals who have worked for U.S. senator Mitt Romney (R). The organization promotes a "conservative and free market viewpoint."[25]
- The AAN is a conservative issue advocacy group that works closely with its sister organization, American Action Forum, which focuses on policy research. AAN's employees are connected to the Conservative Leadership Fund Super PAC.

- The League of Conservation Voters advocates for electing pro-environment candidates, almost all of whom are Democrats.
- Americans for Job Security is a pro-business league based in Virginia.
- 45Committee is a conservative nonprofit group that, according to *The New York Times*, is heavily funded by casino owner Sheldon Adelson.[26]
- Patriot Majority USA is a union-backed, liberal organization that claims to be nonpartisan fighting to "protect American freedom and economically empower all Americans."[27]

GROUP EXPENDITURES

This section examines how Super PACs and dark money groups spend their money. People often associate outside groups with TV ads, but how much of outside groups' budgets goes toward advertising, and what other activities do groups engage in? Data to answer this question are limited, so we conducted our own analysis for the top fifteen dark money groups discussed in the previous section.

Purpose of Super PAC Expenditures

An early study of Super PACs broke down all independent expenditures by Super PACs into fifteen categories. As expected, in 2012, Super PACs spent the vast majority of expenditures on communication activities. Specifically, 87 percent of nonparty independent expenditures went towards advertising (combining TV ads, online activity, radio, direct mail, and other advertising-related expenses). The remaining 13 percent were used for phone calls, field canvassing, wages, campaign materials, polling, travel, and more.[28] No recent systematic analyses of overall Super PAC activities are available to our knowledge, and therefore we are unable to go into more depth here. However, we would expect to find a less lopsided breakdown of Super PAC efforts in recent years and increases in spending with respect to canvassing, events, and travel. The widening scope of Super PAC activities is discussed in chapters 4 and 5.

Ideological Breakdown of Dark Money Spending

For dark money groups, we conducted our own analyses for the fifteen largest organizations between 2010 and 2016 to better understand how more than 50 percent of the dark money groups' activities do *not* constitute political spending, as required by law. Before we present

Figure 3.2 Ideological Breakdown of Dark Money Spending, 2010–18

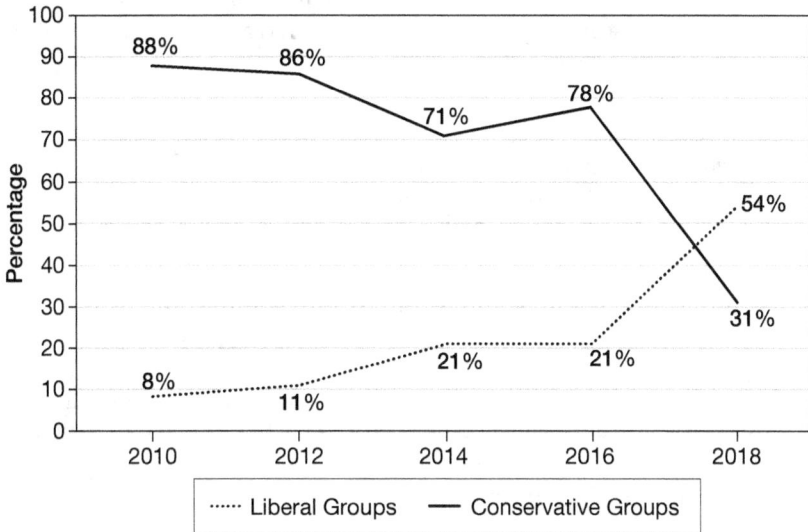

the results, however, we will briefly draw attention to a recent development regarding the ideological leanings of dark money groups and explain the legal context in which nonprofits operate. The previous section explained who the largest politically active nonprofit groups were through 2016, and most of them were conservative. Yet, more recently, liberal groups outspent conservative groups for the first time since *Citizens United*. For the 2017–18 election cycle, liberal groups spent 54 percent of all dark money; conservative groups, 31 percent; and the remaining 15 percent could not be categorized one way or another (figure 3.2). This means that organizations affiliated with both major parties do not shy away from spending money coming from donors who are not publicly disclosed. Overall, contributions to 501(c)(4) organizations totaled more than $1 billion between 2010 and 2018. Additionally, between 2016 and 2018, another $1 billion was spent by partially disclosing groups that are funded by dark money sources or keep some donors hidden.[29]

Political Activity versus Social Welfare

To maintain their status as social welfare organizations, politically active nonprofits have to carefully consider what counts as political activity and what does *not* count. The regularly updated guide *The*

Connection is a valuable resource for nonprofits that explains and summarizes all Internal Revenue Service (IRS) rules as they relate to political activity for nonprofits. The main activities that nonprofits engage in that count as political are

> endorsements of a candidate; publication or distribution of statements in favor of or in opposition to a candidate; direct financial contributions or other support to a candidate, political party, or PAC (other than a ballot measure committee); in-kind contributions to a candidate, political party, or PAC (other than a ballot measure PAC) including, but not limited to: mailing, membership, or donor lists or other resources for fundraising, provision of facilities or office space, staff time, polling results, organizing volunteers for the campaign, opposition research, comparative ratings of candidates, publicizing names of political candidates who support or oppose the organization's position on public issues; membership communications expressly advocating the election or defeat of a candidate; and payment of the administrative and fundraising costs of a political organization.[30]

An important phrase in the preceding list is "membership communications expressly advocating the election or defeat of a candidate" because so much of the dark money is used for political ads. What then are election-related activities that are *not* considered political activities if they are conducted in a nonpartisan manner? Various activities dealing with voter education and engagement activity fall under that umbrella, ranging from issue education, get-out-the-vote drives, and candidate questionnaires and debates to voter registration, provided they are conducted in a nonpartisan fashion. Workshops, publications, and seminars that encourage greater participation in government and politics or campaign practices are also considered nonpolitical activities if they do not explicitly support or oppose a candidate or party.[31] All of the previously mentioned activities are considered issue advocacy and therefore contribute to the social welfare mission of nonprofits.

In addition, some other forms of communication may not be considered political activity. Specifically, communication that identifies specific legislation that the organization hopes to influence is considered nonpolitical. There are also election-related activities that are not considered political, for example, when the communication identifies a candidate solely as a government official who acts on a public policy issue in connection with a specific event. Also, when the communication identifies a candidate solely in a list of key cosponsors of some legislation and if that legislation is the communication's focus, then it does not count as political communication.[32]

The IRS provides a list of factors that tend to indicate that communication from a nonprofit constitutes express advocacy and therefore counts as political activity. Such factors include targeting voters, identifying a candidate for public office and their political position, and not sending out "an ongoing series of substantially similar advocacy communications." However, terms such as *ongoing series* and *substantially similar* are not further defined and can create confusion.[33]

The IRS also allows for a "reasonable person" to judge whether advocacy is either political or nonpolitical, which adds to the ambiguity. Perhaps most problematic is that many forms of communication can reasonably entail elements of both issue advocacy and express advocacy. How should one "political" element of a communication piece be weighed against three or four "nonpolitical" elements because the IRS states that the mere presence of a single factor is not determinative, but the "facts and circumstances" of the activity as a whole are. Classifying all communication as political or nonpolitical for justifying one's 501(c)(4) or 501(c)(6) status is murky and could be based on assumptions disconnected from real-world politics.

To illustrate the claim that efforts to distinguish between express advocacy and issue advocacy may be futile, think of an ad that criticizes a representative for being weak on border security and asks viewers to call the representative's office to complain about his or her policy position. The ad is not using language such as "vote against representative X," but the message is clear, and the average citizen will not notice a meaningful difference between this issue ad and an express advocacy ad while watching TV. For example, the nonprofit group Carolina Rising aired a series of issue ads worth $4.7 million in 2014, criticizing then Speaker of the House Thom Tillis. Because all the ads avoided the magic words and also mentioned policy issues, it reported to the IRS that it had not engaged in any "direct or indirect political campaign activities on behalf of or in opposition to candidates for public office."[34] *The New York Times* called this type of accounting "a new low in campaign finance."[35]

Any discussion of issue advocacy and express advocacy should be placed in the context of what is means to promote social welfare. Organizations that promote social welfare should primarily promote the common good and general welfare of the people in a community as a whole. An organization that primarily benefits a private group of citizens cannot qualify for 501(c)(4) tax-exempt status.[36] In the case of Carolina Rising and other organizations that are operating similarly, one has to ask whether these organizations fulfill this criterion. It seems that certain groups are exclusively or at least primarily acting only on behalf of certain interests in society, political leaders, and ideologically resolute voters, in particular, something the author of *The New York Times* opinion piece also noted. It may be time to think about better guidelines as to how nonprofits need to fulfill their mission so that they truly serve the general welfare of the people.

Nonprofits' Political Spending and Activities

Based on Schedule C of the self-reported annual IRS Form 990, political spending for the largest nonprofits between 2010 and 2016 averaged from 47 percent for 45Committee to 2 percent for the National Rifle Association. Aside from 45Committee, the organizations reporting to spend over 30 percent of their budgets on political activities are: American Future Fund (with an average of 39 percent for the seven-year period), Patriot Majority USA (38 percent), Crossroads GPS (34 percent), AAN (32 percent), Americans for Job Security (31 percent), and the League of Conservation Voters (31 percent). The U.S. Chamber of Commerce, as the largest group, spends an average of 13 percent of its budget on political activities.[37]

Next, we will take a closer look at the 990s to better understand the specific activities dark money organizations engage in, both political and non-political. The 990s requires 501(c) organizations to report more detailed information about its political expenditures. The analysis consists of recording all general revenue as well as all general and functional expense categories for each organization between 2010 and 2017 where the 990s were available. CitizenAudit.Org, GuideStar.org and *ProPublica*'s Nonprofit Explorer served as our sources. We then coded all the descriptions that the organizations provided each year, explaining the mission and kinds of activities each organization said it was involved in. The IRS does not provide a list of activities. Instead, our coding is based on the self-description of each organization's mission and activities. A list of thirteen activities was compiled, and each time an organization said it would engage in one of the thirteen activities, it was coded as a "1," and when said activity was not listed for a specific year, it was coded as a "0."

Overall, the missions and activities can be categorized into three types of activities: advocacy (both issue and express advocacy), legislative work, and activities related to policy research and events. Some activity related to advocacy was reported by 93.3 percent. The only organization that does not engage in advocacy-related activities is the National Association of Realtors, which directly transfers funds to groups it supports. Issue advocacy is the most popular type of advocacy groups report (86.7 percent of groups report that they engage in it). The most commonly used phrases in the 990s that capture issue advocacy are nonprofits' efforts to "educate the public" and "raise public awareness" of policy issues.

Two-thirds of groups report that they create or buy TV ads, and 60 percent of groups say they send out mailings or emails. Of these groups, 40 percent work on legislative proposals and suggestions for how to change existing regulations or offer proposals for new budgetary priorities. The rest of the politically oriented nonprofit activities can be categorized as research and event-related activities. Six groups highlight time dedicated to events and meetings, and five groups discuss their research on policy issues. Overall, none of this seems too surprising, yet the public's and media's focus is usually only on the TV ads and sometimes traditional mailings, not on other types of political nonprofit activities (table 3.1).

Table 3.1   Activities of Top Fifteen Dark Money Groups as Reported to the IRS, 2010–17

	Groups Reporting Activity (%)	Popularity
Advocacy (93.3% of groups)		
Issue Advocacy/Educate the Public	86.7	1
TV Ads	66.7	2
Mailings/Emails/Radio	60	3
Web-based Advocacy	33.3	6
Candidate Advocacy	53.3	4
Legislative Activities (40% of groups)		
Legislative Proposals	33.3	6
Propose Budget Priorities	6.7	13
Work on Regulations	26.7	9
Own Research/Events (46.7%)		
Public Hearings	13.3	10
Policy Research	33.3	6
Investigations	13.3	10
Events/Meetings	40	5
Polling	13.3	10

Source: 990 tax forms from CitizenAudit.Org, GuideStar.org, Nonprofit Explorer by *ProPublica*.

In terms of revenue, twelve of the fifteen organizations almost exclusively (97.5 percent) depend on contributions from individuals and other organizations. The remaining revenue comes from program service (0.08 percent), investment income (2.1 percent), and other revenue (0.3 percent). This breakdown of group revenue is very different for the three membership organizations among the top fifteen, the National Association of Realtors, the National Rifle Association, and the business league Americans for Job Security. They rely heavily on program service (making up 80.5 percent of revenue, including membership fees and grants from other groups), whereas contributions, investment income, and other revenue make up the remaining 19.5 percent.

For general expenditures, there is no reason to separate membership and nonmembership groups. On average, groups spent 6.3 percent of their total expenditures on grants, with substantial variation among the groups (ranging from 0.02 percent to 34.2 percent). Grants can include contributions to other nonprofits that may be used for political spending. Dark money groups routinely claim that the money they transfer to other 501(c)(4)s is for "program support" of other organizations because this is one way for them to fulfill their social-welfare obligation.[38] Salaries make up a little more than 21 percent of total expenditures for the average group. The outliers here are those groups that do not report *any* expenses on salaries, 45Committee and the American Future Fund. How these organizations spend millions of dollars on political activities yet operate without payment of any salaries is unclear. 45Committee is currently being sued by the Campaign Legal Center (CLC) for alleged violations of its 501(c)(4) status, and other prominent organizations (e.g., Crossroads GPS and Americans for Job Security) are also currently involved in legal disputes because of alleged campaign finance violations. On average, fundraising expenditures constitute almost 6 percent of expenses (table 3.2).

A closer examination of the groups' functional expenses reveals that, on average, groups spend more than a third of their total budget (37.6 percent) on the compensation of officers, salaries, employee benefits, and payroll taxes. Lobbying expenditures make up 6.6 percent of expenditures for the fifteen dark money groups. The IRS documents do not break down political versus nonpolitical lobbying, and it is therefore possible that the majority of the lobbying officially relates to specific legislation, which, in turn, can be considered nonpolitical by the groups themselves and the IRS. Office-related expenses

Table 3.2   Sources of Revenue and Expenditures for Top Fifteen
Dark Money Groups, 2010–17

	Average per Year (%)	Three Membership Organizations (%)*
Revenue Source		
Contributions/Grants	97.52	10.61
Program Service	0.08	80.51
Investment Income	2.13	1.57
Other	0.27	7.31
Total	100.00	100.00
Expenses		
Grants Paid	6.33	
Salaries	21.19	
Fundraising	5.83	
Other Expenses	66.65	
Total	100.00	

* National Association of Realtors, National Rifle Association, Americans for Job Security.
Source: 990 tax forms from CitizenAudit.Org, GuideStar.org, Nonprofit Explorer by *ProPublica.*

(supplies, telephone, postage and delivery, equipment rental, bank and credit card fees, printing, etc.) make up 8.5 percent of expenses; travel, 5.7 percent; information technology (hardware, software, tech support services, website design, security, etc.), 5.3 percent; and conferences, 5 percent.

Advertising and promotion, the key category in terms of political engagement, accounts for a fourth of all spending (25.2 percent; table 3.3). This includes amounts paid for electronic and print media, signage, and payments to independent contractors for advertising. Of course, there is a great deal of variation across organizations. For example, in 2012, The American Future Fund spent almost 91 percent of its expenditures on advertising and promotion. That shows how a lot of these expenditures must have been categorized as nonpolitical spending, that is, funds dedicated to issue advocacy.

Implications of Findings

Overall, the results we present for dark money groups show that for some organizations, spending more than 50 percent on expenditures that are explicitly political, as the term is currently defined, might be

Table 3.3   Functional Expenses for Top Fifteen Dark Money Groups, 2010–17 (percentages)

Compensation of Officers	5.37
Other Salaries/Wages	27.59
Other Employee Benefits	2.68
Payroll Taxes	1.96
Management	0.42
Legal	2.37
Accounting	0.31
Lobbying	6.65
Fundraising Services	2.10
Investment Management Fees	0.09
Advertising and Promotion	25.27
Office Expenses	6.11
Information Technology	5.33
Occupancy	2.46
Travel	5.74
Payments for Travel/Entertainment	0.01
Conferences	4.99
Insurance	0.55
Total	100

Source: 990 tax forms from CitizenAudit.Org, GuideStar.org, Nonprofit Explorer by ProPublica.

challenging. Staff, office, and information technology expenditures, as well as expenditures on travel and conferences, do not count as political spending. Some lobbying activities and advertising activities that merely educate the public are also nonpolitical, according to current definitions. An ad that encourages either support for or opposition to a candidate's views or actions may sound like this: "Congressman Smith does not support the Second Amendment and the rights of law-abiding citizens. Call him and tell him that it's time to preserve your freedom." Should that ad count as a political expenditure? Many citizens probably believe that it would be considered political in nature, but some groups claim it as purely educational, whereas others more cautiously operating nonprofits report it as "political spending."

In 2018, a federal district court in Washington, D.C., ruled that *all* "electioneering communications" should presumptively count as political spending and groups that engage in these communications should register as political action committees.[39] Should this ruling, which is currently being challenged, hold up in federal courts, then it would end discussions over issue versus express advocacy ads. Prior to the lawsuit, the FEC reached a deadlocked 3–3 decision on this complaint, as is common for the FEC. Since then, the case is waiting for a hearing and decision by the U.S. Court of Appeals.[40]

The IRS has shied away from scrutinizing dark money groups too closely after public protests relating to the treatment of conservative dark money groups erupted in 2013. That year, the IRS was alleged to have unfairly targeted 250 Tea Party organizations and other conservative nonprofit groups that had claimed tax-exempt status. This created a widely publicized outrage among Republicans and conservative media outlets. Angry voices argued that the IRS had targeted these groups because of their names, which supposedly suggested that they would be political opponents of the Obama administration. Four years later, in 2017, the Treasury's Department's Inspector General for Tax Administration made the case that the IRS had also singled out nearly 150 organizations whose names suggested they were affiliated with liberal organizations.[41]

By then, the damage was long done. The effort to investigate these four hundred organizations may have been the result of pressure by nonprofit organizations, such as the CLC, which had argued prior to the scandal that dark money organizations had been "operating essentially as unregulated committees" and that the IRS was shirking its responsibilities.[42] Since the scandal broke, the IRS has been timid to question the status of dark money groups, and only a tiny number of cases have been investigated. In fact, since 2016, the IRS has not been allowed to issue new rules on political activity that would enable them to regulate the status of nonprofit organizations.[43]

Chapter 7 discusses general ideas for campaign finance reform. For nonprofits specifically, some have suggested that fines should be increased for dark money groups that engage in unethical behavior. That way, more "bad apples" among dark money groups would be deterred from violating federal law. As shown earlier, enforcement by the FEC and IRS is an issue, but even when more serious fines are issued, they may not have the intended effect. For example, when the California Fair Political Practices Commission announced a record $1 million in fines against two organizations, the Center to Protect Patient Rights and Americans for Responsible Leadership in 2013, it was quickly paid with a cashier's check without declaring a source.[44]

At the state level, Montana has pushed for more transparency of dark money spending. Governor Bullock signed an executive order in

2018 that requires groups that receive state government contracts for goods more than $50,000 and new service contracts over $25,000 to disclose their donations if the organization or company spent more than $2,500 in elections during the past two years.[45] This is a sign that states are willing to take initiative if the FEC, IRS, and federal courts are hesitant to take action. However, the key issue raised by our research is that a lot of standard expenditures for groups do not count as political expenditures. Staying below the 50 percent threshold for political expenditures is an expectation that is easy to meet to qualify and keep the status as a dark money group.

"SO WHAT?" EFFECTS ON CANDIDATES AND REPRESENTATION

Now that you have heard about outside group donors and recipients, and what these groups spend their money on, you may ask yourself, "So what; why should I care?" Does all of this have any effect on the candidates running for public office, election outcomes, actual legislation, and the representation of the average voter? Later chapters will offer some answers to these questions, but we can begin to highlight some findings and concerns here.

According to Issue One founder and CEO Nick Penniman, "When outside groups are spending more than candidates are on their own campaigns, we're in the danger zone."[46] He argues that the influx of campaign funds by outside groups comes with a spike in negative advertising. Penniman believes that an avalanche of negativity means that fewer people will run for political office, effective leaders will retire early, and those who decide to run for reelection will often spend too much of their time raising money instead of working on legislation. If those concerns are accurate, then everyone should be worried about the negative consequences for American democracy. That is why Penniman argues that "this startling development should worry Democrats, Republicans, and independents alike."[47]

Are some outside groups really outspending candidates? When outside groups gained prominence in 2010, they outspent federal candidates in twelve federal races, not counting expenditures by party committees. In 2018, that number had grown to twenty-eight, again without including party expenditures.[48] What worries some people is that when outside groups outspend the candidates, then candidates may lose the power to control their campaign's message and the issues and facts that voters should care about when casting their ballot.[49]

We have now had decades of research on the effects of **negative campaigning**—the process of deliberately spreading negative information about your political opponent to damage his or her public image—and even though the evidence about the effectiveness of this strategy is mixed, campaign consultants still believe that portraying your opponent in an unfavorable light is usually better than lifting up your own candidate. So even if candidates want to run a campaign with a positive message, they *can* be drowned out by relentless negativity from the outside, not to mention that negative ads are generally considered more memorable compared to positive ones.

Whether outside groups can influence election outcomes is something we discuss in chapter 6; here, we concentrate on other consequences Super PACs and dark money groups may bring about. In terms of what the effects on legislation are, we briefly talked about the Tax Cuts and Jobs Act of 2017 in the first chapter and the surprising candidness legislators expressed about the pressure they were facing from donors who had helped them to get into or stay in office prior to casting their votes. Interestingly enough, not only were members of Congress outspoken that they did not have much of a choice to pass this major piece of legislation, but so, too, were several Republican donors. For instance, five months prior to becoming law, Republican donor Doug Deason refused to hold fundraisers for Republican candidates and publicly announced that the "Dallas piggy bank" would be closed until the tax reform would be passed. "Get it done and we'll open it back up," Deason said. Deason stood by his word and started to make new financial contributions less than two months after the tax cuts became law.[50]

The pressure from donors to pass tax reform was clearly conveyed not only in closed-door meetings and public statements but also via a large-scale advertising campaign. Two months before the bill became law, dark money groups such as 45Committee, AAN, America First, AFP, and Freedom Partners decided they would run a massive advertising campaign in favor of the law. They were willing to spend at least $43 million in pro–tax reform ads.[51] Despite this tremendous effort to sell the benefits of the tax reform, only 29 percent of Americans had a favorable opinion of the tax cuts at the time of their passage.[52] Some might consider this a story of remarkable attitudinal persistence by the American people because their opinions could hardly be influenced despite extensive public relations efforts.

Groups such as AFP certainly have policy goals beyond tax reform. In 2010, AFP supported legislators financially who successfully fought against a cap-and-trade proposal to reduce carbon emissions put forth by the Obama administration.[53] Also, since its formation, AFP has successfully fought against several attempts to increase the federal minimum wage, both directly via advertising and indirectly by supporting opponents of this idea.[54] Yet megadonors' most powerful direct impact comes in the form of having their "own" representatives control the levers of power. An example of this could be seen in late 2018 when the Trump administration put a former Koch Industries official in charge of research at the Environmental Protection Agency that will decide how the federal government will regulate toxic chemicals that have contaminated millions of Americans' drinking water. These toxic chemicals have been linked to kidney and testicular cancer as well as other illnesses. Resolving this issue could have a serious financial impact on Koch Industries.[55]

The preceding example illustrates the concern that government agencies have the power to advance the interests of an industry or political groups at the expense of prioritizing the interests of the public. When this is, in fact, taking place, this is called **regulatory capture**. When money buys not only *a* seat at the table but also the seat at the *head* of the table, then one can understand fears that conflicts of interest may tilt public policy decisions away from the public interest.

In 2019, we saw another extraordinary example of how dark money groups put pressure on legislators to vote a certain way. In late July, Doctor Patient Unity, a new dark money group without any publicly known donors, started a multimillion-dollar ad campaign, urging vulnerable U.S. senators to reject a proposal intended to cut down on surprise medical bills that are sometimes so high that they lead to private bankruptcies. The Lower Health Care Costs Act would pose a limit on the amount of money health care providers can charge some out-of-network patients when a physician or hospital does not have a contract with the patient's insurer.[56] The ads make the case that a vote for this bill is a vote for the insurance industry, not for patients, and that passage of the bill would result in a doctors' shortage and hospital closures.[57]

These ads were aimed at no less than eleven senators, all of whom are expected to be mired in tough reelection campaigns in 2020. The chances that the bill will become law are considered high, and both Republicans and Democrats were targeted in the TV, digital, and radio ad campaign, even though it is mostly going after Republicans. What this shows is that nonprofits are willing to go after *both* parties if they see their financial interests threatened. Travis Ridout, professor at

Washington State University and co-director of the Wesleyan Media Project, agrees that Doctor Patient Unity is willing to run ads against candidates "if they don't vote in the correct way on this legislation."[58]

There are many legal and ethical issues related to **pay-to-play politics**, situations where individuals or companies make campaign contributions to officeholders or political candidates for public office in the hope of benefiting from legislative and contracting decisions, being appointed to administrative positions, and other favors. Super PACs and dark money groups have further complicated these problems. For example, in 2012, Chevron Corp. made a $2.5 million contribution to the conservative Congressional Leadership Fund (CLF) Super PAC, the largest contribution from a publicly traded corporation to a political group until then.[59] A year later, the consumer advocacy group Public Citizen filed a complaint against Chevron, arguing that the company had violated the Hatch Act, which, among other things, prohibits federal contractors from making campaign contributions. Since Chevron was a public contractor, the violation appeared to be clear.[60] However, the FEC ruled that Chevron's contribution was legal. How come?

It turns out that Chevron U.S.A. is the company that received government contracts, but Chevron Corporation, a different entity, donated to the CLF. Therefore, the FEC did not see any legal violation. Nonetheless, the situation is less obvious when one looks beyond the surface and thinks about the larger implication of this ruling. Chevron U.S.A. is a subsidiary of Chevron Corporation, and Chevron Corporation owns a 100 percent stake in Chevron U.S.A. The same CEO is in charge of both companies, the same mailing address is listed for both corporations, and Chevron Corporation receives the profits that its subsidiary generates. A broader concern could be that others will follow a model after which companies are broken up into two or more units for the purpose of making significant political contributions before or after important contracting decisions are made but where everyone knows where the money is "truly" coming from. "That sort of artificial division of the families of one corporation could cause widespread evasion of federal pay-to-play laws," Craig Holman, government affairs lobbyist at Public Citizen, said about the case.[61]

Another related trend in recent years has been the use by individuals to use **shell corporations** (shell companies)—which exist only on paper without an office and employees, and also without significant business activity—to transfer funds to political organizations. For example, in 2019, real estate developer Stephen Rosenberg created the company SR 2018 LLC, which was then listed as a six-figure donor to the Trump Victory Committee, a joint fundraising group that divides up funds between the Trump campaign and the Republican National Committee. SR 2018 LLC did not report any other business activity until the donation was made.[62] "Disclosure of who is spending money in elections is a vital component of our campaign finance system, but transparency is undermined when a wealthy donor launders their contribution through a shell company," Brendan Fischer, director of the CLC, commented on this trend.[63]

Sometimes concerns arise not over business inactivity of LLCs but over their direct connections to the official campaigns of political candidates. For instance, Trump's campaign manager for the 2020 reelection campaign, Brad Parscale, owns a Delaware-based company, Red State Data and Digital, an LLC with a P.O. box address listed in Washington, D.C. According to FEC records, Red State has received $910,000 from America First Action, the president's official Super PAC. Red State is not allowed to coordinate its activities with the Trump campaign, and Parscale has stated that there "is a perfectly legal and appropriate arrangement, which is firewalled, with zero chance for coordination. . . . Everything is in FEC compliance."[64] Yet, some remain concerned about strategic coordination. "That's why dark money is so dangerous. No one knows what's going on," Fred Wertheimer, president of Democracy 21, a nonprofit organization, said.[65]

Regarding representation, we established earlier in the chapter that megadonors are not representative of the American public at large, neither demographically, ideologically, nor geographically. Is this a problem? The answer depends on who you ask. For some, the funding source is irrelevant. When Jim Bopp, the attorney behind *Citizens United*, was asked whether it matters who is funding outside groups, he responded, "I actually think that the truth doesn't change based on who's funding it. John Gregg is either a pro-life [candidate] or not. What difference does it make who's funding that? The truth doesn't change." Bopp went on to say that voters generally do not care about who is funding campaigns and that disclosure of campaign contributions is completely irrelevant information that only "some left-wing nut jobs" care about.[66] Others express concerns or have found problematic consequences related to representation and trust in institutions, which is examined next.

One consequence related to megadonors and unlimited independent expenditures comes down to seeing more negative public perceptions of institutions, particularly Congress. One study finds that dissatisfaction with representation and disapproval of Congress is a consequence of public perceptions about the improper influence of large, unlimited independent expenditures.

Citizens who are most knowledgeable about Congress are significantly more likely to find unlimited independent spending to be distressing. The authors of said study note that Justice Kennedy's claim in *Citizens United* that "independent expenditures do not lead to, or create the appearance of, *quid pro quo* corruption" are fundamentally wrong in light of the "widespread suspicion" *Citizens United* has created, whereby the American public paints Congress in a bad light.[67]

Other research suggests that the party affiliation of members of Congress can predict how they will represent different income levels in their districts. Specifically, one study finds that individuals with Republican representatives experience an "oligarchic" mode of representation, in which wealthy individuals receive much more representation than those lower on the economic ladder. This is measured by the proportion of bills on which respondents in each income percentile take on the same position as their representatives. In contrast, individuals with Democratic representatives encounter a mode of representation that can be described as "populist," where individuals with the lowest incomes see the best alignment between their positions and those taken by their representatives.[68]

Another study also examined how close legislators' views align ideologically with district constituents and analyzed whether increasing campaign contributions from individuals who reside outside the districts has affected members of Congress' responsiveness. Baker found that legislators who increasingly rely on outside money have progressively become *less* responsive to their constituents. At the same time, outside contributions are associated with a rise in ideological extremism. In sum, outside donors are able to buy additional representation in districts where they do not reside, at the expense of constituents.[69] This is precisely why we speak of outside groups as game changers; they are not only able to influence election outcomes but there is solid evidence that public policy and the representation of constituents are also affected by outside money.

CONCLUSION

Megadonors have a lot in common: professionally, demographically, geographically, and ideologically. More than half of them come from only two sectors of the economy (finance and energy); most are white, male, and older; many of them live in the same neighborhoods of a few large cities; and almost all of them do not want to publicly talk about their political activity. The high concentration of donors coming from the financial and energy sector indicates that regulatory policy goals seem to be of great importance to those willing to spend a great deal of personal resources on political campaigns. Moreover, megadonors are ideologically more extreme compared to the average American. This means the donor class prefers ideological purity over political compromise.

Large individual contributions flow to Super PACs and dark money groups, and these organizations spend the money themselves, or as it is increasingly common, they transfer money across organizations. This makes seemingly financially transparent organizations such as Super PACs less transparent with a higher share of partial disclosure of donors. At the same time, outside groups used to dedicate almost all of their resources toward advertising, especially negative ads targeting political opponents. This is changing as outside group activities have expanded. Our research shows that almost half of all dark money groups engage in both legislative activities (e.g., work on legislative proposals) and conduct their own research or organize political events. Because of nonprofits' expenditures for salaries, offices, information technology, conferences, and more, for most groups, complying with federal law is easy. These expenditures do not count as political activities, even if they may all be related to a political mission.

People have different views on whether the public should have a right to know who the funding sources behind political messages are. For some, this issue is irrelevant because they believe only the content of messages matter. Others are concerned about legislators caving in to the pressure of campaign donors to adopt favorable legislation, people's willingness to run for public office in a highly negative campaign environment, the time legislators need to dedicate to fundraising, and the ability for candidates to get their messages out as opposed to outside groups. Not all nonprofit organizations demanding dark money transparency from other nonprofits are transparent themselves though. The Center for Public Integrity found twenty-one such groups that did not fully disclose their donors.[70] Finally, some scholars have found negative perceptions of Congress related to large campaign donations, new legal loopholes that could open up new paths for influencing political decision making, the ability to buy more representation as members of the donor class, and more extreme position taking among legislators, all as a result of the *Citizens United* and *SpeechNow* decisions.

KEY TERMS

limited liability company   58
negative campaigning   73
pay-to-play politics   75
political spending   60

regulatory capture   74
rollback   55
seed money   54
shell corporation   75

DISCUSSION QUESTIONS

1. Is there reason for concern if megadonors are different from most citizens with regard to their demographics and political ideology? Why do you think certain professional backgrounds, such as finance and energy, are so common among megadonors?
2. Political spending has to make up less than 50 percent of expenditures for nonprofits. This chapter has shown that meeting this threshold is relatively easy for groups. How much political activity should nonprofits be allowed to engage in before they should lose their status as tax-exempt nonprofit organizations, and how should political activity be defined?
3. Do you believe fewer people are running for public office as political campaigns have become more negative in the post–*Citizens United* era? Explain your reasoning.
4. A majority of the American public believes that independent expenditures corrupt politicians or at least give the appearance thereof. Do you agree or disagree? Can you think of specific evidence or examples to support your point of view?
5. One study found that donors who do not reside in the districts where their money is used are able to buy additional representation for citizens with higher incomes. What kind of policies could this affect?
6. Can the American political system still function when legislators are being rewarded for taking on extreme positions? Or does this mean American politics is seriously broken? Explain your reasoning.

ADDITIONAL READING

Baker, Anne E. "Getting Short-Changed? The Impact of Outside Money on District Representation." *Social Science Quarterly* 97, no. 5 (November 2016): 1096–107.

Bramlett, Brittany H., James G. Gimpel, and Frances E. Lee. "The Political Ecology of Opinion in Big-Donor Neighborhoods." *Political Behavior* 33, no. 4 (December 2011): 565–600.

Donovan, Todd, and Shaun Bowler. "To Know It Is to Loath It: Perceptions of Campaign Finance and Attitudes About Congress." *American Politics Research* 47, no. 5 (2019): 951–69.

Miler, Kristina C. *Poor Representation: Congress and the Politics of Poverty in the United States*. Cambridge, United Kingdom: Cambridge University Press, 2018.

Oklobdzija, Stan. "Closing Down and Cashing In: Extremism and Political Fundraising." *State Politics & Policy Quarterly* 17, no. 2 (June 2017): 201–24.

Rhodes, Jesse H., and Brian F. Schaffner. "Economic Biases in Representation: Using New Data to Shed Light on How Wealth Affects Access to Political Representation." February 2014. http://dx.doi.org/10.2139/ssrn.2561423

4

New Trends in
Presidential Campaigns

★ ★ ★

IN 2010, WITHIN TWO MONTHS AFTER the first Super political action committees (PACs) were created, former chairman of the Federal Election Commission (FEC) Trevor Potter was asked about the new role that Super PACs would play in American politics. According to Potter, Super PACs "opened the door to the clearest, easiest way to spend unlimited funds on an election. . . . This is pretty much the holy grail people have been looking for."[1] Presidential elections provide a high-profile venue to see how this "holy grail" of electoral influence is used. This chapter first examines the relationship among presidential candidates, their respective party, and outside groups, specifically Super PACs, in the context of the 2020 presidential election. Then several new trends that are largely the result of the *Citizens United* and *SpeechNow* cases and unique to presidential campaigns are examined. We have seen a host of changes to presidential campaigns in the past ten years:

- The recent movement in the Democratic Party to purify its brand by disavowing Super PACs associated with a single candidate
- Some presidential candidates delaying their official announcements to run for president
- Candidates moving staff back and forth between the candidate's campaign and the outside campaign
- The financial strength of outside groups in presidential primaries
- The increasing use of leadership PACs and joint fundraising committees by candidates to set up presidential runs

- The expansion of outside group activities
- The way Super PACs challenge incumbent presidents during the primaries
- The current dilemma for Republicans wherein outside groups can help a candidate during the primaries but also wound the party's eventual nominee
- The role that campaign field offices have for both parties
- Discrepancies in free media coverage that can help those with fewer resources
- The small donor "revolution" as a countertrend to the rise of megadonors

DEMOCRATIC CANDIDATES, TRUMP, AND OUTSIDE GROUPS IN THE 2020 PRESIDENTIAL CAMPAIGN

Democratic presidential candidates faced rather different challenges regarding outside groups than President Trump did in 2019. While Trump was engaged in feuds with like-minded outside groups (see chapter 1), Democrats were asked whether they supported sympathetic outside groups at all. Some Democrats used the issue to signal that they saw Super PACs as dangerous tools inconsistent with their values and views of how campaigns should be conducted.

In the spring of 2019, End Citizens United, the Progressive Change Campaign Committee (PCCC), and several other groups released a letter asking Democratic candidates to disavow Super PACs and to fight for their demise. Adam Green of the PCCC said that doing so was "in part about purifying the Democratic Party brand."[2] Several Democratic candidates, such as Senator Kirsten Gillibrand (NY), Senator Kamala Harris (CA), and former vice president Joe Biden, publicly stated early in their campaigns that they did not want support from Super PACs. "My values are never for sale. . . . I don't think we should have individual Super PACs, and I don't want one," Gillibrand said at a news conference one day after launching her campaign.[3] A spokeswoman for Biden confirmed the same sentiment shortly after the pro-Biden Super PAC For the People was formed and told the *HuffPost*, he "does not welcome assistance from Super PACs."[4]

However, when asked about support from outside groups in the general election, some candidates backpedaled. For example, Senator Elizabeth Warren (MA), made clear: "They [the Trump campaign] will have PACs and Super PACs and too many special interest groups to count, and we will do what is necessary to match them financially."[5]

Other candidates also were reluctant to commit to any pledges beyond the Democratic primary. Andrew Mayersohn, a researcher at the Center for Responsive Politics, said that he "would be surprised if any [candidates] pledge to reject single-candidate Super PAC support in the general election."[6] Ultimately, the issue might boil down to how Dallas lawyer Marc Stanley, who raised money for President Obama and 2016 Democratic nominee Hillary Clinton, put it: renouncing Super PACs in the general election would be "like bringing a butter knife to a gunfight."[7]

Having support from outside groups to match Trump's campaign financially in the general election reflects one motivation. Yet there is another reason. Steve Elmendorf, a powerful lobbyist who served as deputy campaign manager for John Kerry's campaign in 2004, puts it bluntly: "Any candidate who unilaterally says I won't do Super PACs or I won't do outside groups or I won't do negative ads is probably not going to get nominated by us," referring to affluent donors within the Democratic Party.[8] In other words, there is tension between what some in the Democratic base want to hear versus what potentially supportive wealthy individuals want from a candidate.

Meanwhile, President Trump was dealing not only with "rogue" pro-Trump outside groups, but his personally approved Super PAC, America First Action (AFA), also was in trouble. AFA had planned to raise $100 million in the 2017–18 election cycle but managed to raise only $75 million. Additionally, there were concerns about how AFA was spending its money. Not only did AFA spend $33,000 for one event at a Washington, D.C., steakhouse, but it also paid $120,000 to companies tied to Milwaukee sheriff and Trump supporter David Clarke and spent over $460,000 at properties owned by Trump.[9] There was also frustration about how much AFA was spending on salaries for affiliates of Trump, as well as several hundred thousand dollars in expenses related to "communications consulting" and "strategy consulting" paid to other Trump associates. "There's a perception that people who got fired from the administration or couldn't get administration jobs were just dumped there," a Republican operative who spoke with potential donors to AFA said. He added that "what fundraising they have done they've squandered on parties and other stupid things."[10]

The problems with AFA did not end there. There were other controversial expenses and questions about AFA's leadership. AFA is linked to America First Policies (AFP), a nonprofit dark money group. AFP spent, for example, $100,000 on ads for two Republican congressmen, Representatives Jim Jordan of Ohio and Mark Meadows of North Carolina. Both legislators have been highly supportive of the president.[11] A Republican operative close to the Trump campaign called this expense part of the "general incompetence" of AFA because both Jordan and Meadows represent safe Republican districts. Political insiders assumed that the expense was to signal to other members of Congress that strong Trump supporters would be rewarded.[12]

Complaints about AFA's leadership were common. Grand Old Party (GOP) insiders commented that the president's Super PAC "should be the biggest player in American politics," but instead, the leadership was accused of failing to court moderately wealthy Republicans who could add millions to AFA's coffers. As a result, Linda McMahon took over as AFA's chairwoman in April 2019, after departing as chief of the Small Business Administration. A few weeks in, McMahon told reporters that she was spending half her time on fundraising and the other half on strategy and everyday operations.[13] All in all, Democratic candidates tried to distance themselves from outside groups leading up to the primaries of 2020, while the Trump campaign was watching the operations of its own approved Super PAC and criticizing supportive groups for misusing funds and profiting from the president's name.

The real test for how 2020 Democratic hopefuls are going to deal with Super PACs will come in February 2020. At that time, the Democratic field will have narrowed, with Super Tuesday approaching on March 3, 2020. Fourteen states will hold primaries that day, including California and Texas, where advertising is not only desirable but also expensive. In other words, this will be a time when the candidates could benefit from having a Super PAC the most. When *The New York Times* spoke with donors, strategists, and people close to the Democratic candidates at the end of 2018, they identified Senators Cory Booker (NJ), Kamala Harris (CA), and Kirsten Gillibrand (NY) as the candidates that would be most tempted to use a Super PAC at that stage of their campaigns. Particularly Booker and Harris are known to have ties to wealthy donors, both inside and outside of their home states. According to the *Times*, there were discussions in 2017, long before she had even announced her candidacy, that Harris's former top advisors Brian Brokaw and Dan Newman would lead her Super PAC.[14]

At the time of writing, there is no way to know if Democratic candidates will uphold through the primaries their pledges against Super

PACs. However, what is clear is that future campaigns will provide the same dilemma for Democrats: take advantage of Super PACs and risk losing support from the base or stick to the pledge that one's campaign is not up for sale by special interests. According to Mark Longabaugh, senior adviser to Senator Bernie Sanders (VT), Democratic candidates should stick to principles in the primaries. "You can't on one hand oppose *Citizens United* and the corrupting influence of corrupting money," Longabaugh said, "and on the other hand take that money."[15] At the end, Robby Mook, 2016 campaign manager for Hillary Clinton, is probably correct when he said, "If you're depending on a Super PAC to succeed in the primary, you're probably losing."[16]

NEW TRENDS SINCE *CITIZENS UNITED*

This section summarizes how outside groups have changed the dynamics of presidential campaigns. It also discusses another trend that has arisen largely as a response to the perception that corporate and wealthy donors now play too large a role in campaigns: the small donor movement. Of course, many other major factors—the *fundamentals*—influence the outcome of a campaign that cannot be covered here: the state of the economy, including overall economic growth and changes to real disposable income; the strength of partisanship and the motivation this creates; the ideological positioning of candidates; the popularity of major pieces of legislation or lack thereof; possible scandals; international policy developments; and more. Those elements and how they affect campaigns are important to acknowledge. However, the goal of this chapter is to illustrate the ongoing trends in presidential campaigns since 2010 and to reflect on their implications.

PLAYING THE DELAY GAME

One trend mentioned in the first chapter is that some presidential hopefuls in the post–*Citizens United* era have incentives to wait before announcing their candidacy, especially the "big shots," the perceived frontrunners. Timing the decision to formally announce one's candidacy is a strategic decision. The candidates with the most political connections can use the additional time to set up the "outside campaign" without violating coordination rules. This includes identifying who should lead the candidate's preferred Super PAC, talking to potential donors, and thinking through various "what-if" scenarios. For "long shots," those with a lower chance of clinching the nomination, waiting to make the official announcement may not make sense, as they usually need more time to increase their name recognition, test messages with voters, and hire experienced staff. In that case, the costs associated with a delayed announcement may exceed the benefits, that is, the additional time needed to work on both the candidate's campaigns and the "outside" campaign.

The preceding scenarios described played out in the last couple of presidential campaigns. In 2019, former vice president Joe Biden was the early frontrunner among the Democratic candidates, but he was the last major candidate officially to enter the presidential campaign on April 25, 2019.[17] In this specific case, however, Biden's absence in early primary voting states may indicate that his official reason for the late announcement, uncertainty over whether he wanted to run, could be accurate. "He's prepared, but he's also doing his due diligence," Louisiana representative Cedric Richmond, former chairman of the Congressional Black Caucus who had met with Biden prior to his announcement, said in mid-February of 2019.[18]

Four years earlier, the situation was more obvious. Another well-connected candidate, Jeb Bush, former governor of Florida, waited until June 15, 2015, to formally announce his 2016 presidential bid.[19] A month earlier, on May 13, Bush slipped up when he said in an interview with NBC News, "I am running for President."[20] As a declared presidential candidate, he legally should not have been coordinating with his Super PAC, Right to Rise USA. Yet he openly coordinated with Right to Rise USA until his formal announcement to run for president, raising millions of dollars for the organization and appearing regularly in front of "Right to Rise" banners.[21] Bush also put his name on invitations to hundreds who attended a Right to Rise conference in Miami in April 2015, listing Bush as an honorary chairman of the Super PAC.[22] Through June 30, 2015, Bush's Right to Rise Super PAC was able to raise $102.5 million.[23]

Former Hewlett-Packard CEO Carly Fiorina was another presidential candidate who delayed the formal announcement of her candidacy. Officially, she joined the presidential race on May 4, 2015.[24] However, Fiorina had already created the Unlocking Potential PAC, a Super PAC dedicated to messages that would target "independent female voters."[25] Fiorina had also hired staff, including Sarah Isgur Flores, the deputy communications director for the Republican National Committee (RNC), to work for Unlocking Potential. At that time, Unlocking Potential already announced that Isgur Flores would serve as Fiorina's deputy campaign manager in case Fiorina did run for president.[26] In January 2015, Fiorina had already referred to herself as a "candidate" at the Iowa Freedom when she was interviewed by Fox News.[27]

In sum, there is enough evidence to suggest that some candidates delay their official announcement to run for president for strategic reasons related specifically to Super PACs. The Campaign Legal Center (CLC) offers an analysis of the actions of prospective presidential candidates. The sixty-one-page CLC report takes into account the **advisory opinions** of the FEC, including a detailed description of what the FEC considers "testing the waters" activities of prospective candidates and the legal implications those activities incur. An advisory opinion is issued by a commission or a court that offers advice on how to interpret a law without making a formal, legal judgment. The CLC's report argued that "among the long list of prospective 2016 presidential candidates, only Senator Lindsey Graham and former Senator Jim Webb appear to be complying with the federal campaign finance law requirement that 'testing the waters' activities be paid for with candidate permissible funds."[28]

THE STAFF SHELL GAME

Presidential candidates, naturally, want to be comfortable with the Super PACs to which they are most closely aligned. While Super PACs must avoid consultation, cooperation, and coordination with presidential candidates as they make independent expenditures, candidates have found a way to ensure congruence between the candidates' vision and the activities of Super PACs: by playing what we call the **staff shell game**. The staff shell game means that staff members are moved back and forth between a candidate's official campaign and outside groups. Early in his campaign in 2016, Trump complained that his Republican rivals were "in total cahoots with their [Super] PACs, which they're not allowed to be." He added, "They put their friends in there. One good thing about me: I'm not."[29]

Under current FEC rules, there must be a **120-day cooling-off period** between the time a staffer or consultant can be employed by a candidate and the time they can work for an outside group.[30] This rule ensures that organizations can make expenditures that are deemed independent of the candidates. As it stands, staffers and consultants can work for outside groups within the same election cycle, a policy that increases the probability of coordination between outside groups and candidates. For other guidance regarding cooling-off periods, one can look at some states' **revolving door** policies. The revolving door refers to the movement of high-level employees in the public sector to private-sector jobs and vice versa. Florida passed the strictest state-level policy on lobbying restrictions via a ballot initiative in November 2018. Starting at the end of 2022, a six-year cooling-off period will go into effect.[31] Whether a stricter cooling-off period for presidential staffers and consultants is desirable to avoid possible coordination between candidates and outside campaigns remains debatable.

The movement from campaign or legislative staff to an outside group and vice versa is not the exception, but the norm. For example, Buffy Wicks left Priorities USA Action, a Super PAC supporting Hillary Clinton, as the executive director in May 2015 to work directly for the Clinton campaign. A Clinton official commented at that time, "We are recruiting Buffy for a senior-level role on the coordinated side of the campaign."[32] After the cooling-off period, in the spring of 2016, Buffy Wicks then became the state director for Hillary for California.[33] Mike Murphy, who ran Jeb Bush's campaigns since 1998 and was Bush's favorite strategist until he declared his candidacy in 2015, represents another example. Murphy led Right to Rise, Jeb Bush's Super PAC in 2015 and 2016. "He's a good friend and I'm going to miss him," Bush told the media two days before announcing his candidacy.[34]

THE *NEW* MONEY PRIMARY

In 2004, Michael Goff published a book titled *The Money Primary: The New Politics of the Early Presidential Nomination Process*. Sixteen years later, the book remains relevant. Goff argues that early fundraising strength in the primaries means candidates can buy viability and demonstrate strength. He claims that money can buy those factors—advertising, travel, events, research, consultants, and so on—that lead to media coverage and public attention. More publicity allows candidates to raise more money, which, he claims, is ultimately a predictor of success.[35] With highly active outside groups, the cost of campaigning has increased substantially since *Citizens United*, which means that the **money primary** (also known as the *invisible primary*)—the time between setting up one's candidacy and the start of the actual primaries—has increased in importance. For example, given the prominence of outside money in the 2016 presidential election, several Republican candidates tried to win the support of two megadonors, Charles and David Koch, a process that some members of the press have called the "Koch primary."[36]

The presidential campaigns of 2012 and 2016 support Goff's argument that the money primary matters as a sign of candidate viability. One detailed analysis of the 2012 election shows that "it was money spent by Super PACs that allowed the race to go on as long as it did. Super PACs provided Romney's rivals with more than enough resources to wage a viable campaign, to stay in the race longer, and to give Republican voters in many more states a choice and more of a say in who their nominee would be."[37] The same case can be made for Trump's rivals in 2016. However, although money still begets money and fundraising strength still signals viability, the case that money is a predictor of a campaign's success has lost a lot of its explanatory power in the past two decades. For instance, Trump won the 2016 presidential nomination despite significant disadvantages to many of Republican rivals in both fundraising and outside spending. Moreso, between the fall of 2015 and March 31, 2016, Republican Super PACs spent $29.8 million *against* Trump, followed by $8.5 million Super PAC spending against Senator Marco Rubio from Florida and $6.1 million against Senator Ted Cruz from Texas.[38] Yet Trump compensated for the fundraising deficit with an ability to generate free media coverage, which is discussed in chapter 6.

Although now a quasi-litmus test for Democratic presidential candidates exists to renounce outside groups during the primary phase, Republican candidates are unlikely to do the same in the future. A **litmus test** in this context is a fundamental question asked of a political candidate whereby the answer to which determines whether someone might be willing to support a candidate. In fact, for any Republican presidential candidate to take a general stand against Super PACs would seem strange because it would contradict the support for free speech rights, something Republicans usually advocate. Consequently, one can only speak of an ongoing shift toward outside spending in presidential primaries for Republican candidates. In 2012, Republican donor and chair of several finance committees, Barry Wynn, explained on the Fox Business channel the old versus the new process for Republican candidates who want to jump-start their presidential campaigns:

> But this [Citizens United] has really changed entirely the way fundraising is done. If you go back and look at what we were doing before the decision [Citizens United] two years ago, we would always form finance committees, and the finance committees may consist of 50 people. They

would go out and have events for the presidential candidate, and they would bring in maybe a hundred people. They would give $2,000 and you would have $200,000 per event. You do 50 of these and you raise ten million dollars, and that ten million dollars would really be the seed capital to crank up the campaign—hire staff, and begin the campaign efforts around the country, and going to the early primary states and hire staff. Now the candidates have to look at that and say: do I really have the time to do that? Do I need to go to Iowa to the coffee shops, to New Hampshire and the coast and eat shrimp with the folks in Charleston, South Carolina? And if I'm going to spend my time doing that, I don't have time to go around the country to these 50 events and raise ten million dollars. So it'd be easier to call four people, have them give two and a half million dollars a piece through the Super PAC, and that way you've got your ten million dollars. Even though it's uncoordinated, it's still a part of your campaign. . . . Now you actually have two campaigns. You have the Super PAC campaign that essentially is working—not coordinating—for the candidate and actually against another candidate, but the Super PACs are not really working with the campaign. They are a separate campaign run by professionals though, so they know how to coordinate without talking to each other.[39]

According to Wynn, a presidential campaign consists of two campaigns: the "coordinated" candidate's campaign and the uncoordinated Super PAC campaign. Although uncoordinated, the Super PACs Wynn references are nevertheless affiliated with a single candidate; therefore, the term "single-candidate Super PAC" is often used in that context. In 2010, only twenty-two single-candidate Super PACs were involved in federal elections. By 2018, that number had reached 259, and 2,654 Super PACs overall were active at the federal level that year (see figure 4.1).

More specifically, how important are outside groups, particularly Super PACs, compared to the candidate's campaign? In terms of overall spending, Super PACs have proved to be significant. Consider the 2016 presidential campaign. Outside groups supporting former New Jersey governor Chris Christie raised and spent almost $23.9 million on his campaign. Nearly three-quarters (74 percent) of the total came from outside groups, and only about one-quarter (26 percent) from his campaign. Similarly, Jeb Bush's campaign raised only a little under 22 percent of the money toward his campaign, while 78 percent came from outside groups. Marco Rubio's campaign raised just less than one-third (32 percent) on its own, while a little more than two-thirds (68 percent) came from outside. Wisconsin's governor Scott Walker's campaign, which did not last long, was

Figure 4.1 Number of Super PACs Involved in Federal Elections, 2010–18

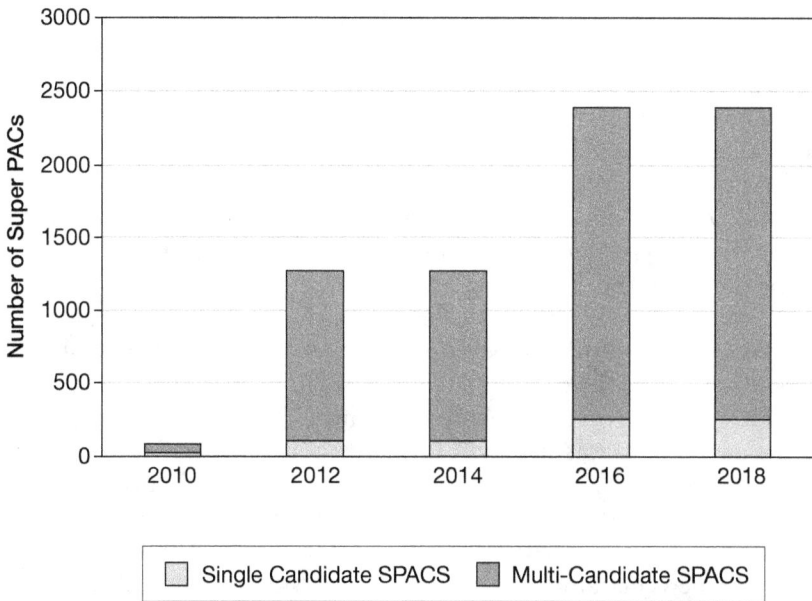

75 percent outside money. Ted Cruz's campaign, on the other hand, was able to raise the majority of funds, 62.5 percent, on its own without outside groups.[40] Most of these examples illustrate a shift toward reliance on outside funding, but they have another commonality: outside money did not buy success—all these candidates lost.

Yet money is not insignificant either. Outside groups are particularly dominant at the early stages of fundraising in campaigns. In the first half of 2015, almost $4 out of every $5 raised on behalf of Republican presidential candidates went to independent groups, not the official campaigns. The opposite was true for Hillary Clinton and her Democratic contenders, where 80 percent of the contributions went directly to the campaigns.[41] At that time, one of the most well-known national experts on campaign finance, Michael Malbin, executive director of the nonpartisan Campaign Finance Institute, commented on the Republican primary: "It's pretty clear that the Super PACs are playing an unprecedented role. This whole development to me is staggering. You're in a fundamentally different system than twelve years ago or eight years ago."[42]

THE PRESIDENTIAL PRIMARY VACUUM

According to calculations by Demos, a New York City–based think tank with election reform as one of its priorities, the *Citizens United* decision has had more impact on spending in presidential campaigns than any other court decision. As a result of *Citizens United*, approximately $690 million in campaign spending was added to the presidential primaries and general election in 2016.[43]

Seventeen Republican candidates were running for president in 2016 before Donald Trump became the Republican nominee and eventual winner of the 2016 presidential election. As usual, the RNC did not endorse a specific candidate during the primary, and the result was that Super PACs stepped into this vacuum. For eleven of the seventeen candidates, outside spending proved to be their primary source of funding. Only six candidates were able to raise more money than outside groups did.[44]

How does candidate spending in the 2012 presidential election compare to outside spending? In 2012, outside spending made up about 42 percent of all spending in the presidential election, leaving 58 percent to the candidates. During the presidential primaries, Romney's Republican competitors raised 64 percent of the money spent, while 36 percent came from the outside.[45] Mitt Romney, who unofficially clinched the Republican nomination in April 2012, received $42.9 million of outside spending through April 20, 2012, from his Super PAC, Restore Our Future.[46] His campaign spent $78.4 million during that time frame (through March 31, 2012).[47]

This does not mean the RNC is sitting on the sidelines while Republicans are choosing their nominee. For example, in 2012 the RNC used independent expenditures that almost exclusively went toward attack ads against Obama. Throughout the 2012 presidential campaign, the RNC used 94 percent of its independent expenses, $42.2 million, on anti-Obama attack ads.[48] Even if the RNC had wanted to make larger direct contributions to any of their presidential candidates or the eventual Republican nominee, it could not do so legally. A national party committee can only give up to $5,000 per election—where the primary and general elections count as separate elections—directly to a federal candidate. A drop in the ocean. The rationale for such a low contribution limit is that parties "have the potential to corrupt candidates beholden to them."[49]

During contested primaries, candidates cannot rely on party support. Parties may focus on the opponent, assuming there is an incumbent running for reelection, but will wait before offering any candidate-specific support until there is an official nominee. This vacuum has opened an opportunity for outside groups to fill the vacuum, and they certainly are taking advantage of it.

The Increasing Importance of Leadership PACs

In October 2013, CBS's *60 Minutes* aired a story titled "Washington's Open Secret" about **leadership PACs**. As discussed in chapter 1, leadership PACs are committees that make independent expenditures, are controlled by candidates or officeholders, but the expenditures themselves cannot support one's campaign. Legislators use leadership PACs to make contributions to other lawmakers, but they also use them for personal noncampaign expenses. The *60 Minutes* segment was the public's introduction to this special type of PAC. In the story, investigative journalist Peter Schweizer argued that, because legislators can use funds from leadership PACs for personal use, they are a form of political "slush fund."[50]

Presidential candidates are using leadership PACs to jumpstart their presidential bids. For example, in January 2015, prior to announcing his presidential candidacy, New Jersey's governor Chris Christie's closest allies formed the Leadership Matters for America PAC.[51] Christie served as honorary chairman of the committee.[52] Although the leadership PAC was legally prohibited from directly supporting Christie's campaign, it proved to be an important organizational vehicle. Specifically, Leadership Matters for America's expenses mostly went toward administrative assistance (largely travel and legal services), fundraising, consulting services, and research (particularly polling).[53] All told, Leadership for America spent almost $3.5 million in the 2016 election cycle in support of Christie.[54]

How does the help from Christie's leadership PAC compare to his campaign expenditures for the presidential nomination? Christie's campaign raised $8.4 million. Put differently, Christie's leadership PAC alone raised about 40 percent of what his official campaign raised in 2015–16. Leadership PACs can accept $5,000 per year from individual donors or other political action committees. Aside from offering organizational assistance to presidential candidates, leadership PACs use the contributions they receive to support other political candidates and their political party, which can then lead to reciprocal contributions, direct contributions to the candidate, or support by outside groups. In the 2012 presidential election, various leadership PACs contributed $372,900 to Romney, showing that a well-established network of political friends can help candidates despite the relatively low contribution limits.

Rubio's Reclaim America PAC, another leadership PAC, contributed $290,000 to federal candidates and party committees during the 2016 election cycle.[55] This included $10,000 to the early voting state parties in Iowa and New Hampshire. Meanwhile, Rick Perry's leadership PAC, RickPAC, gave $10,000 to the Republican Party in New Hampshire and $5,000 to South Carolina Republicans.[56] "This is a good way to build name identification in critical states that helps down the road," according to Viveca Novak, editorial and communications director at the Center for Responsive Politics.[57] Overall, leadership PACs can serve as the architecture for presidential campaigns, and they can serve as a "warm-up to the main attraction," political science professor Anthony Corrado told the *Los Angeles Times*.[58]

In an article about the Democratic presidential candidates in 2019, *Politico* examined how Democrats used leadership PACs during the 2018 midterm elections. The analysis broke down the proportion that the candidates spent in support of others and contrasted it with the percentage spent on themselves (for travel, staff, consulting, and other services). Biden's leadership PAC spent the lowest percentage on others (25 percent; $603,000) and 75 percent on himself. Among the top-tier candidates, Senator Elizabeth Warren spent the highest percentage on others (85 percent, $1.2 million), followed by Senator Bernie Sanders (46 percent; $124,000), and Kamala Harris (37 percent; $680,000). This distribution of Biden's expenses in 2018 has been interpreted as a sign that he may have used about $1.8 million in leadership PAC money to set up his presidential campaign.[59]

Interestingly, Biden used the money for a specific purpose: digital consulting and web services. In other words, Biden's campaign sought to develop more sophisticated online fundraising tools. Unsurprisingly, he ran a small donor online contest in 2018, which seemed to serve as a trial balloon for other small donor fundraising efforts in 2019 and 2020. Last, Senator Harris's preparation for her presidential run also stands out. Harris spent a large portion of her funds on consulting services and fundraisers to foster relationships with big donors. She also took twenty-six trips to seventeen states on behalf of House and Senate candidates in 2018 and to early primary states.[60] Overall, Harris's strategy to focus more than others on traditional fundraisers with big donors may point to a calculation that small donors can be more extreme in their political views, which would make them more likely to contribute at higher rates to well-known progressive candidates such as Senators Warren and Sanders.

PLAYING PINBALL WITH JOINT
FUNDRAISING COMMITTEES

A **joint fundraising committee** (JFC) can be created by two or more candidates, PACs, or party committees to raise money for campaigns, and it splits the proceeds and expenses based on a mutually agreed-on formula. A donor still needs to abide by contribution limits for each of the participants in a JFC, but donors are able to write one large check instead of several smaller checks. Prior to *McCutcheon v. FEC* (2014), checks to JFCs were subject to aggregate contribution limits, but those limits have since been lifted.[61] Joint fundraising committees are particularly popular during presidential election years: their breakout year was 2008 when they raised $509 million, which was more than double in 2012 with $1.1 billion, and $1.2 billion in 2016.[62]

The Center for Public Integrity and *Politico* shed light on joint fundraising committees in 2017 with an investigation into how these committees operate. The investigation discovered that a lot of money is initially given to state parties who then transfer the money to the national parties. State parties are legally allowed to transfer unlimited hard money to their national allies. For example, in the 2016 election cycle, when Hillary Clinton's main joint fundraising committee received contributions, it allocated the money between Clinton's campaign committee, the Democratic National Committee (DNC) and a number of state-level Democratic Party committees. State Democratic parties then send the money to the DNC, allowing the national committee to receive significantly more cash than would have been possible under existing federal contribution limits. Republican state parties also sent the vast majority of money they received from JFCs to the RNC; in fact, the states' parties that received money from the Trump Victory JFC sent more than 90 percent of those funds to the RNC.[63]

Daniel Weiner, senior counsel for the Brennan Center for Justice, has compared the process of legally sending the money back and forth between committees, particularly party committees, to a game of pinball. Brendan Fischer from the CLC calls the current practices that both major parties are engaged in a "form of legalized money laundering."[64] Those who do not take issue with this practice can argue that parties are simply trying to compensate for unfair restrictions for political parties compared to the unlimited expenditures that are legal for Super PACs. Overall, joint fundraising committees are just another weapon in what has become an arms race for more campaign dollars.

OFFICIAL PARTY COMMITTEES

In 2014, political parties benefited from another campaign finance decision by the Supreme Court. In *McCutcheon vs. the Federal Election Commission*, the Court ruled in a 5–4 decision that aggregate contribution limits are unconstitutional because they violate the First Amendment (see chapter 2). In the 2013–14 election cycle, there was a $123,200 hard money (i.e., cash) limit for aggregate contributions to federal candidates and political parties.[65] The Supreme Court ruled this limit unconstitutional, and suddenly, there was less competition among the party committees within each party. There used to be a zero-sum game; for example, if individuals maxed out their contributions to the DNC with $32,400 in 2013–14, then they were not able to give to the Democratic Congressional Committee or the Democratic Senatorial Campaign Committee. Since *McCutcheon*, individuals are able to give the $32,400 to all national committees and $10,000 each to all fifty state party committees.

Despite the controversial ruling, the DNC's and the RNC's fundraising efforts peaked in the pre–*Citizens United* era and have never fully recovered. The DNC set its record in 2004 with $404.7 million and was able to approach similar levels ($372.1 million) only in 2016. In 2019, the DNC is far behind the 2015 benchmarks, showing that it is struggling in an environment where many Democratic donors prefer to give to Super PACs or directly to the candidates instead of to official party committees. The RNC raised $444.7 million in 2008, experienced a few downswings in the interim, but then set a new record for the midterm elections in 2018 with $324.8 million.[66]

SUPER PAC ACTIVITIES WITHOUT COORDINATION

The FEC defines **coordinated communications** as communication "made in cooperation, consultation or concert with, or at the request or suggestion of, a candidate," a candidate's committee or agents of the committee, or a political party committee or its agents.[67] So the art of the game for presidential and congressional candidates has become how to send helpful directional signals to Super PACs without consultation, cooperation, or coordination with these groups. Doing so has led candidates to disclose information (broadly defined) to the public that they would not share otherwise in an effort to help outside groups and their activities. One can think of this as a **signaling game**, where signals are actions that more informed participants (candidates) use to convey information to less informed participants (outside groups).

For example, candidates sometimes provide outside groups with **b-roll footage** on YouTube and other websites, showing them on the campaign trail—giving speeches at events, showing enthusiastic crowds, shaking hands, or visiting corporations. B-roll material is supplemental film footage that is often presented without sound. Outside groups can then use the footage to produce ads of their own, creating a consistent visual message. For example, when Marco Rubio ran for president in 2016, he used a Vimeo account to post b-roll footage that was then picked up by his Super PAC.[68]

Outside groups initially focused on TV advertising after the *Citizens United* and *SpeechNow* decisions, and traditional TV advertising is still the largest expense for them today. However, since 2015, outside groups have become more involved in other campaign functions: canvassing, voter registration, data collection, selling merchandise, email lists, opposition research, and organizing campaign events—all without violating coordination laws. We presented some examples of how outside groups are getting more involved in these activities in the first chapter.

Former governor of Ohio John Kasich had a Super PAC in the 2016 election cycle that serves as an example of what to expect in the future. New Day for America worked closely with a data analytics firm, Applecart, to mine a range of sources such as local news reports and even yearbooks to identify personal networks and people who have influential relationships with highly coveted voters.[69] Such advanced ground games will continue to evolve, especially as data analytics becomes more complex and capable. Even if such new Super PAC activities were to violate federal coordination rules, the "likelihood of the laws being enforced is slim," Ann M. Ravel, said in an interview, who, at that time, was the chair of the FEC. "I never want to give up, but I'm not under any illusions. People think the FEC is dysfunctional. It's worse than dysfunctional."[70] The causes of the FEC's dysfunction and possible solutions are discussed in chapter 7.

In part, the move from TV commercials to digital ads and the ground game has been driven by the surging costs of TV commercials, which, in turn, is a result of the spike in outside groups competing with each other and the overall rising costs of campaigning. By law, candidates are guaranteed the lowest advertising rates, whereas Super PACs must pay market-based prices. What is less well known is that all advertisers, including candidates and Super PACs, pay the same rates for digital ads.[71] Even with Super PACs doing more of the traditional and digital campaign activities that candidates and political parties are usually associated with, there are limitations on what Super PACs can do. "There were things we couldn't do. We could do a whole bunch—pay for media, the ground game, but we couldn't pay for candidate travel" or fees to get on primary ballots, according to Austin Barbour, who served as chief strategist for Super PACs supporting Rick Perry.[72] Peter Pasi, a Republican digital consultant, added, "I think people are finding out the hard way that campaigns still matter. You still need to keep the lights on; you still need to pay people."[73]

SUPER PACS VERSUS INCUMBENT PRESIDENTS DURING THE PRIMARIES

Although Democrats are generally opposed to using Super PACs in their primaries, the sentiment is not the same for accepting Super PAC help against an incumbent president while the Democratic candidates are still battling it out. The reason for this is time. By the time the Democratic National Convention ends on July 16, 2020, the nominee will have fewer than four months to run his or her campaign against President Trump. Brad Parscale, President Trump's campaign manager for the 2020 election, has been open about the advantage this provides to the incumbent president. "It's much more efficient two years out to try to find a possible voter, a possible donor. It's just a considerable advantage that the other side won't have because you just can't replace time."[74]

Although there was not an incumbent president running for reelection in 2016, the 2012 presidential election offers the same picture. Super PACs played the early political **attack dogs**—individuals or groups known for harsh and personal attacks against others. In 2011, before the primaries had even begun, Republican outside groups had already spent $18 million on attack ads against President Obama, more than twice as much as all Republican candidates combined at that point. The ads focused on Obama's track record as president, including his perceived failure to create enough jobs. In addition, Republican strategist Karl Rove posted an online video from his Super PAC, American Crossroads, where he tried to fire up the Republican base: "We say it every election, but this time it's true: 2012 is the most important election in 100 years, and I don't say that lightly. . . . We've got to fight to save our country."[75]

THE REPUBLICAN CONUNDRUM: SUPER PAC HELP VERSUS DAMAGED GOODS THEORY

Super PACs are known for their negative campaigning. For Republicans running for president, the ads Super PACs run show deficiencies in other candidates' records and character, thereby making one's campaign more appealing. At the same time, candidates can tell the media that they cannot be held accountable for any Super PAC actions because the Super PACs have to act independently. Of course, the most popular target of criticism is a campaign's frontrunner at any given time. According to political scientist Samuel Popkin, there are two winners in every presidential election campaign: the *inevitable winner* at the beginning of a campaign—such as Rudy Giuliani or Hillary Clinton in 2008—and the *inevitable victor* after it is all over.[76] Popkin uses the word "inevitable" for both winners and victors because that is how media pundits, political strategists, and other experts portray them, with post hoc rationalizations as to why the eventual victors were inevitable. To what extent Super PACs have brought down the early "inevitable winners" needs scholarly attention once there are enough cases to analyze. In early 2019, Biden was the "inevitable winner" among Democratic candidates, with a large lead in various polls, even without having officially entered the race at that point. Whether he will also become the inevitable victor is unclear at the time of this writing, but Popkin's theory would suggest otherwise. In fact, Popkin argues that it is particularly difficult for "successors"—as he calls former vice presidents—to win the nomination.

That said, although President Trump was not an inevitable winner in 2016, he was already the frontrunner a few weeks after he entered the race in June 2015, and he was able to sustain his lead all the way to the nomination. In Trump's case, the issue was a different one: almost everyone underestimated his staying power. For example, a month after Trump declared his presidency, Rick Wilson, a well-known Republican political consultant, told the *Guardian* that Trump was experiencing "a celebrity political bubble."[77] Wilson continued: "He is an entertainer. He is a showman. He is a clown in a fancy hat, strutting the stage for a few minutes, and then the serious actors will come on the stage in a little while."[78] Wilson's prediction proved wrong: Trump was not only able to secure the Republican nomination, but he was also able to win the presidency.

Either way, more often than not, inevitable winners at an early stage—another example would be Howard Dean in 2004—turn out *not* to be the inevitable victors in presidential primaries. Although Super PACs may help a primary campaign, possibly even all the way to a nomination, there is often a price to pay in the general election. In 2012, former presidential nominee John McCain expressed concerns about the role that Super PACs play for the eventual party nominee, "I think there's reason to be concerned about it," McCain said on ABC's *This Week*, referring to the intense negativity in the Republican presidential primary race. "I've been in very tough campaigns. I don't think I've seen one that was as personal, and characterized by so many attacks, as these are. Frankly, one of the reasons is the Super PACs."[79]

The DNC and Democratic Super PACs watched the 2012 Republican primary carefully. Rick Perry accused Romney of saying "whatever [he] need[ed] to say for whatever office [he's] running for," and Newt Gingrich claimed Romney would "say almost anything" to win the nomination. Rick Santorum said that Romney would "pander" to voters without a vision for the country. Republican Super PACs used this theme in their ads, and later, the DNC, President Obama, and Democratic Super PACs reinforced this narrative, saying that Romney did not have core values.[80]

Mark McKinnon, a campaign consultant, suggests that Super PACs have created a system of "mutually assured destruction," because "no matter who wins, they will have been so thoroughly nuked no one can govern because they'll be completely radioactive."[81] In all, Super PACs can support and amplify a candidate's message, but some argue they may turn a party's presidential nominee into **damaged goods**—someone whose reputation has been severely damaged throughout the primary process, thus reducing the chances of winning the general election.

COORDINATED EXPENDITURES AND THE PARTIES' GROUND GAME

Political parties have three ways to support federal candidates financially: they can make (1) direct contributions, (2) independent expenditures, or (3) coordinated expenditures. **Coordinated expenditures** allow the parties to pay for goods or services in coordination with a candidate without giving the money directly to the candidate or candidate committee. For example, a party can pay for a candidate's campaign bill, which would be treated and reported as a coordinated party expenditure, while a check payable to the candidate committee would be treated as a contribution.[82] The amended Federal Election Campaign Act of 1974 allows for coordinated party expenditures to acknowledge the special role that political parties play in organizing elections and to avoid their marginalization in campaigns.[83] Therefore, the Federal Election Campaign Act included a provision to allow parties, but not others, to spend on behalf of their candidates in coordination with them.[84]

For presidential candidates, the FEC uses the following formula to calculate the maximum amount political parties can spend on coordinated expenditures: the national voting age population multiplied by 2 cents multiplied by the price index, which accounts for an annual cost-of-living adjustment. Based on this formula, the coordinated party expenditure limit for presidential candidates in 2012 was $21,684,200 and $23,821,100 for 2016. In 2012, the RNC spent the maximum allowed on coordinated expenditures to support Romney, and the Party allocated an additional $42 million on independent expenditures to help him attack President Obama.[85] Entering the final stretch of the 2016 election, the RNC spent only $321,531 on independent expenditures against Clinton but spent $20.3 million on coordinated party expenditures.[86]

In 2016, the Republican Party had a lot of trust in its own *ground game*. The political ground game centers around **canvassing**, which involves direct contact with voters to identify supporters, register those who are not, and to persuade undecided voters. For example, in early 2016, the RNC announced it would hire an additional 392 staffers and 98 new offices across 11 battleground states, including Florida, Pennsylvania, Michigan, and Wisconsin, states Trump won by small margins.[87] In the past ten years, we have seen a resurgence of elite-based campaign mobilization, organized by the leadership of both parties, through campaign field offices.[88]

RNC-sponsored campaign field offices were a focus of Reince Priebus, RNC chair from 2011 to 2017. According to Josh Kivett, the RNC's southeast regional political director, having new field offices in battleground states "was the culmination of a four-year process." Priebus "had a strategic vision for a data-driven, permanent ground game," Kivett told the *Orlando Sentinel* after the 2016 election.[89] Kivett also shared that the RNC has divided Florida into 254 unique "turfs," each staffed by people with deep knowledge of those communities who understand the challenges and opportunities in each area. In many of these areas, in 2016, "they didn't run into the Clinton ground game, or the Democratic ground game," Kivett said.[90]

THE SMALL DONOR REVOLUTION

There is a new dynamic in American politics that stands in stark contrast to the increasing reliance on megadonors, namely, the substantial growth in small donors. Although Republicans are currently in the process of establishing one common platform for small donors, ActBlue has monopolized the market for Democrats in processing small donations. In 2004, ActBlue processed less than $1 million; in 2014, $334 million; in 2016, $781 million; and in 2018, $1.6 *billion* in cash donations. The $1.6 billion in 2018 came from five million people, and the average contribution was 40 dollars. In 2018, 60 percent of the ActBlue donors were women. The contribution numbers for 2018 will likely be shattered by November 2020, should the current trend hold. "If you were concerned about an undue influence by large donors, then the ActBlue story is an unalloyed good for the system," Malbin told the *New Yorker*. "But it does have this other side. It fits in with and contributes to a nationalization of an already polarized politics."[91]

More than half the money fourteen Democratic candidates raised from individual donors during the first quarter of 2019 came from donors giving $200 or less each. Four years earlier, less than a third of the donations came from these small donors.[92] Some refer to the increasing reliance of political candidates on small contributions as the **small donor revolution**.[93] There are at least two important implications of this new trend. First, there is no evidence that average citizens are "throwing in the towel" in light of megadonors collectively contributing hundreds of millions of dollars. Although there is concern that *Citizens United* has created political apathy and cynicism, the small donor revolution offers a powerful counterargument. In an era of strong partisanship, people want to be stakeholders, and making small donations creates a buy-in of the political process.

Second, fundraising is not a zero-sum game where campaigns gain contributions from one group at the expense of other segments in society. Two particularly significant increases in overall campaign spending at the federal level were seen in 2012 and 2018. Although campaigns are getting more expensive, Democratic presidential candidates in particular need to find the right mix of small donors and big donors without having to sacrifice support from one specific group. Although Republican presidential candidates can more heavily rely on outside groups and megadonors during the primary phase without facing retribution from voters, they also are increasingly engaged in securing small donations from supporters.

In fact, President Trump has made clear that having a successful Republican equivalent to ActBlue is a priority after several failed attempts in the past. On June 24, 2019, Trump tweeted that he was pleased to announce the launch of a new platform called WinRed. "This new platform will allow my campaign and other Republicans to compete with the Democrats [*sic*] money machine. This has been a priority of mine and I'm pleased to share that it is up and running!"[94] A few days earlier, Karl Rove expressed relief in an opinion piece in the *Wall Street Journal*, saying that the "GOP is finally imitating ActBlue," but he also warned that WinRed's processing fees should go toward "enhancements, algorithms, and list building, rather than big consulting fees and salaries."[95]

President Trump's previous success with small donors is seen as paramount for the success of WinRed. Republican strategists hope Trump can strengthen his small donor base going into the 2020 election and that the personal information that donors provide can be used for appeals to donate to other campaigns. Even though the technology behind WinRed is sophisticated, the key factor to making the platform successful is an "old-fashioned" email list.[96] What about Super PACs—will they integrate WinRed into their fundraising efforts? According to the president of the Congressional Leadership Fund Super PAC, Dan Conston, the answer is yes. Conston's Super PAC would "be adding small dollar fundraising" into their GOP campaigns.[97] To what extent small donors are willing to contribute to Super PACs in the coming years remains to be seen.

There is no doubt that more Americans are making political donations now compared to twenty or thirty years ago. According to surveys conducted by the American National Election Studies, the share of Americans who say they have donated to an individual seeking office within the past year doubled from 6 percent in 1992 to 12 percent in 2016. Meanwhile, the share of those who have donated to parties has also increased, rising from 4 percent to 9 percent across the same period, while the share making donations to outside groups continues to be between 3 percent and 6 percent. However, not everyone is equally likely to contribute. People with higher incomes, advanced education, and older individuals are more likely to make political donations. [98] Although there is no systematic data at this point, this could mean that white and older candidates could benefit the most from this new small-donor trend.

In fact, there are ongoing discussions in the Democratic Party about how fair the rules are that allow candidates to qualify for debate participation in the primaries. For the 2020 election cycle, the DNC established both polling and fundraising thresholds—a steadily increasing minimum number of individual donors—that candidates have to meet to get on the debate stage. Steve Phillips, an African American activist and civil rights lawyer, argues that the current fundraising requirements are unfair to black voters because the "pool of people who have discretionary income to be donors is overwhelmingly, if not disproportionately, white."[99]

One of the consequences the current fundraising rules create is that candidates buy ads that focus on qualifying for the debates, instead of more substantive ads with higher information value that would explain stances on policy issues, character, or shortcomings of the current president. For example, Senator Gillibrand bought online ads that stated, "Enter to win a whiskey with Kirsten" with the title "Contest: Join Kirsten for a drink!"[100] Also, the candidates are running these ads in their home states and in areas that are unrepresentative of the country, such as parts of California and New York that are well known for fundraising successes. Last, there is so much concern about the fundraising requirements among candidates that "campaigns are spending upward of $40 on average for every email address of a prospective small-dollar donor, an unsustainable ratio that has forced cutbacks on hiring, candidate travel and organizing support on the ground in key states."[101] These developments show that there is now so much emphasis on raising money from small donors that discussions of policy have become an afterthought, something proponents of more democratic discourse in political campaigns will despise.

According to one survey, 27 percent of Americans said they will make a political contribution by Election Day 2020. Among self-identified Democrats and Republicans (excluding Independents) that number is even higher; 34 percent of Democrats and 33 percent of Republicans said they planned to make a political donation (or had already made a contribution by June 2019) by November 2020.[102] The reality of such giving levels remains to be seen; however, if actual participation rates are anywhere close to these expressed intentions, then the result would be a new record of individual donations.

CONCLUSION

Much has changed in the way presidential election campaigns have been conducted since *Citizens United*. Initially, presidential candidates from both parties accepted the new, dominant role of outside groups, especially during the primaries. This is the result of outside groups' ability to raise a lot more money for unlimited independent expenditures than candidates can, who are hamstrung by low cash contribution limits ($5,600 for individuals who want to give directly to candidates in the 2019–20 election cycle who are competing in primaries and general election). As a result, the first presidential election after *Citizens United* saw a 594 percent increase in independent expenditures from the 2008 election ($144 million that year) to $1 billion in 2012,[103] and independent expenditures have continued to grow since then. Today, as a sign of concern about this trend, Democratic presidential candidates vow to wait until the general election before they accept help from Super PACs and other groups.

Simultaneously, *Citizens United* has impacted various strategic decisions candidates make: the timing of when to officially start their campaign, moving staff in and out of the campaign team, how to use leadership PACs and joint fundraising committees most effectively, how much they want to help outside groups indirectly or offer them opportunities for political action (by sharing b-roll footage online, staging campaign rallies, etc.), the solicitation targeting of large versus small donors, and how those candidates with fewer resources can try to compensate for a lack of financial resources (e.g., somehow attracting free media). In general, political campaigns have become increasingly more expensive since *Citizens United*, and outside groups can create increased viability for candidates who otherwise would have faded sooner. They can also do the "dirty work" for candidates, with their focus on negative messages about their opponents, without the accountability candidates face. Still, outside groups' activities feed into the public's perception that there is too much money in politics and that politicians are up for sale, given that outside groups presumably want something in return for the millions of dollars they are spending.

Citizens United has also greatly affected political parties. Although parties were first seen as the losers of the Court's decision, they have adapted greatly, especially regarding congressional races, as the next chapter will demonstrate. Concretely, the leadership of the major parties has created its own Super PACs, and they are highly successful in raising funds for House and Senate campaigns. The *McCutcheon v. FEC* decision in 2014 has also helped parties since it eliminated biennial aggregate contribution limits. Major donors prefer to contribute to federal candidates and national party committees instead of state parties. But now a donor can give the federal limit of $10,000 to every single one of the fifty state parties. Last, the parties have invested a lot of resources into the battleground states. This investment is giving them a sustained presence in those states.

Because presidential campaigns are becoming increasingly expensive, conventional wisdom is that presidential campaigns are *least* likely to be affected by money. Money matters most when people know less about the candidates and when there is a higher chance of creating a significant resource advantage for one side. That is not the case in general election campaigns for the presidency, where both sides will have a lot of resources, and voters will have the most information about the candidates.

KEY TERMS

120-day cooling-off period   87
advisory opinions   87
attack dog   98
b-roll footage   97
canvassing   101
coordinated
    communications   96
coordinated expenditures   100
damaged goods   100
earned media   159
joint fundraising committee
    (JFC)   95
leadership PAC   93
money primary (invisible
    primary)   88
signaling game   96
small donor revolution   102
staff shell game   87

DISCUSSION QUESTIONS

1. Do you believe that the restrictions on staff moving from a campaign to a Super PAC are not strict enough, too strict, or are they okay where they are? Do you think these cooling-off periods can be effective? Explain your reasoning.
2. How is money a sign of candidate viability in presidential campaigns? How do Super PACs affect candidate viability?
3. Should presidential candidates vow to not accept support from Super PACs until after the presidential primaries? Can help from Super PACs at an early stage make a difference?
4. Do you think Super PACs and dark money groups can damage a party's presidential nominee during the primaries so that it may negatively affect the nominee's chances of winning the general election?
5. Do you consider the small donor movement a meaningful countertrend to the rise of megadonors? Explain your reasoning.

6. Based on what you have read, do you believe that the FEC guide-lines regarding the coordination between candidates and outside groups should be modified? If so, should they be strengthened or loosened?

ADDITIONAL READING

Gulati, Girish J. "Super PACs and Financing the 2012 Presidential Election." *Society* 49, no. 5 (September 2012): 409–17.

Hansen, Wendy L., Michael S. Rocca, and Brittany Leigh Ortiz. "The Effects of Citizens United on Corporate Spending in the 2012 Presidential Election." *The Journal of Politics* 77, no. 2 (April 2015): 535–45.

Hansen, Wendy L., and Michael S. Rocca. "The Impact of Citizens United on Large Corporations and Their Employees." *Political Research Quarterly* 72, no. 2 (June 2019): 403–19.

Sebold, Karen and Andrew J. Dowdle. "Can 'Letting in Sunlight' Lead to Accidental Sunburn? The Unintended Consequences of Campaign Finance Reform on the Financing of U.S. Presidential Candidates." *Election Law Journal* 17, no. 3 (September 2018): 209–20.

Smith, Jeff and David C. Kimball. "Barking Louder: Interest Groups in the 2012 Election." *The Forum* 10, no. 4 (February 2013): 80–90.

Vandewalker, Ian. "Shadow Campaigns: The Shift in Presidential Campaign Funding to Outside Groups." Brennan Center for Justice, 2015. https://www.brennancenter.org/sites/default/files/publications/Shadow_Campaigns.pdf.

5

New Trends in Congressional Campaigns

★ ★ ★

MUCH HAS CHANGED FOR CONGRESSIONAL CAMPAIGNS since the U.S. Supreme Court ruled in favor of unlimited independent expenditures. Since 2010, we have seen an influx of money into congressional campaigns in the form of outside spending, and that means an increased ability to advocate for and fight against candidates and their messages. Money can buy visibility, highlight legislative records, and point out flaws in candidates, potentially affecting one's chances to win political races.[1] Over the past ten years, outside groups have assumed some of the roles previously ascribed to political parties and traditional political action committees, including aggregating funds collected from individuals, providing some of the information voters rely on when choosing candidates, and setting the national political agenda.[2] Additionally, more congressional campaigns are financed by a donor class who resides outside the districts where their money is sent, campaigns are getting more negative, and more specific campaign activities, such as opposition research, voter mobilization, the redistribution of campaign funds to other organizations, and fundraising are conducted by outside groups, are largely out of the public's sight.[3]

Before delving into the consequences of the *Citizens United* and *SpeechNow* decisions for congressional campaigns, a snapshot of the financial picture from the 2018 midterm election can illustrate some of the changes taking place:

- The most expensive midterm election in U.S. history was that of 2018, with total spending exceeding $5.7 billion (a 50 percent increase in spending over 2014). The previous record for a midterm election was set in 2014 with $3.8 billion in overall spending (figure 5.1).[4]

- Nonparty outside spending increased by 84 percent compared to 2014 to almost $1.1 billion (figure 5.2).[5]
- Successful challengers for seats in the U.S. House of Representatives raised and spent, on average, $4.6 million. This does not represent the majority of campaign spending in those races though. On average, an additional $5.2 million was spent in the form of independent expenditures by party leadership Super political action committees (PACs) and nonparty outside groups in these races, bringing the total to almost $10 million per candidate.[6]
- For challengers who beat incumbents in the U.S. Senate, about $42.5 million was spent per race. On average, candidates spent $13.5 million, and nearly $29 million came from spending in the form of independent expenditures. Roughly $20 million came from independent expenditures made by political parties, and almost $9 million came from outside groups.[7]
- There were record levels of spending in several individual races. Candidates and outside groups spent $209 million in Florida's U.S. Senate race, while the candidates in the Texas U.S. Senate race spent $125 million. Nine of the ten most expensive House races in history took place in 2018.[8]
- Of the $4 billion in individual contributions given to candidates, outside groups, and party committees, $2.9 billion came from donors who contributed more than $200.[9]
- An analysis of independent expenditures shows groups supporting Democratic candidates outspent Republican efforts two to one in the last seven days (October 29–November 4, 2018), $82.4 million to $40.5 million, leading up to the election. The advantage was clear in both the House ($43.7 to $20 million) and the Senate ($38.7 to $20.5 million).[10]
- In the ten most expensive general election races in both House and Senate races, there was an identical breakdown between candidate and outside group spending: 51.8 percent of all spending came from candidates and their campaigns, and 48.2 percent from independent groups. One can speak of resource parity between candidates and groups in these races. However, groups spent very little in the Texas Senate race, which means that outside spending dominated six of the ten races for the U.S. Senate seats. In those six races, almost 62 percent of all campaign spending came from outside groups.[11]

Figure 5.1 Total Midterm Election Spending, 2010–18

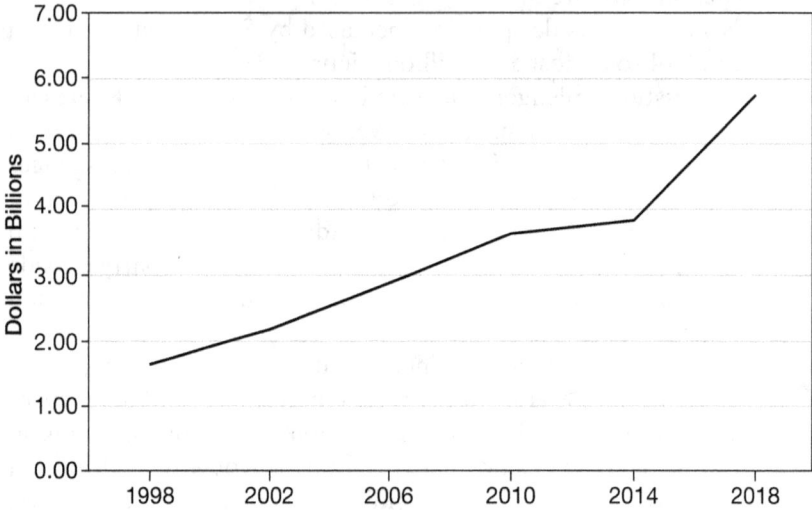

Figure 5.2 Nonparty Outside Spending in Midterm Elections, 2010–18

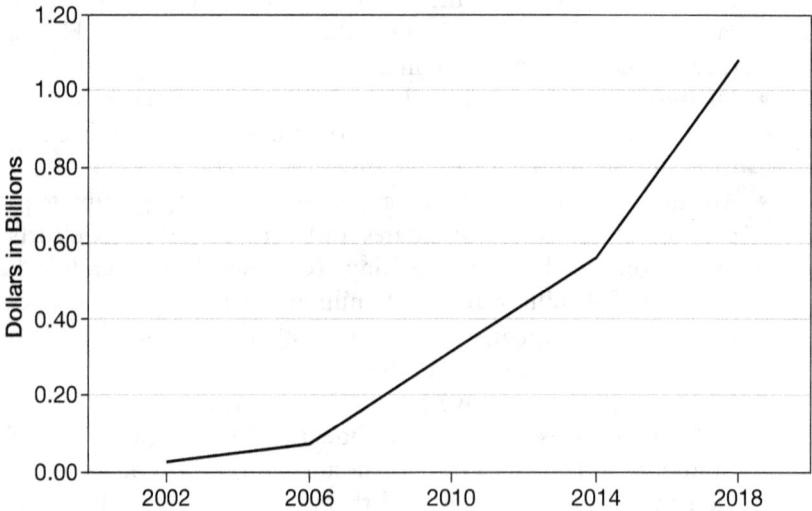

These statistics provide a glimpse into the current spending trends in congressional campaigns. The next section turns to a discussion of what we know more generally about congressional campaigns as well as campaign spending and its effects. After the literature review, recent trends and insights involving outside groups in congressional campaigns are highlighted.

WHAT WE KNOW FROM THE LITERATURE

A large body of research has been conducted in an effort to better understand when and how political campaigns matter. Although media pundits and those involved in campaigns often highlight how much campaigns matter, political scientists have shown that statistical modeling without specific campaign variables can be helpful in predicting elections, particularly presidential elections. Standard non-campaign variables included in these models are the state of the economy (e.g., changes to gross domestic product, real disposable income, and unemployment), presidential popularity, and the number of terms a party has been in the White House.[12] These models also show that citizens primarily engage in retrospective evaluations before casting votes. **Retrospective voting** stresses the past performance of a political party, legislator, or an administration. However, the research also shows that **asymmetric information**—when voters know more about one candidate than the opponent—allows for campaigns to matter.[13] This kind of asymmetry is least likely for presidential campaigns but more likely for congressional campaigns, the focus of this chapter.

Typically, incumbents benefit from asymmetric information during the early stages of campaigns. Incumbents are more familiar to voters, either through media coverage, social media, materials received by the incumbent—congressional officeholders enjoy the **franking privilege**, that is, the ability to send out mailings without postage—or via personal interactions. This familiarity gives incumbents an early advantage because it usually comes with a degree of public appreciation and respect. In the meantime, challengers need to make a convincing case as to why the incumbent should be defeated; they need to introduce themselves to as many voters as possible, and they need to leave the impression that they will be a good replacement. The "burden of proof," so to speak, is upon the challenger's campaign.[14] All of this takes time and money, which is why outside groups can play a crucial role in campaigns, particularly for challengers.

There is no doubt that the **incumbency advantage**—the structural advantages that officeholders enjoy, ranging from district offices and staff to fundraising advantages and committee assignments that can help bring benefits to the district—is a factor in congressional campaigns, and for state offices, as studies have shown. One study found that the significance of the incumbency effect has grown over time; it was four times greater in 2000 compared to the 1950s.[15] However, **political polarization**—the divergence of political attitudes to ideological extremes—has become so strong in the past two decades that the incumbency advantage has significantly decreased since then.

In fact, one scholar found that by 2014, the incumbency advantage was back to the 1950s levels. The study attributes this weakening of the incumbency status to "an increase in party loyalty, straight-ticket voting, and president-centered electoral nationalization,"[16] all of which are attributed to the widening partisan divide in the U.S. electorate. Although the percentage of persuadable voters is greater in congressional elections compared to presidential elections, mobilizing a party's core supporters is crucial in a polarized political environment. This is why there are now more volatile **wave elections**—where, at the federal level, one party picks up twenty or more seats in the House of Representatives—from one election to the next. Still, challengers need to make themselves known. People are unlikely to vote for someone they know nothing or little about, and that requires challengers to introduce new information to voters, which, in turn, can influence their vote.[17]

In terms of congressional campaign spending, the following summarizes decades of research on this issue:

> Early studies tended to find that spending by challengers was far more effective than incumbent spending. More recent work argues that in principle campaign spending is equally productive across candidates, but that there are strongly diminishing marginal returns to campaign spending. Since most challengers spend less than incumbents, their spending is marginally more effective, even though the underlying "production function" that transforms money into votes is not different for challengers. Further, the best efforts at identifying the treatment effect of money in congressional races yield fairly similar substantive results: candidate spending has very modest to negligible causal effects on candidate vote shares.[18]

The **law of diminishing marginal returns** means that adding an additional factor of production (in this case campaigning, which requires money) results in smaller increases in output (the vote share). Researchers have found that campaign spending has only modest effects on election outcomes but that it is more effective for challengers than incumbents because they often have less money to spend. Nevertheless, some scholarly disagreement remains about how spending matters for incumbents compared to challengers and to what degree spending matters overall.[19] The basic conclusion that campaign spending in congressional races has even a modest effect has been questioned in a recent, methodologically sophisticated study. The study concludes that "political expenditures are rarely pivotal in determining election outcomes."[20]

The idea that spending more money causes someone to win a political race is certainly too simple. In fact, when incumbents spend unusually high amounts of money during their campaigns, then the chances of them losing the election increase.[21] Having a significant war chest—money set aside for a campaign—is certainly desirable for incumbents, but when they need to spend unusual sums of money on their campaigns, it is usually a sign of desperation, indicating that they are trailing in polls. When incumbents are in danger of losing reelection and opponents "smell blood," an influx of money by individual donors, the parties, and outside groups can pour in. In the 2018 midterm elections, such an inflow of funds was true both for struggling incumbents and for their challengers.

Earlier studies have shown that an incumbent's campaign spending makes no obvious difference once a challenger's spending taken into account. In other words, the challenger's spending is what makes a difference in congressional campaigns because it may decrease the incumbent's vote share.[22] But that insight has been questioned in more recent studies. One study comes to the conclusion that "the impact of campaign spending on election outcomes, *regardless of incumbency status* [emphasis added], is small but positive."[23] Nevertheless, if we accept the more common notion that challengers' spending is at least marginally more effective than that of incumbents, then *Citizens United* could be interpreted positively for challengers because it has allowed them to identify outside groups who are willing to spend large sums of money on their behalf, an important condition to run a competitive campaign. It also means that new spending limits would not put incumbents and challengers on equal footing.[24]

Others disagree with this interpretation of *Citizens United*. One study found, on average, that incumbents outraise challengers by a 4:1 ratio. The analysis demonstrated that having *low* contribution limits reduces the incumbency advantage and therefore helps challengers. Lower contribution limits also prevent incumbents from accumulating considerable war chests that may deter challengers.[25] Others point to another possible consequence for challengers post–*Citizens United*. One study concludes that raising spending limits leads to more expensive races, which means fewer candidates will run for office. Those candidates who ultimately decide to run for office increasingly come from wealthy backgrounds. Overall, this helps incumbents in solidifying their electoral advantages.[26] Put differently, incumbents may benefit from more campaign spending, but it may also contribute to a decrease in **descriptive representation**—a situation where constituents share certain characteristics, such as financial backgrounds, race, and gender, with their representatives. In other words, according to the study cited earlier, expensive campaigning means that more millionaires and billionaires, who may not have much in common with their constituents, are running for public office.

There are other, more critical scholarly voices, who argue that most academics cannot see the forest for the trees: one study argues that "money's independent influence on elections remains powerful."[27] This analysis found a strong and consistent relation between major party candidates' shares of the two-party vote and their proportionate share of total campaign spending across all House and Senate elections between 1980 and 2014. The analysis demonstrates the same uniform pattern: the more money members in both parties spend on their campaigns, the higher the proportion of votes they receive. The authors are unusually frank in their conclusion: social scientists need to stop "behaving like ostriches" and "recognize what everyone else does: that we live in a money-driven political system."[28] The authors even accuse congressional and campaign finance scholars of providing cover for the leaders of both major parties to dismantle the campaign finance system. Ultimately, they ask, why do "all those nice people in expensive suits and dresses keep pouring money into the political system" if it does not affect election outcomes?

We agree that congressional and campaign finance scholars have been timid in their conclusions about the effects of money. Some of this seems related to complicated methodological issues in establishing *causal* relationships between money and winning elections. Students who want to dig deeper into these issues will quickly encounter a common statistical problem in the social sciences that also applies to studying campaigns and elections: **endogeneity**. This problem happens when an independent (explanatory) variable in an empirical model correlates with the model's error term, which prevents us from making causal claims. Without getting deeper into the statistical discussion and the efforts to work around the causality issue, we concur with the critical voices mentioned earlier that well-heeled donors would not flood the political system with money if their

return on investment—the return on a particular investment (in this case, electoral success and desirable, subsequent policy decisions) relative to the investment's cost (in this case, financial support)—would not be significant for them.

This investment approach has been used by political scientists who study the effects of lobbying on securing tangible benefits, such as federal contracts. These studies have found strong evidence that lobbying can come with tremendous returns for those who make the investment. For example, a recent study by Dusso, Holyoke, and Schatzinger found that for every dollar larger corporations in certain industries spent on lobbying Congress and the bureaucracy, they could expect an increase in contracts of about $300 and $900, respectively.[29] To summarize, there is good reason to look at financial commitments to the political sector from the perspective of a rational investor who will only make or continue to make considerable campaign contributions if the returns exceed the investment.

CONGRESSIONAL CAMPAIGN TRENDS SINCE *CITIZENS UNITED*

Since 2010, outside groups have influenced congressional campaigns in several major ways. The trends will be described in the following sections, summarized as follows:

- Outside groups play an increasingly crucial role in funding congressional elections; the funds for campaigns are coming more and more from sources outside of the affected congressional districts.
- A focus on competitive races and the partisan composition of Congress is enhanced.
- Super PACs increasingly specialize in specific aspects of political campaigns beyond advertising without the public's awareness.
- Partially disclosing Super PACs are particularly successful in their fundraising efforts.
- Organized blitz campaigns and continuous ad firestorms by independent groups increase.
- Outside groups contribute to the growing political polarization in Congress as well as wave elections with fewer swing voters.
- Some of the most successful "outside" groups are either guided or run by political parties; in fact, party leadership Super PACs have become the biggest players in Washington, D.C.

INDEPENDENT EXPENDITURES

The changes that took place in congressional campaign finance between 2016 and 2018 were dramatic. In 2016, the average winner of a race for a seat in the House of Representatives spent $1.5 million. In 2018, successful challengers, on average, raised $4.6 million, while defeated incumbents raised $3.7 million. More interestingly, the candidates themselves did not raise the majority of funds in those races. On average, successful challengers were helped with $5.2 million in party and nonparty independent expenditures, while the supporters of defeated incumbents spent $3.9 million in the form of independent expenditures. We saw the same pattern in open-seat races where, on average, Republicans saw $400,000 and Democrats $500,000 more in spending via independent expenditures per race than the candidates themselves spent. Overall, we saw a record in the number of House races with more than $5 million in independent expenditures: forty-one, almost double from 2016, as figure 5.3 shows. In 2010, there were only three such races. In 2018, seventy-three House races saw $1 million or more in independent expenditures, compared to 40 in 2016.[30]

In the Senate, there are too few cases from which to conclude any definitive trends, but according to the Campaign Finance Institute there were six races with independent expenditures of $50 million or more. This compares to only four such races in 2016, and none in 2010 (see figure 5.2). Eleven races saw $10 million or more in

Figure 5.3 Independent Expenditures on the Rise: $5+ Million Races for U.S. House Seats

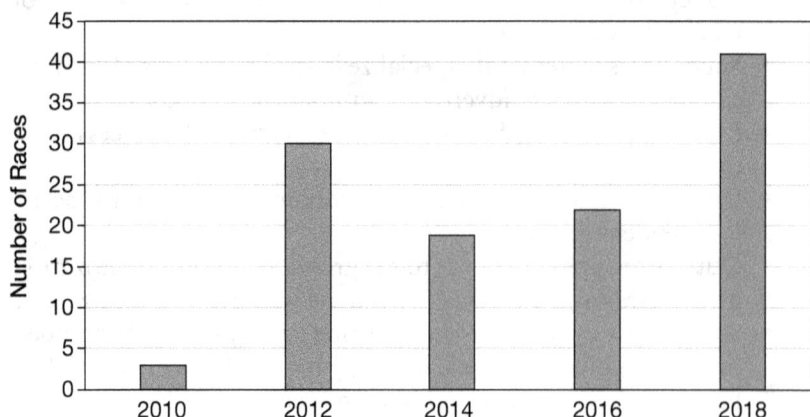

Figure 5.4 Independent Expenditures on the Rise: $50 Million Races for U.S. Senate Seats

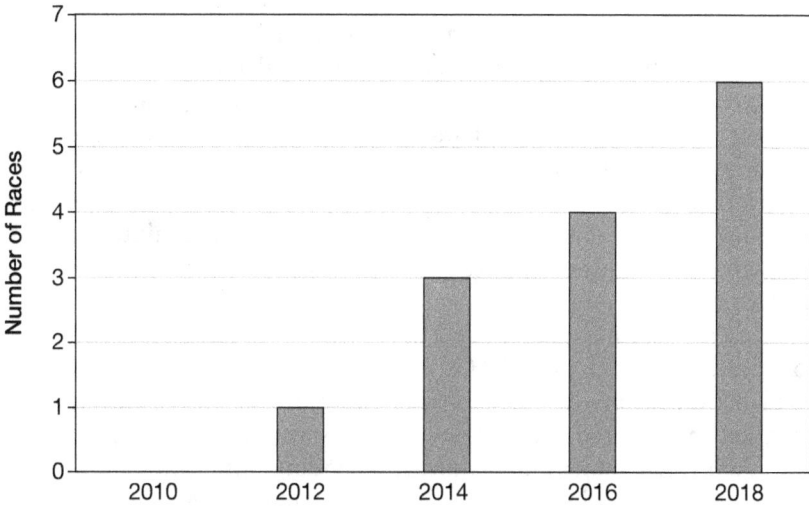

independent expenditures in 2018, compared to nine in 2016. Overall, independent expenditures by party leadership Super PACs was higher than nonparty groups.

THE ELECTORAL STRATEGY: A FOCUS ON COMPETITIVE RACES AND THE IDEOLOGICAL COMPOSITION OF CONGRESS

In the pre–*Citizens United* era, scholars who studied organized interests in political campaigns focused on the role and actions of traditional PACs. PACs are still active today and can make hard money contributions up to $5,000 per candidate and election. These political committees can also make independent expenditures but are more limited than Super PACs because of the contribution limits they must follow while raising money. Both PACs and Super PACs are required to report their donors and spending, with the caveat that Super PACs can accept contributions from dark money groups who do not have to disclose their donors.

There are three basic types of PACs: **ideological PACs** represent mostly organizations that focus on a single issue—for example, abortion, gun rights, or lesbian, gay, bisexual, transgender, and queer rights—with the goal of influencing the composition of Congress. Put simply, a $1,000, or even $5,000, contribution will not fundamentally change someone's mind on these issues. Therefore, ideological PACs prefer to use an electoral strategy to try to influence the policy agenda with the ultimate goal of producing beneficial policy outcomes for their group. **Access-oriented PACs** (also known as pragmatic PACs or investor PACs), on the other hand, use contributions to facilitate relationships with lawmakers. Last, **mixed-strategy PACs**, such as trade associations, use a combination of both strategies: show support for sympathetic candidates and donate to incumbents to maintain access to them.[31] This raises the question: how do Super PACs fit into these categories?

Researchers have concluded that Super PACs act most similarly to traditional ideological PACs. They are concerned about the partisan composition of Congress and therefore act more like parties than access-oriented PACs. Dwyre and Braz categorize Super PACs and their independent expenditure spending into four categories: candidate-specific Super PACs, pragmatic mainstream Super PACs acting like political parties with a focus on likely election winners, ideological Super PACs, and access-oriented Super PACs. They analyzed all 856 active Super PACs from the 2012 election cycle that filed reports with the Federal Election Commission (FEC) and found that almost two-thirds of Super PACs (64 percent) were candidate-specific, organized to advocate for just one candidate. Those Super PACs were more or less evenly distributed across presidential, Senate and House races. The rest were multicandidate Super PACs, most of which were party-like PACs, focused on competitive races to help their party win a majority. More than three-fourths (77 percent) of all Super PAC disbursements went toward independent expenditures, and the rest toward operating expenditures, hard money contributions, and transfers to other committees.[32] Nothing has fundamentally changed in the last couple of years that would suggest that this composition of Super PACs has changed considerably in the past few years.

Super PACs rely heavily on megadonors. For example, in the fourteen months leading up to the 2016 election, 41 percent of all Super PAC funds came from just fifty donors and their relatives.[33] Super PAC donors want their money to go toward competitive races. Although individual donors may have an interest in one specific congressional district, large donors ultimately want to keep or flip congressional majorities. These megadonors also make a lot of direct contributions to candidates for federal office. Until the end of the first quarter in 2018, two-thirds of the roughly $750 million in individual contributions to House candidates came from donors outside the candidates' districts. Additionally, in forty of the most competitive House races, more than 75 percent of the individual contributions came from donors who resided outside the districts.[34]

Some data from races for state-level offices can also illustrate in the concentrated nature of independent expenditures, showing that a significant part of campaign spending comes from individuals who do not reside in districts where the money is used. For example, in the 2015–16 election, 91 percent of independent expenditures at the state level came from only 300 individuals. However, that money was spent in 2,300 races. At the same time, 23 percent of all independent expenditures went to 10 races out of 4,300, where data were collected.[35] All told, this type of disbursement in independent expenditures shows both the breadth and depth of such spending. There is an influential, engaged class of donors who are contributing widely both to outside groups and to federal candidates and who are focused on giving to out-of-jurisdiction candidates. This illustrates just how influential the recent elimination of aggregate contribution limits can be in allowing a small number of donors to be much more influential.[36]

Traditionally, congressional incumbents are the main beneficiaries of hard money contributions by large donors. Because money is drawn to power, not all incumbents benefit equally: congressional party leaders, committee chairs, and policy architects are able to raise more money than others.[37] Also, those in leadership positions are able to collect large sums from party committees and leadership PACs.[38] Although this preferred way of direct giving to powerful incumbents has not meaningfully changed since *Citizens United*, the main criterion for Super PACs and their independent expenditures remains the competitiveness of races. This is certainly not surprising in a political environment where elites are ideologically highly polarized and the stakes associated with changes in political power are high. A recent study by Rocca and Clay confirms this: "The likelihood that a Super PAC invests in a race is strongly determined by the electoral context, even after controlling for the legislative influence of the incumbent member of Congress."[39]

The trends outlined earlier may lead one to believe that nonpartisan groups who just want to educate voters cannot be effective in such an environment. However, this is not the case. Voters can be susceptible to nonpartisan messaging in this polarized era, even in highly competitive congressional districts, as a real-world student project has shown. The student-based, nonpartisan voter mobilization coalition in Indiana's highly competitive Second Congressional District communicated nonpartisan get-out-the-vote messages through door-to-door canvassing had a powerful effect on getting people younger than thirty to vote. These young, potential voters were least likely to be contacted by partisan campaigns.[40] In other words, whether such nonpartisan efforts come from the campaigns themselves or from outside groups, campaigns and groups are well advised to talk directly to young voters rather than relying on digital and traditional advertising campaigns.

ORGANIZATIONAL DIVERSITY AMONG SUPER PACS AND ITS IMPACT

Not all Super PACs share the same characteristics; in fact, there are major differences in how individual Super PACs operate. Research has shown that some active Super PACs are similar to leadership PACs, think tanks, consulting firms, and party committees given their focus on research, redistribution of resources, and voter mobilization. Others spent big portions or even the biggest part of their budgets on salaries, fundraising, and organizational maintenance.[41] Herrnson, Heerwig, and Spencer point out that most of these organizations operate in a way that avoids public attention.[42] We believe that this observation is important because it speaks to the confusion, skepticism, and cynicism that this lack of knowledge creates in the public. Who can you trust when you do not know who is doing research for candidates and groups and who is paying the staff for doing the research?

Herrnson, Heerwig, and Spencer have examined other differences among Super PACs and have made the following observations. Between 2010 and 2016, almost one-fifth (18 percent) of all Super PACs made independent expenditures only in House races, 13 percent exclusively in Senate races, and 11 percent focused solely on presidential elections. Of all Super PACs, 17 percent spent funds on both House and Senate races, and 41 percent made no independent expenditures.[43] During that timeframe, 19 percent of all groups only supported Democratic candidates, 34 percent only helped Republicans, while 5 percent were bipartisan. The remaining 41 percent did not make independent expenditures.[44] The authors also found that partially disclosing Super PACs—because of dark money contributions—are financially much better positioned than fully transparent Super PACs, raising about twice as much as fully disclosing multicandidate Super PACs. Multicandidate Super PACs help many candidates—incumbents and challengers—in their campaigns, and they are generally most successful in raising funds, even compared to incumbent-only focused Super PACs. However, single-candidate Super PACs heavily support incumbents. That makes it harder for challengers to compete.[45]

In addition, the authors find that presidential-race only and Senate-race only Super PACs raise more than twice as much as money as House-only Super PACs. At the same time, experience matters for fundraising success. Older, more experienced Super PACs raise more than three times as much as single-year organizations. Super PACs that make independent expenditures receive almost twice as much in funds as those that do not. Last, hybrid "Carey" committees (see chapter 1) constitute 8 percent of all Super PACs. These committees often started as traditional PACs, and they raise both hard money for candidates and soft money for independent expenditures.[46] Although the media usually does not distinguish between different types of Super PACs, different organizational characteristics of Super PACs are associated with different Super PAC missions and different levels of fundraising success.

ORGANIZED BLITZ CAMPAIGNS AND CONTINUOUS AD FIRESTORMS

Chapter 6 discusses the political advertising trends for outside groups since the *Citizens United* decision in great depth. At this point, however, we highlight two general methods outside groups have used widely in congressional campaigns since 2010. First, groups increasingly take out a concentrated number of ads—on TV and/or online—within a short timeframe in connection with events close to Election Day, often in coordination with other groups. These **organized blitz campaigns** aim to mobilize and energize voters. Blitz campaigns are not to be confused with a **moneybomb**, a term used to describe an intense fundraising campaign that usually takes twenty-four hours or less, often carried out at the end-of-quarter fundraising deadline. Blitz campaigns are particularly important in an era of high political polarization where a significant **enthusiasm gap**—the difference in expected turnout among the supporters of the major parties—can foreshadow the direction an election will likely take. Also, outside groups engage in sustained advertising efforts over several months or longer that cross electoral as well as legislative goals and timeframes. We call this type of advertising campaign a **continuous ad firestorm.** Continuous ad firestorms are symptomatic of the **permanent campaign,** the idea that separating a legislator's term into time dedicated to governing and separate time for campaigning is a fool's errand. An example of each type of ad campaign is discussed in the following subsections.

Organized Blitz Campaigns

When Justice Brett Kavanaugh was confirmed to the U.S. Supreme Court on October 6, 2018, after a close 50–48 vote following much controversy, emotions among critics of the confirmation ran particularly high. During the confirmation process, Kavanaugh had been accused of instances of sexual assault, and one of his accusers, Christine Blasey Ford, testified before the Senate Judiciary Committee. Kavanaugh strongly denied the allegations. When the Senate decided to confirm Kavanaugh despite the allegations and a follow-up supplemental investigation by the FBI, liberal groups organized a digital blitz campaign. According to a *USA Today* investigation, within hours after the confirmation, up to 4.4 million left-leaning candidate and group ads appeared on Facebook, surpassing conservative-leaning ads five to one. Although candidates also launched ads, most of the ads came from outside groups.[47]

At that time, one of the organizers, Liz Jaff from Be A Hero PAC, a hybrid PAC/Super PAC, said that people were "mad" and that the blitz campaign would mobilize voters in the 2018 midterm elections. Other organizations that led the charge were MoveOn.org and NARAL Pro-Choice America. "It's incredibly painful to think of the suffering that we know Brett Kavanaugh and his appointment will bring about for millions of Americans," NARAL's ad stated. "But we will not forget this pain—not tomorrow, not next week, and not in November," the ad continued. Overall, the ads targeted different demographic groups but used similar language: "Furious, "outraged," and "disgusted" were frequently used in the ads to describe the Senate's confirmation.[48]

According to Justin Schall, a Democratic consultant, Facebook is a powerful tool in campaigns because it allows tailored messages to be targeted precisely to specific voters. For example, in the case of Kavanaugh, the outside groups were able to target certain clusters of suburban women who may have been likely to be "put off" by Kavanaugh's confirmation.[49] Schall argues that Facebook is an effective campaign tool because it allows for the transfer of emotions into action. Democratic political strategist Alex Kellner added that it is particularly important to "rile up the base" in midterm elections when turnout is crucial.[50] Overall, the takeaway message from this example is a different one, however: the more than four million appearances of liberal ads on people's screens were dominated by outside groups, not candidates. People may not always realize this when they see messages on their screen, but because of their coordinated efforts outside groups are frequently the ones who are able to capitalize the fastest when controversy and emotions erupt.

The degree to which outside groups and candidates will be able to use Facebook to target individuals in the future will partially depend on citizens themselves. In July 2019, Facebook announced that the company was adding a transparency tool that would allow people to see why they are seeing an ad (e.g., the personal interests and hobbies that users publicly disclosed and that were matched to a specific ad), how the ad is linked to a data broker or ad agency, and how to opt out of targeted ads. When users select "Why am I seeing this ad" in the dropdown menu of an ad, they can see this information.[51] Only time will tell how much citizens will use the new opt-out tool for targeted ads. Of course, advertising will be less effective should a larger proportion of users not allow for targeted advertising in the future. The new tool also allows Facebook users to suggest certain topics they would not like to see in future ads. However, adding "politics" or "political campaigns" to the list of topics one does not want to see is not a guarantee that such ads will not appear on someone's news feed. "You may still see ads related to this topic, but we'll use your input to improve the ads you see," Facebook tells its users.[52]

Candidates' Greatest Fear: Facing the Late "Ad Bomb"

What is the greatest fear congressional incumbents face in their reelection campaigns? Former senator Evan Bayh was asked this question during an interview with Senator Arlen Specter from Pennsylvania for a PBS pilot about the role of money in politics, and the discussion turned to Super PACs. Harvard law professor Lawrence Lessig has paraphrased Bayh's response:

> The single greatest fear of any incumbent is that thirty days before an election, some anonymously funded Super PAC will drop $1 million against him. When that happens, there's little the incumbent can do. He

can't then turn to his largest contributors—by definition, they have all maxed out and can't, under the law, give any more. So in anticipation, the incumbent must line up support—or let's call it protection. In light of the risk that the incumbent will be targeted, the incumbent needs a kind of assurance: If she needs a defense, there will be the resources to defend her.[53]

According to Lessig, the assurance that someone will come to protect a candidate in case of a late ad bomb could come in the form of *Super PAC insurance*, the idea that an incumbent or challenger will be offered resources to immediately counter a late "ad bomb." Scholars have proposed different variants of how this concept could work. Super PAC insurance is discussed in more detail in chapter 7.

Continuous Ad Firestorms

The Republican tax reform signed into law in December 2017 offers an opportunity to present an example to discuss a continuous ad firestorm. Between July 2017 and June 2018, the dark money group American Action Network (AAN) more than tripled its already significant media efforts from the prior year with two goals in mind: first, to help pass the tax bill, and second to support continuously those legislators who voted for the bill in their reelection efforts in the 2018 election. All in all, the 501(c)(4) group spent more than $27 million on media advocacy in that timeframe, on "issue advocacy and mobilization," according to the AAN's tax records. In other words, the group avoided the *magic words* discussed in chapter 2 to avoid the risk that the expenditures might fall under express advocacy. In addition, the 990s—tax forms filed by tax-exempt groups—reveal that the group also funneled $15.8 million of its contributions to one of the two Republican leadership Super PACs, the Congressional Leadership Fund (CLP), in the form of a grant.[54]

Of the $51 million in contributions and grants the group received in 2017, $16 million came from an unnamed donor. Although the AAN can claim it helped pass the Tax Cuts and Jobs Act, it could not prevent almost half of the forty-nine Republicans they supported following the tax vote from losing their House seats in 2018. Although the AAN tried to sell the benefits of the tax reform and the accomplishment of passing the bill with a host of ads in those Republican-held districts, it was not enough to prevent midterm losses.[55]

SUPER PACS DISCLOSING THEIR
DONORS *AFTER* AN ELECTION

One of the legal directives guiding outside group politics is that Super PACs need to disclose their donors, except for the grants received from dark money groups. However, one of the trends among Super PACs in recent years has been to delay the disclosure of a group's contributions, often until after the election. This, of course, runs counter to the U.S. Supreme Court's majority opinion in *Citizens United* whereby citizens and shareholders would be able to hold Super PACs accountable because of their "prompt disclosure of expenditures."[56] The Court argued that in the Internet age, citizens should be able to "see whether elected officials are 'in the pocket' of so-called moneyed interests" and act accordingly.[57] In 2015, Justice Kennedy, who wrote the majority opinion in *Citizens United*, was asked about this section of the decision. He said that disclosure is "not working the way it should" in a time when instant online reporting would not be a problem.[58] In reality, sixty-nine Super PACs delayed the disclosure of their donors in the 2018 election cycle, according to an analysis by *Politico* and *ProPublica*. For the congressional primaries and special elections alone, that added up to more than $15 million of delayed disclosures.[59]

How is this done legally? *Politico* explains one common strategy:

> Start a new Super PAC after a deadline for reporting donors and expenses, then raise and spend money before the next report is due. Timed right, a Super PAC might get a month or more undercover before being required to reveal its donors. And if a Super PAC launches right before the election, voters won't know who's funding it until after they go to the polls. The strategy—which is legal—is proving increasingly popular among Democrats and Republicans.[60]

In other words, some Super PACs wait so long in the election cycle to file their new existence with the FEC that voters will not know who sponsored their messages until *after* the election. These late-forming outside groups are called **pop-up PACs**. Another method to avoid revealing Super PAC donors before an election is to go into debt for advertising and other activities but then fundraise later to pay off the debt. Some of these other activities include mailers and phone calls. This is what a Super PAC called Sunshine PAC did when it blitzed the Sixth Congressional District in Illinois in a seven-way Democratic primary in March 2018, with $130,000 for mailers and phone calls. The Sunshine PAC revealed its donors only after the primary.[61] Other groups simply do not file required disclosure forms on time, a violation of campaign finance law. Brendan Fischer from the Campaign Legal Center commented on these cases when he said that "these operatives may view the FEC as so dysfunctional that they can ignore their most basic legal obligations and get away with it."[62]

In fact, the FEC has decreased its issuance of fines recently. One report found that in 2018, the FEC was on pace for its second-lowest penalty total in twenty years.[63] At this juncture, the FEC seems to have set its sights on going after the most egregious campaign finance offenders. One of the most prominent examples is the case of the American Conservative Union and two affiliated groups who agreed to pay a $350,000 fine, the largest post–*Citizens United* penalty imposed by the FEC, after they made a $1.71 million contribution illegally to a Super PAC called the Now or Never PAC.[64] Even if the FEC were to go after the Sunshine PAC that did not file its FEC forms, the maximum penalty for such a violation is $17,000, hardly a slap on the wrist for extremely wealthy donors. As a matter of fact, risking a small fine may well be part of some PACs' strategy: almost no one will hear or care about an FEC fine and the subsequent disclosure of donors until after an election, when it is unlikely ever to matter again.

EFFECTS ON POLITICAL PARTIES

How have all these developments affected political parties? In the first chapter, we raised a few questions, which are addressed here: are outside groups complementing, competing, or replacing parties in the support of preferred candidates? Specifically, do outside groups follow the lead of parties or do they prefer more extreme candidates? Do outside groups affect both parties in the same ways or indifferent ways? There are certainly many questions worth exploring regarding changing party-group relations.

Currently, Super PACs are greatly expanding their range of campaign activities. We now rarely blink an eye when we hear that the Democratic super PAC For Our Future is rolling out a $90 million grassroots turnout operation in the key swing states for the 2020 election.[65] Or that two Republican Super PACs, the Great America PAC and Committee to Defend the President, are coordinating their efforts in a $1 million voter mobilization effort whose goal is to register one million conservative voters before November 2020.[66] Parties once conducted these activities, but now outside groups are performing them, even though such efforts may still be guided by political parties.

To what extent are outside groups competing against parties? As an example, fundraising can be examined. We saw in the first chapter that the Trump campaign is concerned that donors are giving to outside groups instead of donating directly to the reelection campaign. Research shows that donors who used to give regularly to the parties, sometimes described as *habitual donors*, now provide significant support to outside groups instead. The result is that parties need to spend more money for each dollar they are raising; especially those donors who gave regularly to the Democratic Party have become less loyal.[67]

What happens when outside groups—including traditional PACs—differ with their party over which candidate they support? Between 2012 and 2016, this happened forty-five times in races for the U.S. House of Representatives. The interest group's preferred candidate won twenty-three of them (51 percent). Super PACs supported 91 percent of the winning candidates and 50 percent (11 candidates; 22 candidates total) of those who lost. In other words, in the current era of triumvirate campaigns, outside groups are quite capable of successfully fighting against a party organization's consensus candidate.[68]

Other trends have been affecting parties since 2010. When outside groups are strongly involved in congressional primaries, we have seen that female candidates have benefited from this on the Democratic side, while it has limited the opportunities for Republican women. Experienced Democratic candidates but inexperienced Republican candidates are advantaged in those situations. Additionally, when there is heavy outside group involvement, winning candidates are less likely to be moderates.[69] Figure 5.5 shows that significant political spending by single-candidate Super PACs in primaries has more than quadrupled between 2014 and 2018. Political parties are generally staying out of internal contests in congressional primaries, and this vacuum has been filled by outside groups.

Overall, there are elements of competition between outside groups and parties, as well as areas where outside groups have become surrogate actors for political parties. However, when tensions rise between the two because of how candidates position themselves ideologically, then outside groups may decide to call their own shots by supporting a different candidate. Parties have adjusted to this new campaign environment. One way they have done so is by having networks that not only work across actors within a congressional district,

Figure 5.5 Single-Candidate Super PAC Spending in Senate and House Primaries, 2012–18

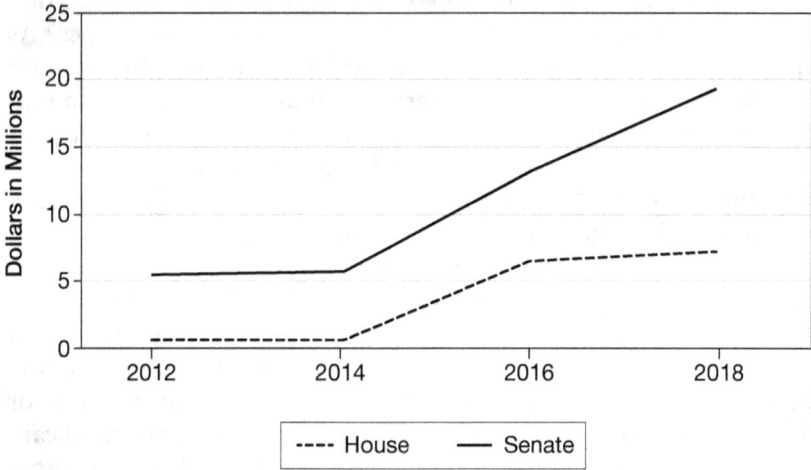

horizontal networks, but by building networks that "operate with fluidity across state boundaries,"[70] that is, vertical networks. In sum, party-group relations are changing, and groups are taking on more traditional party functions. Yet, parties have found other ways to maintain their prominence by adjusting their strategies, as the next sections demonstrate.

The New Party Super Weapon: Party Leadership Super PACs

The main challenge for political parties in campaigns is that the *Citizens United* and *SpeechNow* decisions allow for unlimited independent expenditures by organizations that excluded parties. The FEC rules state that independently made expenses for communication cannot be made "in consultation or cooperation with . . . a *party committee* or their agents" (emphasis added).[71] This begs the question: what else have parties done to cement their role in the triumvirate campaign era? Journalistic op-eds sometimes depict parties as the losers of the current campaign finance laws, but academic research sees parties flourishing in this new environment. How?

The national Democratic and Republican leaders did not take long to create their own Super PACs once *Citizens United* and *SpeechNow* were decided. The Democratic Party's leadership created the House Majority PAC and Senate Majority PAC as affiliated

Super PACs. Republicans leaders formed the CLP and Senate Leadership Fund (SLP). All four of them are Super PACs, but they are not officially party Super PACs because party committees cannot make independent expenditures (see the FEC rule discussed earlier). However, a closer look at who started, and is affiliated with, these Super PACs reveals that **party leadership Super PACs** is an appropriate term for these Super PACs: for Democrats, Speaker of the House Nancy Pelosi is affiliated with the House Majority PAC and former senator and majority leader Harry Reid is affiliated with the Senate Majority PAC.[72] For Republicans, the Congressional Leadership PAC was known as the "Boehner PAC"[73] in the early years, nicknamed after former Speaker of the House John Boehner. It then became known as Paul Ryan's Super PAC,[74] who served as Speaker of the House until January 2019. The CLP currently does not list its leadership on its website.[75] The SLP was initially led by Steven Law, Senate Majority Leader Mitch McConnell's former chief of staff,[76] and is currently led by Mike Duncan, former chairman of the Republican National Committee.[77]

How successful have the parties' leadership Super PACs been in raising money and spending them on independent expenditures? The CLF only raised $11.3 million in the 2011–12 election cycle, almost half of which came from Miriam and Sheldon Adelson.[78] However, for the presidential election in 2016, the CLF was able to increase its commitments significantly by spending a little over $50 million. During the most recent midterm elections in 2018, the CLF spent $158.7 million on Republican candidates. In other words, the extended party network is now fighting fire with fire when it comes to competing against other Super PACs. The SLP took longer to get off the ground. It was formed in 2015 and has close ties to American Crossroads, another Super PAC affiliated with Republican consultant and policy advisor Karl Rove. The SLF spent $114.2 million in the 2016 elections and even increased its spending for the midterm elections in 2018 to $127.3 million.[79]

Unofficial Democratic Party Super PACs have also shown tremendous growth in recent years. The House Majority PAC spent $35.7 million in 2012, $55.7 in 2016, and $95.6 in 2018. In the meantime, the Senate Majority PAC went from spending $42.1 million in 2012 to $91.2 million in 2016 to $165.6 million in the 2018 election cycle.[80] What does all of this tell us? It means that political parties needed a couple of years to set up new campaign finance structures, but they have recovered with Super PACs that are run by, or at least affiliated with, each party's leadership. In fact, the four largest Super PACs in 2017–18 were the four unofficial party Super PACs discussed earlier (figure 5.6). Party leadership Super PACs are now the biggest insiders in Washington playing the "outside" game.

Yet, the four unofficial party Super PACs get surprisingly little attention in the media or from the public. Instead, single-candidate Super PACs receive the bulk of media attention. For example, in 2018 the New Republican Super PAC supported a single candidate, former governor Rick Scott from Florida, who ran for a seat in the U.S. Senate in 2018 (see chapter 6). He won with 50.05 percent of the vote, and the New Republican PAC spent almost $34 million

Figure 5.6 Ten Largest Super PACs, 2017–18

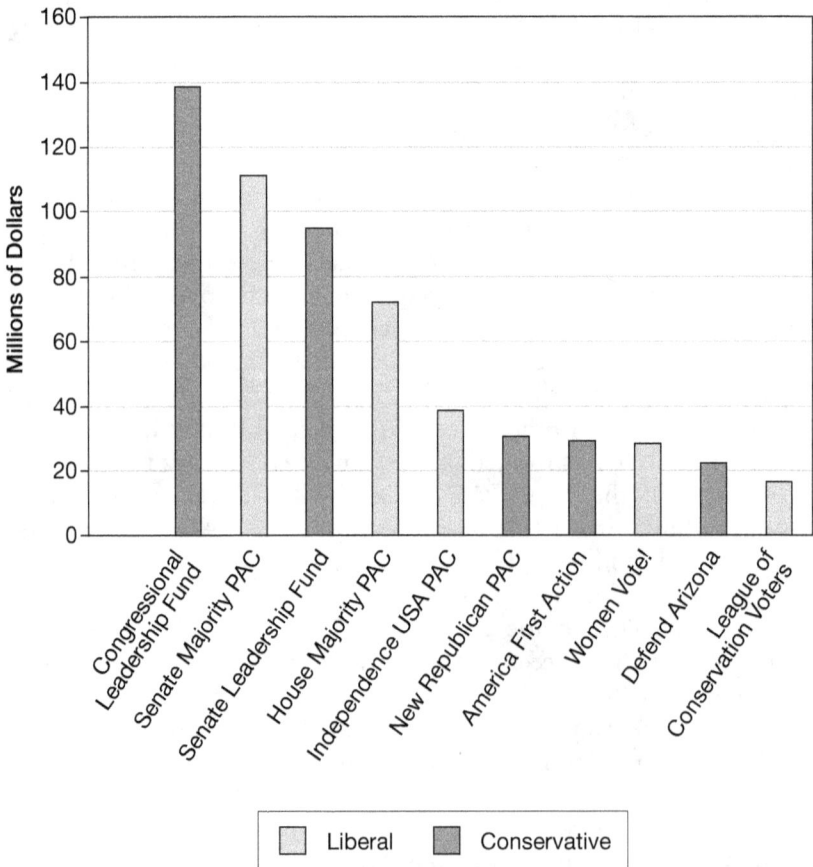

in its successful efforts to support Scott.[81] Despite the media's focus on single-candidate Super PACs, the biggest Super PACs today are quasi-party committees, which speaks to the resilience of political parties. These "quasi-party" Super PACs are vote maximizers; they are focused on winning majorities, not pushing the most extreme candidates or single issues.

What about the traditional party committees? The National Republican Campaign Committee (NRCC) and the National Republican Senatorial Committee (NRSC) are the official fundraising arms of the Republican Party exclusively dedicated to electing Republican legislators to the U.S. House of Representatives and U.S. Senate. Collectively, the NRCC and the NRSC have been able to raise more money in each subsequent election cycle since 2008, including midterm elections. In 2012, the committees collectively raised $272.7 million; in 2016, $308.9 million; and in 2018, $357.2 million. In other words, the NRCC and NRSC combined are currently raising money at similar levels compared to the RNC.[82]

The Democratic Congressional Campaign Committee (DCCC) and Democratic Senatorial Campaign Committee (DSCC) represent the equivalent to the NRCC and NRSC on the Democratic side. Combined, the DCCC and DSCC have generally outraised its Republican counterparts. Fundraising for both campaign committees slowed immediately following *Citizens United* but reached new heights in 2014 ($375 million), 2016 ($399.8 million), and 2018 ($445 million). All told, the national party committees do not have the same level of influence they once had. The RNC, however, appears to be returning to its 2008 levels whereas the DNC has been struggling recently. All of the campaign committees are raising more money with each election cycle, showing that *McCutcheon* has strengthened the parties' campaign committees to continue to play an important role in financing political campaigns in America.

OUTSIDE GROUP EFFECTS

There is only limited research on the effects of all the observed outside spending in congressional elections over the past ten years. This is surprising given the statistics we presented for the 2018 election, where outside spending matched or even exceeded candidate spending in the most competitive House and Senate races. One problem that can explain the paucity of studies is the statistical problem mentioned earlier in this chapter: endogeneity. In fact, some scholars have argued that independent expenditures should be viewed as an endogenous variable, meaning that they are a factor that arises from within campaigns.[83] One study has found limited, yet statistically significant, effects of outside spending in congressional campaigns. This is because Super PACs and dark money groups often support those candidates who outspend their opponents significantly (with diminishing marginal returns, as discussed earlier), or outside groups on both sides neutralize each other.[84] However, outside groups have the ability to target voters within subgroups of the population, which makes it possible for these subgroups to turn out to vote at a higher rate than they would have without these additional efforts.[85] Overall, outside groups have been found to adopt autonomous yet complementary strategies in the electoral process.[86]

As the next chapter discusses in more depth, Super PACs and dark money groups are primarily working against candidates they do not want to see elected rather than promoting their preferred candidates. As a result, candidates may have to respond to the criticisms raised by outside groups, or they can feel inclined to run a more negative campaign themselves, either personally or via their own Super PACs. Overall, this cycle of negativity can reduce a candidate's ability to control the message they want to convey and instead shift the messaging power to Super PACs. However, proponents of *Citizens United* can make the case that outside groups are shedding light on issues that otherwise would not be raised. This can increase candidates' accountability and improve the representational relationship between incumbents and constituents.[87]

In addition to the organizational diversity of Super PACs discussed earlier, *Citizens United* brought us another concrete outcome: group diversity in terms of political goals.[88] Although nonpartisan organizations represent only a small minority of organizations, they certainly exist. For example, Amazon founder and CEO Jeff Bezos made headlines in 2018 when he made his first major political donation, $10 million, to the With Honor Fund, a Super PAC that backs veterans of both major parties running for the House of Representatives.[89] Another example is the Mayday PAC, a Super PAC created by Harvard law professor Lawrence Lessig, whose goal it is to elect candidates who will work toward substantial campaign finance reform. Other types of new Super PACs are ideological in nature and may represent the vision of single major donors (e.g., Liberty for All and Ending Spending) or challenge the party establishment (e.g., FreedomWorks and Senate Conservatives Action Fund).[90] The latter can be seen either as adding much needed new voices in politics that better represent the views of those who were not recognized enough in the past, or they could be viewed as orchestrated efforts by elites that do not speak for larger segments of society.

Finally, and perhaps most importantly, research points to additional advantages for congressional incumbents in the post–*Citizens United* era. There has been a growth of single-candidate Super PACs at the congressional level, and there is some evidence that this type of Super PAC favors incumbents. Boatright, Malbin, and Glavin theorize that single-candidate Super PACs are funded by networks of large donors who are well connected to powerful incumbents. "This does represent a shift in political power," they conclude. The authors also point out that Super PACs funded by one or a handful of megadonors hardly mobilize activists and that this is not their motivation. Those donors are motivated to win elections and wish to exert influence or even control over the recipients of the donations. Super PACs offer a much better tool for individuals interested in impacting group spending compared to traditional interest groups and campaign committees.[91]

CONCLUSION

Several new trends were identified in this chapter: the rise of outside groups in funding congressional elections, sometimes exceeding candidate spending in competitive races; their sharp focus on competitive elections with an eye of changing and keeping congressional majorities, contributing via negativity to a more polarized Congress; the increasing specialization and scope of Super PAC activities; the rise of partially disclosing Super PACs due to funding from dark money groups; common types of outreach efforts; the meteoric rise of party leadership Super PACs; and the overall effects of Super PACs for congressional campaigns, particularly primaries and incumbents. "The Super PAC stuff has changed the whole dynamic," a former legislative director told journalist Patricia Murphy from *Roll Call* about congressional campaigning.[92] In the post–*Citizens United* era, members of Congress are spending more time than ever fundraising, particularly to meet with billionaires in hopes of securing funds from supportive outside groups. Murphy added that a lobbyist told her, "There are no real limits anymore. You used to be able to tell people, 'I'm maxed out.' But that's out the window."[93]

One also needs to think about other political developments that work in conjunction with the rise of outside groups. Party elites are weaker when there is a disconnect between them and the party's base. One can argue that we have seen such a division in both parties in recent years. For the Republican Party, issues such as immigration and trade come to mind, contributing to the rise of President Trump. For Democrats, the ascent of the progressive wing of the party can illustrate such a divergence.

Moreover, party elites have lost power because of how voters use media to get information. "Parties once had the power to restrain the impulses or the sovereignty of the individual voter," Steve Schmidt, John McCain's campaign manager in 2008, said in an interview. "They could communicate in a hierarchical, top-down way, and it was more often than not received as credible. . . . People trust people like them, and consume news through social media, and through websites and blogs and Twitter and all manner of other sites, where their opinions are validated, not challenged."[94] When parties lose the grip on messaging, it opens the door for more extreme political positions who may voice their discontent via well-funded Super PACs.

KEY TERMS

access-oriented PAC   118
ad blitz   xxx
asymmetric information   111
continuous ad firestorm   122
descriptive representation   114
endogeneity   114
enthusiasm gap   121
franking privilege   111
horizontal network   127
ideological PAC   117
law of diminishing marginal
   returns   112

mixed-strategy PAC   118
moneybomb   121
party leadership Super
   PAC   129
permanent campaign   122
pop-up PAC   125
retrospective voting   111
return on investment   115
spending blitz   xxx
vertical network   128
war chest   113
wave election   112

DISCUSSION QUESTIONS

1. Why do you think is there not more evidence in academic studies that campaign spending is a major factor in explaining electoral success? How do large donors see a return on their investment?
2. How do the trends described in this chapter affect incumbents compared to challengers? Have we seen a shift in power?

3. Do you consider it a problem when more campaign funds are not raised within the district where they are used, but from a small elite who finances out-of-jurisdiction candidates via outside groups? Explain your reasoning.

4. Do you believe that outside groups contribute to the polarization in American politics? Explain your reasoning.

5. What do you consider the key changes the increased activity of outside groups has brought to congressional campaigns? Are they problematic or positive?

6. How has the rise of Super PACs and dark money groups in campaigns shifted the balance of power between candidates, political parties, and outside groups?

ADDITIONAL READING

Baker, Anne E. "Are Federal PACs Obsolete?" *Interest Groups & Advocacy* 7, no. 2 (May 2018): 105–25.

Baker, Anne E. "Do Interest Group Endorsements Cue Individual Contributions to House Candidates?" *American Politics Research* 44, no. 2 (March 2016): 197–221.

Boatright, Robert G., Michael J. Malbin, and Brendan Glavin. "Independent Expenditures in Congressional Primaries after *Citizens United*: Implications for Interest Groups, Incumbents and Political Parties." *Interest Groups & Advocacy* 5, no. 2 (May 2016): 119–40.

Herrnson, Paul S., Jennifer A. Heerwig, and Douglas M. Spencer. "The Impact of Organizational Characteristics on Super PAC Financing." In *The State of the Parties: The Changing Role of Contemporary American Political Parties*, edited by John C. Green, Daniel J. Coffey, and David B. Cohen, 248–62. New York: Rowman & Littlefield, 2018.

Rhodes, Jesse H., Brian F. Schaffner, and Raymond J. La Raja. "Detecting and Understanding Donor Strategies in Midterm Elections." *Political Research Quarterly* 71, no. 3 (September 2018): 503–16.

6

Political Advertising in the Post-*Citizens United* Era

★ ★ ★

DURING THE 2018 REPUBLICAN PRIMARY for U.S. Senator from Arizona, a little-known pro-Democratic Super PAC called Red and Gold ran attack ads against GOP front-runner Martha McSally.[1] McSally was certain to be a greater threat than other primary candidates in the general election, so pro-Democratic groups ran ads attacking her before she was officially the nominee. Outside groups can try to boost perceived weaker candidates, hoping for an upset victory in the primary, but even if the frontrunner secures the nomination he or she is then "wounded" going into the general election. Either way, the group leaves its mark.

The ads against McSally targeted her record on health care, claiming that she voted five times to raise costs on people over fifty, a key voting demographic in Arizona. One of the ads stated, "They tax your pay; they tax your car, and just about everything you buy. Now, Congresswoman Martha McSally wants to tax your *age*. You heard right. McSally voted to let health insurance . . . charge people over 50 [years old] five times more." The other ad made similar claims but ended with the accusation that McSally "puts Washington [D.C.] ahead of Arizona."[2]

After the primary, the pro-Democratic Senate Majority PAC, affiliated with the Democratic Party's leadership, was revealed as the source of the ads' funding.[3] After McSally secured the Republican nomination, liberal megadonors George Soros and his son donated another $600,000 to Red and Gold for general election ads.[4] All told, Red and Gold spent nearly $1.7 million, exclusively against McSally.[5]

The 2018 Arizona Senate race serves as a typical example to illustrate political advertising trends that have arisen in the post–*Citizens United* era. Money is funneled from several sources, including unknown donors and existing Super PACs, to an unknown group with an innocuous-sounding name. That group then floods the airwaves and online media with attack ads. Candidates and the general public alike shake their heads trying to figure out exactly what is happening and why some unfamiliar group is suddenly "meddling" in the election.[6] When reporters attempt to uncover the sources of the funding, the spokesperson for the group—assuming one can be contacted—refuses to reveal donor information until the Federal Election Commission (FEC) requires it.[7] As is common, the truth is not discovered until after the election, if ever. Finally, like many outside groups who appear only for one election cycle, Red and Gold has vanished, leaving few tracks. In the next election cycle, new groups pop up with new names, produce more ads, and again no one discovers valuable information about the groups until the election is over.

* * *

Because political advertising is the single largest expense category in elections, understanding how those resources are used is crucial to developing a complete picture of campaigns in the post–*Citizens United* era. This chapter examines the role of political campaign communication, with an emphasis on how the laws and Court's rulings described in chapter 2 are changing the ways in which candidates, parties, and outside groups advertise. This chapter covers the following:

- Political advertising spending trends of outside groups by election since 2010
- How the *Citizens United* and *SpeechNow* rulings have allowed many groups to advertise anonymously. Dark money has led to dark advertising, which prevents voters from learning valuable information and holding anyone accountable
- The ways in which digital media are changing the political advertising game, including astroturfing and microtargeting
- The "tone" (positive, contrast, negative, attack) of political advertising
- A discussion about the effects and implications of political advertising
- How free media coverage can counter the impact of paid ads in an era of increased independent expenditures

OUTSIDE GROUP ADVERTISEMENTS IN
FEDERAL ELECTIONS SINCE 2010

This section provides a snapshot of the overall involvement of outside groups' political advertising. We begin in 2010, the first election affected by the *Citizens United* ruling.

Several trends are evident and can provide insight into how the U.S. Supreme Court's rulings have changed the "game" of political advertising. With few exceptions, both the number of overall ads and the money spent have increased since 2010. Similarly, the percentage of overall ads aired by outside groups has increased (see figure 6.1), while the percentage of ads by candidates and parties has declined.[8]

2010: Congressional Midterm Elections

The year 2010 broke political advertising records. Approximately 1.6 million ads aired, which was a 36 percent increase from 2008. The total estimated cost in 2010 was $735 million, an even larger increase (61 percent increase) from the previous election cycle. Outside groups aired nearly 14 percent of the total number of ads; in 2008, outside groups aired only 5 percent of the total ads. At the same time, the total percentage of ads that candidates aired dropped by 7 percent.[9]

Figure 6.1 Percentage of Ads by Outside Groups, Presidential and Congressional Elections, 2000–16

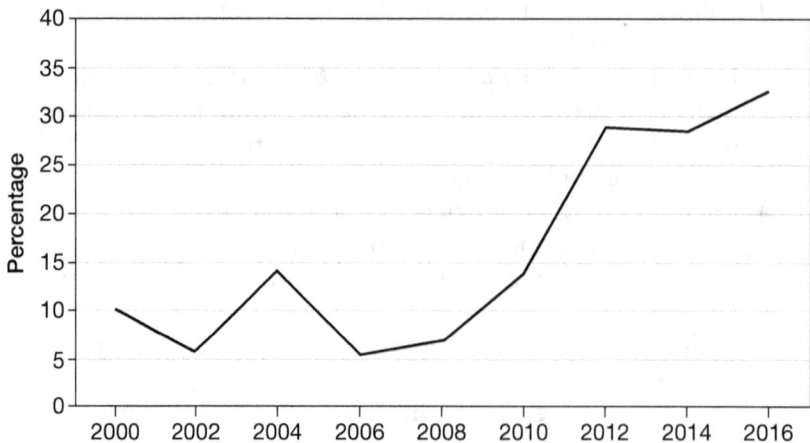

2012: Presidential and Congressional Elections

As most scholars and pundits predicted, 2012 saw the most money spent and the most ads aired to date. There were more than 3 million ads aired between the beginning of 2012 and Election Day. This was a 33 percent increase from 2008. The total cost was a staggering $1.92 *billion*, an 81 percent increase from the previous presidential election cycle.[10] This was due in no small part to the removal of regulations in the ways that outside groups could now spend on advertising as well as the removal of previous constraints of airing ads throughout the previously forbidden blackout periods.

Independent groups played a significant role in the advertising. Compared to the prior presidential election cycle in 2008, there were *sixteen times* (an increase of 1,600 percent) the number of ads aired by outside groups.[11] Independent groups spent an estimated $360 million on the presidential race alone in 2012.[12] In the South Carolina Republican presidential primary, independent groups spent twice as much as the candidates themselves.[13] By 2014, such a ratio would no longer be an anomaly confined to one state.

2014: Congressional Midterm Elections

The overall trend of total volume of political ads ended in 2014, except for an increase in advertising for Senate races.[14] The total number of ads for U.S. Senate seats increased from the previous election cycle by 55,459, which was not as significant as the previous two election cycle increases: from 2008 to 2010, ads increased by 195,047, and from 2010 to 2012, there was an increase of 136,213 Senate ads. In similar fashion, although the trend was showing ever-increasing negative advertising, 2014 saw that trend end as well. Yet, one factor stood out: the percentage of outside group ads for U.S. Senate and House races exceeded 25 percent (25.7 percent, to be exact) for the first time. In the 2014 election cycle, outside spending exceeded the candidates' spending in nine U.S. Senate and nineteen House of Representatives elections.[15] This was, therefore, "The Year of the Outside Group" in political advertising, according to the Wesleyan Media Center.

Later in the report, the same researchers also declared 2014 "The Year of Dark Money."[16] This was because more than 35 percent of outside group ad spending were from groups that do not disclose donors, and an additional 6.4 percent of the ads were from groups that only partially disclose their donors.[17] In several Senate races, outside groups spent even more than the candidates themselves. In Colorado, Crossroads Grassroots Policy Strategies (Crossroads GPS) spent $6.5 million in favor of Cory Gardner, the Republican candidate, while the Gardner campaign spent $5.2 million. In North Carolina, a pro-Democratic group, Senate Majority PAC, spent $9 million while the Republican candidate spent only $5.4 million.[18]

2016: Presidential and Congressional Elections

In 2016, outside groups aired 28 percent of all the ads in federal elections.[19] Groups paid for and aired 38 percent of all the ads for U.S. Senate races, continuing the trend that groups are becoming increasingly significant players in federal elections.[20] Even more to the point, groups set their sights on competitive Senate races to attempt to wrest control of the body from the other party. For example, groups paid for nearly half of all the ads aired in Nevada and Pennsylvania.[21] Compared to the Senate races, outside groups made up a smaller share of expenditures for ads in House races that year.[22]

The 2016 Presidential Election

No consideration of federal elections in 2016 would be complete without discussing the most unusual presidential race in recent history: Donald Trump's defeat of Hillary Clinton. Clinton not only significantly outspent Trump insofar as traditional TV ads were concerned ($257 to $91 million) but also failed to air ads until the last week of the election in several states that she lost by small margins, such as Wisconsin and Michigan.[23] Clinton aired more than 402,000 ads to Trump's 120,908. Oddly, Trump aired even fewer ads than did Bernie Sanders (128,494), who, of course, did not air any ads in the general election.[24]

Ads aired over broadcast networks tell only a fraction of the story about advertising's impact on the 2016 presidential election. There are two other considerations, both of which are discussed in subsequent sections of this chapter. First, free media attention helped Trump overcome the spending gap. Second, there exists the possibility that digital advertising (both Trump's and outside groups') and other online methods of campaigning played a much larger role in the election than we yet know. Trump's campaign spent heavily on digital advertising, especially in states he won by small margins.[25] Additionally, although a clearer picture is emerging, and is examined later in the chapter, we still do not know the full extent of the Russian government's efforts to manipulate the U.S. electorate in Trump's favor via online and other social media accounts. Not until recently have the prominent Internet and social media companies begun to reveal anything about political advertising expenditures and sources, which is briefly be outlined after the 2018 elections are described next.

2018: Congressional Midterm Elections

In 2018, the Wesleyan Media Project reported that there were more dark money ads overall than in any of the previous four election cycles for House and Senate races. At the same time, the percentage of dark money ads for House and Senate races composed 11.2 percent of all ads, which was an increase from 7.1 percent in 2016, but down from approximately 14 percent in the 2012 and 2014 election years. In 2018, more than one-fifth (22 percent) of all ad spending for U.S. House of Representative elections was from outside groups; in 2016, it was 15 percent.[26] Significantly, however, these numbers are only from national broadcast (over-the-air) TV networks and national cable buys but do not include any local cable or digital ad buys.

For the first time since *Citizens United*, dark money groups ran ads in favor of Democrats running for the House at a higher rate than for Republicans. Of group ads on behalf of Democrats, 25 percent came from dark money sources, whereas 12 percent of the group ads on behalf of Republicans were from dark money groups. For Senate candidates, the percentage of dark money ads were about the same for both parties but were higher overall than for House races. Roughly one-third of ads sponsored by an outside group for Senate races on behalf of both major parties were from a dark money source.[27]

* * *

Thus far, we have examined how much money has been spent in the most recent elections. The trends typically show that elections not only are getting more expensive and are producing, airing, or displaying more ads in more media categories but specifically that the percentage of advertising from independent groups is increasing. Additionally, dark money sources are producing more ads overall in most races. This leads us to new questions about political advertising in the post–*Citizens United* era: To what extent is anyone accountable for the content of these ads? Whose voices are truly being heard?

ANONYMITY AND ACCOUNTABILITY

Americans for Job Security, American Future Fund, Partnership for America, Club for Growth, Priorities USA, Alliance for Freedom, Common Sense, Action Now Initiative, Fund for the Public Interest,

Citizens for a Strong America, and Center for American Progress Fund. Can you tell which of those groups back Republicans? Democrats? Can you tell without any other information which groups are ideologically libertarian, conservative, liberal, or progressive? A quick perusal of the lists of Super political action committees (PACs), 501(c)s, and 527s will reveal that most of the names of the groups are inoffensive and ambiguous. This is no accident. According to political scientist Darrell West, groups that run ads "have clear partisan interests and therefore are not seen as credible by reporters, legislators, or the public."[28]

Interest groups understand that one of the most significant aspects of effective persuasion is how an audience values and trusts a source. Many special interests lack credibility in the public realm because voters are savvy to their motives, but what if those special interests could hide behind groups that appear to be something they are not? The names of most of these groups are designed to sound inoffensive and agreeable, using words with generally positive connotations such as "freedom," "progress," or "security." The names that groups choose are significant because, except for some forms of digital advertising, they appear visually on the ad somewhere, sometimes accompanied by audio.

Discerning the ideological position of most groups from the names alone is often impossible. In some cases, the names of the groups may even suggest the exact opposite mission than the group's true agenda. Take the example of the now-defunct National Wetlands Coalition, which sounds like a conservation group concerned about the environment but was funded by oil companies and real estate developers who sought to deregulate environmental protections for projects such as pipelines and other development on wetlands.[29] A more recent example is Americans for Responsible Leadership, which, according to the Center for Responsive Politics, is funded almost exclusively (more than 97 percent of its total funds) by the Koch Brothers via yet another group with an innocuous name, The Center to Protect Patient Rights (CPPR). The CPPR could only be traced back to a post office box in Phoenix, Arizona; it served as a financial conduit for a network of nonprofits but did not perform any "social welfare."[30] In fact, since 2008, CPPR has given more money (more than $165 million) to other politically active nonprofits than any other organization.[31] The CPPR provided grants to many other groups; all except one of them was a 501(c)(4), with equally anodyne names: American Future Fund, Concerned Women for America, and American Commitment, among others.[32] Interestingly, the CPPR changed its name in 2014, perhaps in response to articles outing its machinations, to American Encore, yet another generic name.[33] This ability to cloak partisanship and ideology, or even intentionally mislead the public, is one of the most effective tools that outside groups possess, and the advantages of doing so are most obvious in political advertising.

Astroturfing

In addition to using misleading names, some of these groups also are **astroturfing**,[34] which is a deliberate attempt to appear as though they are a grassroots social movement, a group of everyday, concerned citizens who happen to share a common goal and have thus united in action. The reality in most cases is that the organization is funded by a relatively small number of corporations and megadonors, as chapter 3 illustrated. Crossroads GPS, the dark money "sub-Super PAC" of American Crossroads, is one clear example because the "GPS" part of the name stands for "Grassroots Policy Strategies." Another group is called "Save our Tips," which sounds like a concerned group of waiters, waitresses, taxi drivers, and other service workers but is funded by restaurant owners who do not want minimum-wage laws applied to waitstaff.[35]

Featured in two documentaries, *Toxic Hot Seat* and *Merchants of Doubt*, one of the more notorious astroturf groups was Citizens for Fire Safety. When the state of California was reconsidering its law requiring flame retardants in furniture, the three largest manufacturers of the chemicals (Chemtura, Albemarle, and ICL Industrial Products) created a fake organization to make it appear as though firefighters, doctors, and concerned parents supported a continuation of the flame-retardant laws.[36] The people behind these groups are masterful manipulators who are, via grassroots-sounding names and carefully constructed advertising campaigns, able to deceive the public into thinking they are comprised of thousands of concerned, everyday citizens, when, in fact, they are often funded by corporations and a few megadonors.

Such groups are becoming increasingly common in digital forms as well, which is known as **digital astroturfing**, posting memes and other forms of disguised advertising. Kovic et al. define digital astroturfing as a "form of manufactured, deceptive, and strategic top-down activity on the Internet initiated by political actors that mimics bottom-up activity by autonomous individuals."[37] The authors further argue that digital astroturfing is distinct because, unlike regular astroturfing that can include "varying degrees of genuine grassroots components," digital astroturfing is entirely fake.[38]

One of the most active dark money groups, the pro-Democratic Majority Forward, ran a series of digital ads during the 2018 midterms that were disguised as a grassroots movement. Majority Forward, unknown to the general public, created a Facebook page called "The Tax Scam," which was disguised as a group of people who were opposed to the tax cuts Trump was proposing at the time. The ads ran with taglines such as "82 percent of the Benefits Go to the 1 percent," "The Tax Bill Is Rigged for the Wealthy," "$1.5 Trillion in Debt and You're on the Hook," and "Out-of-State Billionaires Are Making You Pay For Their Tax Cuts."[39] According to Facebook, the ads ran for approximately two weeks without a disclaimer such as "paid for by." The absence of any disclaimer may have increased the likelihood that the ads could have been mistaken as authentic posts by an "autonomous" individual or group. Other similar Facebook pages and ads have popped up since the 2018 midterms as well under names such as "Stand up America" and "Americans for Tax Fairness."[40]

Deception in the Content of Group Ads

Many groups have adopted ways of deceiving the public by hiding their identities and motives, but what about the actual content of the political advertisements? Kenneth Winneg et al. studied the 2012 presidential campaigns, including the Republican primary. They discovered that outside groups spent approximately $300 million on TV advertising, about 25 percent of which contained at least one "deceptive claim."[41] Additionally, the ability to hide funding sources seems to correlate with how deceptive the content tends to be. Groups that were not required to disclose donors were more likely to use deceptive claims, especially in the primary phase of campaigns.[42]

Following the trends seen elsewhere, groups were more deceptive earlier in the election process. Various pro-Republican groups, for example, were more deceptive during the primaries but became less deceptive in the general election when the only target against whom negative ads could boomerang would have been the party's nominee, Mitt Romney. Winneg et al. suggest this was because "attacks perceived as illegitimate risked a backlash among those whose ballots Republicans needed in order to win the White House."[43] The main pro-Obama group, Priorities USA Action, on the other hand, spent more on deceptive ads after the primary, which may have been "a function of Democratic confidence that the group's tactics would not redound against" Obama.[44]

Groups that do not disclose donors, as well as the timing of when groups used more deceptive advertising content, can be understood in the context of avoiding backlash. A well-documented **backlash effect** exists, wherein voters may hold the attacker accountable for creating and sponsoring the ad.[45] This is why corporate America, for example, typically is hesitant to donate directly to candidates or to groups that are required to disclose donors. Shortly after the *Citizens United* ruling, the state of Minnesota passed disclosure laws. When Target and Best Buy donated money in 2010 to MN Forward, a group that supported a social conservative for governor, gay rights activists and others staged protests in Target stores. There are more ways now for corporations and individuals to avoid detection, as chapter 3 demonstrated; thus, we currently have only limited knowledge of who funds most 501(c)s.[46]

Why Disclosure Matters

Why does it matter if an ad does not reveal its funding sources or appears to be from a type of source that it is not? Although the scholarship is still in its early stages about this question, several studies suggest that potential voters believe ads from "unknown" sources much more than ads from the candidates.[47] Additionally, candidates avoid the backlash effect to a greater extent when viewers are unfamiliar with the sources behind the ads. One reason wealthy individuals and large, for-profit corporations, are now donating in larger sums is because they also can remain in the shadows, avoiding potential fallout from a negative ad. Thus, both candidates and the funding sources (whether an individual or a corporation) do not need to worry about the consequences of the public's perception of the ads.

This explanation is also the most likely for why most 501(c)s that partake in political advertising are typically short-lived. According to tracking data, the overwhelming majority of groups participate in only one election cycle and then either disappear or morph into a different group. Fewer than 10 percent of all groups participate in more than two election cycles.[48] Additionally, nearly 80 percent of all groups who participate in political advertising exist for only one election cycle.[49] In all likelihood, this short life cycle is to prevent discovery by watchdog groups and investigative journalists and to keep voters in the dark. In the unlikely event the public finds out who the donors were, the potential for any impact would already be passed.

DIGITAL POLITICAL ADVERTISING

Digital advertising, which includes any ads found in online sources such as websites, blogs, social media platforms, or apps, is much harder to catalog and study, but what is known is that the amount spent on online ads continues to increase. Approximately $1.4 billion was spent on digital political advertisements in 2016, which was a 789 percent increase from 2012.[50] In 2014, digital advertising was estimated to make up only 1 percent of all political advertising expenses, but estimates are that in 2018 approximately 20 percent (about $900 million on digital ads) of political advertising was spent on digital media.[51] Between May 2018 and May 2019, approximately $615 million was spent on political ads on Facebook alone.[52] About $400 million of that was spent between May 1, 2018, and Election Day, November 6, 2018. More than $200 million was spent in the six months after the election, indicating that political advertising in the digital realm has become an ongoing practice. Google, the parent company of YouTube, reported that nearly $85 million had been spent on political ads from May 31, 2018, to June 1, 2019.[53] Both Facebook and Google now have "transparency" websites in the wake of criticism about Russian interference in the 2016 elections, likely as a response to ongoing public discussions and as a strategy to avoid stricter regulations.[54]

Significantly, **disclaimer notices**, statements that identify who paid for and authorized the ad, that have long applied to TV, radio, and print electioneering ads did not apply to digital ads until December 2018, when the FEC released an opinion that nonprofits ought to display a disclaimer.[55] Despite this, an investigation by *ProPublica* found that only a small percentage of ads on Facebook contain any disclaimer, likely because of the inefficacy of FEC enforcement.[56]

Aside from the overall increase in the use of digital ads, there are several other techniques as well that campaigns and groups are using. The following sections explain native advertising and microtargeting.

Native Advertising

Advertising is becoming more sophisticated in the digital arena. One of the newest trends in political campaigns is producing **native advertisements**, also called "sponsored content." This form of advertising is camouflaged to blend into its surrounding habitat. For example, an ad for a candidate on a news or political website is written to mimic a news story or editorial content from the original source. The Bernie

Sanders campaign produced this type of ad in 2016. On the popular website *Buzzfeed*, the Sanders campaign ran an ad that was titled "15 Reasons Bernie Sanders is the Candidate We've Been Waiting For."[57] The ad looks and reads as if it were written by a member of *Buzzfeed*'s staff and therefore seems like an endorsement from a media outlet when, in fact, it is not.

The Obama campaign in 2012 ran a native ad on *Buzzfeed* as well. Following Mitt Romney's now-infamous gaffe during the second presidential debate that he had "binders full of women," the Obama team ran an ad with what looked like an editorial headline: "What Mitt Romney's 'Binders Full of Women' Says about His Views." Below the headline, the text read: "No policies. No Solution. Mitt Romney's only answer on equal pay for women was 'binders full of women.' Watch and see why Mitt Romney's wrong for women."[58] Directly below the text was an embedded video advertisement produced by Obama for America that included a clip of Romney's gaffe from the debate.

These ads often deceive people. In one study, fewer than 8 percent of college students correctly identified native advertisements as promotions, mistaking them as news or editorial content.[59] In another study, 41 percent of the participants identified the material correctly as an advertisement.[60] There are, therefore, legal and ethical issues related to this category of advertising. **Truth-in-advertising** laws prohibit false and misleading advertising in the commercial realm, and the Federal Trade Commission (FTC) has acknowledged the misleading nature of native ads.[61] For that reason, the FTC recommends calling attention to the content by noting that it is a "paid advertisement" or "sponsored content." Of course, truth-in-advertising regulations do not apply to political ads because such ads are protected under the First Amendment (see chapter 2), so the FTC has no control over them. Moreover, the issues related to native advertisements are exacerbated when the sources are dark money groups. If nondisclosing groups can take advantage of camouflaged ads that also require no disclosure, voters will find it doubly difficult to determine the funding source(s) of the message.

Microtargeting
As social media platforms, data collection, and data analytics have become increasingly sophisticated, so, too, has the ability of advertisers to target increasingly more carefully selected audiences. In the late 1990s, several campaigns experimented with "banner ads," which

were ads that typically ran at the top or bottom of a web page. The ads could be tailored according to some basic demographic tendencies for the audience who was known to frequent that website or read that publication. The ability to do this is an example of **narrowcasting**. For example, readers of the *New Yorker* tend to be affluent, highly educated, and knowledgeable about public affairs, so advertisers could carefully target that audience.[62]

The level of sophistication today makes the banner ads of the late 1990s look rudimentary by comparison. **Microtargeting**, by contrast, has the capacity to target individuals with specific, customized messages. When users create a Facebook, Twitter, or other social media account, they often disclose a wealth of information: age, race, gender, zip code, marital status, where they went to high school and/or college, and so on. Then, many of these platforms also ask users to select, or "like," interests they may have. These interests could be relatively general (sports, politics, country music) or quite specific (a particular sport, a particular politician, or a particular musical artist). All these data are later used to target specific users on the platform.

Trump's 2016 campaign used extensive microtargeting on Facebook. Brad Parscale ran Trump's 2016 digital advertising campaign and is Trump's campaign manager for his 2020 reelection bid. Parscale says he tested fifty to sixty thousand variations of Facebook ads every day during the 2016 campaign. Using databases that contained "detailed identity profiles" on 220 million people, Parscale and his team claim to have created "over 5.9 million ads between [the nominating] convention and Election Day."[63] The following is how he described the campaign's use of data for microtargeting ads:

> When you decide you're going to run for President of the United States, now you have hard-matched data with consumer data, matched with voter history, matched with very comprehensive polling data from all over the country. By the time all those pieces are put together, then you can actually pull out an audience. You can say, "I want to find everybody in this portion of Ohio that believes that the wall [U.S.–Mexico border] needs to be built, that thinks that possibly trade reform needs to happen," and so we want to show them [an ad] on trade and immigration.[64]

Microtargeted ads also employ subtle changes, such as a different font or color scheme, that the creator believes might be more persuasive to a specific person or small group. For example, Parscale explained, "we might write 50,000 ads that only have very, very small nuances changed about them."[65]

Near the end of the campaign, when nearly every poll showed Trump was likely to lose, the campaign reportedly switched to a different strategy: to attempt to depress voter turnout. A senior campaign official told reporters that they had "three major voter suppression operations underway," which were designed to target "idealistic white liberals, young women, and African Americans."[66] The campaign targeted its late-game digital ads to cultivate despair and apathy among specific categories of likely Democratic voters. Combined with the efforts of domestic and foreign operatives and saboteurs—but invisible at the time to the public—that strategy may have paid off.

Foreign Dark Money and Digital Advertising

The Russians seem to have followed the Trump campaign's digital advertising strategies.[67] Although illegal for foreign entities to donate to candidates or to produce electioneering communications,[68] the Russian Internet Research Agency took advantage of loopholes and oversight to disseminate more than eighty thousand posts of digital advertisements that reached an estimated 126 million people via astroturfing and **sock puppets,**[69] which are fake online accounts meant to look like the accounts of real people.[70] Russia's efforts have often been referenced as deriving from a "troll farm," but such a label dangerously minimizes the actions of the Russian government. "Trolling" is not to be confused with digital astroturfing. **Trolling** is "malicious, disruptive or disinhibited online behavior by individuals who engage in the activity . . . of their own individual volition."[71] Trolling is not, however, "initiated on behalf of political actors," nor is it "manufactured," and it is only "somewhat deceptive."[72] The Russian government coordinated a top-down strategy meant to achieve a certain political outcome; it was not merely trolling, even if the efforts at times employed the techniques of Internet trolls.

In all, more than half of the ads the Russians ran focused on stirring racial tension and getting minorities to vote against Clinton or to not vote at all. For example, users on Facebook who were within twelve miles of Buffalo, New York, were shown ads that allegedly came from a Facebook group called Blacktivist, promoting a protest event about an African American woman who died in jail in that geographic location.[73] Blacktivist also endorsed Green Party candidate Jill Stein as an attempt to draw votes from Clinton. Other ads by a group calling itself Woke Blacks aimed to "chip away at Clinton's . . . lead among African-Americans."[74] Another Russian account on Facebook was called United Muslims of America, who posted that they were "boycotting" the election, refusing to vote for Clinton because "she wants to continue the war on Muslims . . . and voted yes for invading Iraq."[75] Pro-police ads and other postings were made under a group the Russians called Back the Badge; the postings were meant to stir tensions between those who were concerned about instances of excessive use of police force and those who wanted to defend the police.[76] Ads about immigration, some under the Facebook page name Secured Borders, targeted Facebook users who had "liked" Fox News hosts.[77] A foreign entity was able to run ads microtargeted at those whom they believed would be deceived into thinking the ads came from other like-minded individuals.

Other ads were more obviously political and were clearly aimed at harming Clinton's reputation and likability. Likely following the lead of Trump's many "Lock her up!" chants during rallies, several Russian ads contained images of Hillary Clinton behind bars.[78] One of the more outrageous Russian ads, posted under the group name Army of Jesus, showed an image of Satan arm wrestling Jesus. The caption of the image displayed a dialogue between Satan and Jesus. Satan said, "If I win, Clinton Wins!" and Jesus replied, "Not if I can Help it!" Below the image was a request to "Press 'Like' to Help Jesus Win!"[79] Even after the election, the Russian agency continued to run microtargeted ads.[80]

What started in the 1990s as "banner ads" on certain websites has become increasingly more sophisticated as data-mining firms have access to user data on many social media platforms and apps. Every time users interact with platforms such as Facebook, Twitter, Instagram, and YouTube, they provide invaluable data that ultimately can be used to manipulate them. As people watch fewer TV programs in real time and have multiple ways to avoid advertising during shows and televised sporting events, the importance of digital advertising will continue to increase. Currently, the technology is far ahead of both the law and the public's awareness of how advertisers are attempting to influence them.

THE TONE AND CONTENT OF POLITICAL ADS

There are many ways to categorize the tone of any given message, but for the purposes of this chapter, and based upon what prior scholarship has analyzed, we can think of ads as having three general tones: positive, contrasting, and negative. **Positive ads** are designed to make viewers feel good about a candidate, whether about her experience, voting record, or character. **Contrast ads** draw comparisons that show why one candidate is better or worse than another; this can be based on any number of differing ideas, such as experience, accomplishments, or fitness for a given office. **Negative ads** provide a message against an opponent in some manner, pointing out a deficiency in experience, a bad track record of supporting or opposing certain policies, or character flaws. But not all negative ads are equal, so we also consider a subset of the negative ad: the attack ad.[81]

Although much of the literature on political advertising uses "negative ad" and "attack ad" synonymously, there is value in distinguishing them and discussing attack ads as a more precise subgenre of negative ads. **Attack ads** are distinctly personal and harsh, more along the lines of the ad hominem fallacy than negative ads more broadly.[82] Think of attack ads as personal insults that are irrelevant to how a person might do his or her job, whereas a merely negative ad at least has some relevance to the fact that a candidate will have lawmaking powers. Arguably, then, attack ads possess less worth in a democratic society. Negative ads, on the other hand, may be more valuable because they have the potential to inform the public about a candidate in some meaningful way. Some scholars even argue that negative ads have the benefit of informing voters and holding politicians accountable for their past actions.[83]

Some general conclusions can be made about negative advertising. First, most people claim to dislike negative ads.[84] This is particularly true of attack ads.[85] Second, negative ads and attack ads can be risky, especially for candidates to use, because of the backlash effect. Creating and airing ads perceived as unfair or too personal can, therefore, end up helping the target of the ad. Despite the alleged unpopularity of negative ads, they also tend to be more memorable.[86] This has some potential to mitigate fading effectiveness, which may further explain why the majority of ads are negative or attack ads.

In a larger sense, negative ads once were believed to reduce voter turnout. This is known as the **demobilization hypothesis**. The argument was that too much negativity caused potential voters to have a "weakened sense of efficacy" and to become "cynical about the responsiveness of public officials," which, in turn, caused them to stay at home.[87] Although some studies have shown that voters may feel more cynical about politics or more distrustful of their government because of negative ads, the demobilization hypothesis has been countered by dozens of subsequent studies, and now the consensus is that negative advertising does not appear to reduce voter turnout and may even increase turnout for three possible reasons: (1) negative ads can contain useful information that creates more knowledgeable voters, who, in turn, are then more likely to vote; (2) negative ads can create stark contrasts, and when voters have more distinctive candidates, they are more likely to vote; and (3) negative ads are more likely to result in stronger emotional reactions, which also possesses the potential to get people to the polls.[88] We hasten to add that these studies have not taken into account the types of digital astroturfing and microtargeting that were discussed previously. Future research could make new discoveries about these ads in relation to turnout.

Tone and Content in Outside Group Ads

As figure 6.2 illustrates, the trend in the post–*Citizens United* era is an increasing amount of money spent *against* candidates. This is a significant shift in overall tone from prior eras. During the 1984–1992 period, for example, independent groups spent three times as much on ads supporting a candidate than in opposition.[89] Research comparing the tone and content of political advertising has discovered that outside groups, especially those that do not disclose their funding sources, air a much higher percentage of negative and attack ads. In

Figure 6.2 Nonparty Independent Expenditures, Money Spent for versus against Congressional Candidates, 2000–16 (adjusted for inflation)

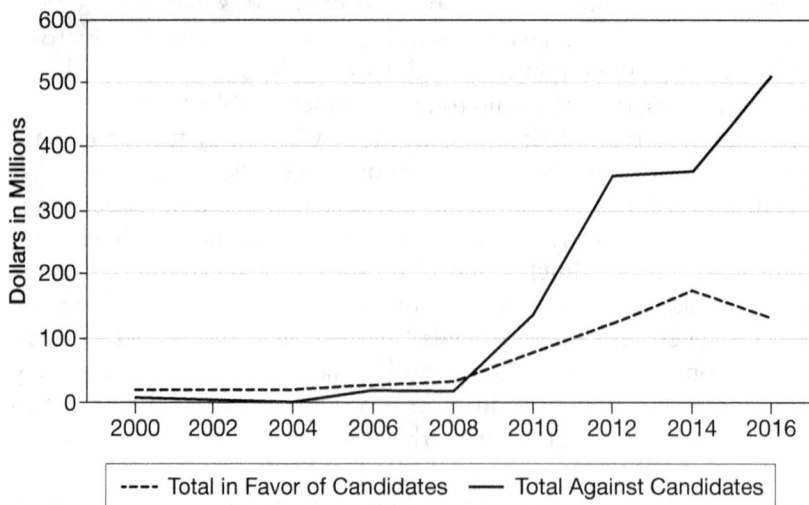

both 2010 and 2012, more than 70 percent of all independent expenditures were made to oppose a candidate.[90] In 2010, ads by independent groups were 2.5 times more likely to be negative than candidate ads.[91] The Wesleyan Media Project analyzed the tone of the ads in the 2012 federal campaigns from September 1 to Election Day and discovered that ads by interest groups were more frequently negative. Ads aired by outside groups were negative 83 percent of the time. Party and PAC ads were negative slightly less often (78 percent). Yet the most significant and telling contrast is that official ads by the candidates' campaigns were negative less than half as often as those by groups (39 percent). Specific to the 2012 presidential election alone, group-sponsored ads were negative 85 percent of the time, whereas the party-sponsored and candidate-sponsored ads were negative only 54 percent and 51 percent of the time, respectively.[92]

The most likely explanation for why candidates' ads are negative less often is because of the potential for a backlash effect. Outside groups appear much more immune to such an effect. Voters do not typically hold candidates responsible for the attacks made by others.[93] This is why one scholar has dubbed Super PACs a candidate's "alter-ego."[94] Despite playing this surrogate role as attack dogs, outside groups tend to remain loyal when it comes to staying on topic with the campaigns of their preferred candidates.[95]

Attack ads are also more effective when sponsored by unknown groups, according to one study. Brooks and Murov created a fictional set of candidates and ads to test whether sponsorship of an ad influenced its effectiveness. The experiment was designed to measure both persuasiveness and backlash. If the persuasiveness of the ad was greater than any backlash against the attacker, then an ad would be considered at least somewhat effective. An additional variable was whether the ads appeared to have been sponsored by the candidates themselves, by an independent group, or completely unsponsored. They found that candidates are "punished" substantially for attack ads—a confirmation of the backlash effect found in prior studies—but that the persuasiveness of the ads was rather constant regardless of sponsor. Still, that means that an attack ad "by an unknown independent group is more effective than an identical ad sponsored by a candidate in the eyes of the public overall."[96] Other research has found that letting outside groups do the "dirty work" for candidates not only allows candidates to avoid the backlash effect but that candidates also can directly benefit from this in their standing among voters because voters often do not connect group ads to candidates.[97]

Case Study: The 2018 Florida Senate Race

As Election Day of the 2018 midterms neared, control of the House of Representatives was becoming increasingly likely to switch to the Democratic Party.[98] Republicans and their supporters focused a lot of their energy on maintaining control of the Senate, and many outside groups turned their attention—and financial clout—to several crucial Senate races. One of the main targets of those groups was incumbent Florida senator Bill Nelson. The former governor of Florida Rick Scott was running against Nelson. Unseating an incumbent, even in a swing state, would not be easy, and it certainly would not be cheap. In fact, the 2018 Florida Senate election currently holds the unofficial record for being the most expensive U.S. Senate race in U.S. history. Estimates put the cost at more than $200 million.[99] Outside groups funded approximately $87 million of that total.[100]

One of the biggest spenders in the campaign was the New Republican Political Action Committee, a Super PAC that Rick Scott himself controlled in 2016 to help elect Donald Trump.[101] In 2018, the Super PAC spent nearly $30 million in advertising to help get Scott elected. In just the final week of the campaign, the Super PAC spent $11 million, almost all of it on TV ads attacking Nelson.

One thirty-second ad, "Generations," shows three women and an infant sitting at a table in a cafe. The youngest woman is looking at her cell phone; she is watching an ad in favor of Bill Nelson. With a tinge of disgust in her voice, she says to her mother and grandmother, "These political ads; have you seen this one?" while tilting her phone so they can see the screen. The mother replies, "Bill Nelson's been running for office almost as long as I've been alive." The grandmother adds to the conversation, calling into question Nelson's mental health: "And the things he's been saying lately? Poor man seems more and more confused." The daughter asks, "What has he ever done, anyway?" The mother replies, "I can't think of one thing." But the grandmother can: "He's cut my Medicare and raised taxes." The daughter seems convinced: "I won't vote for anyone who hurts you [the grandmother] or us [presumably all of them, including the infant]." The grandmother ends the ad by saying, "Bill Nelson has been in Washington way too long. It's time we bring him home."[102] This ad employed both negative and attack methods. In addition to claiming that Nelson raised taxes and made cuts to Medicare, the ad's condescending manner ("poor man") implies that Nelson has lost his mental faculties ("seems more and more confused").

The Super PAC also ran two fifteen-second attack ads. One was called "Lining,"[103] and it accused Nelson of being an "empty suit," an insult that can mean a person is ineffective, incompetent, or a "phony." The ad begins with an image of a men's suit jacket; on the lapel are three campaign buttons, two for Nelson and one with an image of Hillary Clinton. The narrator says, "We know Bill Nelson is an empty suit, but look inside." The suit opens, showing its lining. The white text on the screen says, "Bill Nelson votes with his party 89 percent of the time." The screen view pans slightly upward, revealing the inner pocket of the suit, which has an image of a 1040 federal tax form sticking out of it. The text on the screen to the right of the tax form reads, "Bill Nelson voted to raise taxes 375 times." The narration "Bill Nelson's suit is empty, but it's lined with danger that hurts Florida families" concludes the ad.

Another fifteen-second ad was called "Puppet."[104] It begins with an image of Bill Nelson as a marionette, with circuslike music playing in the background. The narrator asks, "Why are Democrats spending almost $50 million to reelect Bill Nelson?" And then he answers his own question: "They control this confused puppet nearly 90 percent of the time." After repeating the claims about raising taxes 375 times, the image on the screen shows Senate minority leader Charles Schumer, Hillary Clinton, and Nancy Pelosi above a stage labeled "Democrats' Puppet Show" With this image on the screen, the narrator concludes, "Bill Nelson: Washington Democrats' ole-reliable puppet."[105]

These ads contained rather harsh and personal attacks against a candidate, accusing him of being mentally deficient, an "empty suit," and a mere "puppet." In an incredibly close race that triggered a recount, Rick Scott defeated Bill Nelson. Out of more than 8.1 million votes, Scott won by a margin of only 10,033 votes.[106]

Case Study: Outside Groups against Trump 2020

Nearly a year before an official Democratic opponent was running against President Trump, negative ads already were airing during the summer of 2019. Priorities USA, a pro-Democratic Super PAC, was spending millions on digital ads in media markets just ahead of where Trump was campaigning. About a week before Trump's reelection launch rally in Florida, Priorities USA ran a series of ads on the websites of many of the state's most prominent newspapers. The Super PAC also announced its intentions to pay for more than $100 million worth of ads in other key swing states, such as Wisconsin, Michigan, and Pennsylvania, through the Democratic primaries.[107] Incumbents enjoy significant advantages in elections, but perhaps outside groups are game changers with their abilities to neutralize, or at least reduce, those advantages. The ads will be described to illustrate the common roles of surrogate attackers and loyal issue advocates that outside groups play in a campaign.

Several of the ads focused on health care, continuing with a key theme Democrats believed helped them in the 2018 midterms.[108] A mother worried that her son, David, might not be able to afford insurance because of a preexisting condition narrates one fifteen-second ad. Following the narration is the text, "Trump's Economy Isn't Working For Us." A thirty-second ad features "John" and "Deborah." John is identified as a veteran, and Deborah is identified as a registered nurse. After they express an inability to afford health care, Deborah says, "I'm sure he [Trump] doesn't run into anybody on his golf courses or in his hotels that have the issues that 70 or 80 percent of our country has."[109] Such a claim falls into the category of a personal attack because it calls into question a person's motives rather than a policy stance or voting record.

Another ad focused on economic issues and jobs. "Chuck," who is identified as a steelworker, tells the audience, "Trump came to Carrier [manufacturer of heating and cooling equipment in Indiana] and told them he was saving all the jobs, and that was bull#*^t. . . . People cheered, people clapped, people cried. They wanted something to believe in." But then Chuck says that he "had to tell the people their jobs were going to Mexico." The ad concludes with an attack-oriented remark: "All Trump cares about is cutting taxes for the people at the top—the same companies who are shipping our jobs out of this country."[110]

One final ad, "Trump's America," contained both health care and economic issues. The ad begins with a farmer saying, "Trump's trade war is costing me." The ad abruptly shifts to Deborah, who remarks, "The president has put my kids one medical emergency away from bankruptcy." While Deborah is saying this, the ad quickly switches to a black screen with large white letters that say, "WE GET SCREWED." An unidentified businessman says that "he's struggling to keep his business afloat," while Trump is saying, "It's the best it's ever been." Then we hear Chuck's aforementioned "bull#*^t" line, and the ad concludes with his exhortation, "Working people gotta fight back."[111]

* * *

The case studies illustrate the main roles that outside groups fulfill when advertising on behalf of their preferred candidates or party. Outside groups, especially those who keep their donors a secret, use negative ads more frequently than do candidates. Dark money groups can get away with harsher personal attack ads because they are largely immune to any backlash effect. Voters tend not to punish candidates for the ads of outside groups. Additionally, outside groups nearly always fall in line with candidates' issues, as demonstrated by New Republican PAC's focus on tax hikes and Majority Forward's and Red and Gold's emphasis on health care.

DOES POLITICAL ADVERTISING MATTER?

The answer to this question is complicated and has many conditions and exceptions. Ask several dozen political scientists or communication scholars, and there will likely be a dozen different answers. Some scholars contend that ads have no effect on elections, while others suggest that ads can have "substantial persuasive effects."[112] Another article about campaign effects sums up the scholarly consensus in the following way: "the prevailing scholarly consensus on campaigns is that they have minimal effects."[113] Yet, if that is true—if political advertisements have only *minimal* effects—then why do candidates, parties, and groups continue to spend the largest percentage of their budget on advertising alone in any given election cycle?

The answer may be as simple as concluding that *minimal* effects are all they hope or expect to attain. When many elections are decided by small margins in several key swing states or districts, "minimally effective" advertising may be enough. In 2016, the Clinton campaign seems to have made significant missteps by largely ignoring campaigning and advertising in several states, presumably operating under the assumption they had already won those states after analyzing internal and public polls. Wisconsin stands out as a prime example. Clinton did not campaign there in the general election despite losing the primary to Sanders and did not run advertisements in Wisconsin until the last few weeks. She lost by a small margin of only 22,748 out of nearly 2.8 million votes cast. The margin of victory was less than 1 percent (0.7 percent).[114]

On the other hand, Spenkuch and Toniatti recently have argued that advertising can alter "the partisan composition of the electorate." They suggest that many previous studies may not have found any significant effects because the "mobilizing and demobilizing effects of political ads tend to cancel out." They conclude by suggesting that even if political ads do not have a lasting impact on voters' beliefs, that "partisan imbalances in political advertising have the potential to decide close elections."[115]

Additionally, there is some evidence that political advertisements, when targeted and designed in certain ways, can have the desired effects. This is particularly true in the primary phase of campaigns.[116] Such a finding seems to match up with other trends in the post–*Citizens United* campaign era. Outside groups have indeed seen some of their greatest impact in primaries, as was also noted in chapter 5. One reason for this appears to be that would-be voters cannot rely on "partisan cues" in the primary phase, and therefore ads by outside groups are potentially more effective.[117]

Outside groups also tend to advertise earlier in the election process.[118] This may be because voters' minds are often made up long before Election Day, but it could also be because outside groups do not qualify for the lowest available advertising rates like the candidates do, and as the election nears, air time typically costs more. Groups have probably figured out that their dollars are spent more effectively in primaries and earlier in the general election.

Voters are not a monolithic bloc where everyone has an equal chance of being affected. Research has shown that independent voters and those with low political involvement are most influenced by Super PAC ads. Citizens with lower levels of political knowledge have a lower affective attachment to political parties, which makes them more susceptible to new information, particularly in primaries.[119] This offers yet another reason why outside groups are so active in competitive primary races.

However, spending earlier rather than later might also diminish the potential effects of groups' advertising. This is because the effects of political advertising also tend to be short-lived, even though some research has shown that "advertising advantages do correlate with movement in the polls."[120] This is often referred to as an **effects decay**. Studies suggest that, immediately following an ad, candidates might see a small percentage of increased support, but the support fades quickly. For example, one study showed a pro-Obama ad to potential voters. A survey revealed a 2.8 percent increase in the respondents' "intention" to vote for Obama. Yet a follow-up survey after the election found that only about half of those same respondents actually reported voting for Obama.[121] Another study, which examined Rick Perry's gubernatorial reelection campaign in 2006, showed similar strong effects initially that decayed almost completely within a week or two.[122]

Political advertising also has its smallest effects on the presidential election because most voters are already quite familiar with presidential candidates by the time the general election rolls around. Advertising has more significant effects on congressional, particularly House, races,[123] where candidates may be less well known. Because incumbents have the advantage in terms of name recognition and voter familiarity, challengers' campaigns and advertising typically have greater potential to matter.[124]

FREE MEDIA COVERAGE

Paid-for advertising can be countered without additional funding. One reason why money is less powerful in predicting the victor in a presidential primary or even in the general election is the ability of candidates to generate free media coverage in today's campaigns. The biggest expense category in presidential campaigns is advertising. However, with the rise of social media, candidates can speak to voters directly, which, in turn, can create a great deal of **earned media** (or free media), publicity gained organically through content that is deemed newsworthy. Earned media cannot be bought or owned. More specifically, **free media value** is the approximate amount of money that candidates would be willing to spend if they had to purchase the otherwise free news coverage they generate.[125]

In the twelve months leading up to November 1, 2016, Media-Quant estimated that Donald Trump received the highest free media value at $4.96 billion, far more than Hillary Clinton's free media value of $3.24 billion.[126] Clinton would have had to raise and spend an additional $1.72 billion to match the kind of additional free media coverage that Trump was able to generate. His rallies, among other events, garnered major media coverage, partly because of some of the more contentious claims he made, and, probably more importantly, because of the media's fascination with the novelty of a celebrity businessman running for president.

Furthermore, the way Trump communicated on Twitter allowed him to increase his number of followers leading up to the election. By Election Day 2016, Trump's Twitter following had increased to 13 million compared to 10.3 million for Clinton, a net advantage of 2.7 million followers.[127] Twitter alone brought $236 million additional free attention for Trump compared Clinton, according to estimates.[128] Other measures of media and citizen attention confirm how Trump dominated both his primary foes and Clinton in various ways on the Internet and on social media platforms. For example, Trump was the most Googled presidential candidate, and he also received the most mentions of any candidate on Facebook. Overall, Google trends analysis shows that online interest in candidate Trump was three times higher than that for Clinton.[129]

What does all of this mean for political candidates in general? Political scientist Peter Francia speculates that Trump's "use of social media and his ability to generate free media may end up changing the way future presidential campaigns are conducted in the years to come."[130] However, being controversial for the sake of free media coverage is probably not a formula most candidates are eager to embrace, despite it being mutually beneficial for candidates and media outlets, as Francia points out. The real challenge for candidates is how to be newsworthy without resorting to eyebrow-raising statements. The ways candidate and later President Trump has used Twitter to engage in a direct conversation with citizens, including retweeting ordinary citizens, serving as an original news source, and being perceived as authentic, are the elements future candidates may want to emulate the most. In fact, the "de-professionalization" of social media use may be one of the lessons that future candidates should pay attention to.[131] In other words, having staff post carefully crafted, yet "boring," social media messages that come across as disingenuous is not a way to connect with voters.

CONCLUSION

Kyrsten Sinema defeated Martha McSally for the U.S. Senate in Arizona, but the contest was so close that the race was not called until one week after election day. Initial results showed McSally in the lead, but as early and mailed-in ballots were counted, Sinema pulled ahead. She won by 1.7 percent of the vote.[132] Political advertising likely only has minimal effects if candidates and outside groups are able to raise similar amounts of money, but as seen throughout this chapter minimal effects are sometimes enough. In the case of Sinema, effective ads early in the campaign may have made the difference. Is it possible that outside groups and outside money in Florida, Arizona, and elsewhere were just enough to tip the scales? Outside groups appear to think so; otherwise, they would be unlikely to spend millions attempting it.

This chapter has illuminated the largest expense category of political campaigns: advertising. The focus was on how political advertising is changing in the post–*Citizens United* era. Significantly, spending on political advertising by outside groups, particularly spending that is difficult or impossible to trace, has increased substantially since 2010.

That money is changing the nature and content of political advertising in several important ways. First, because some groups can hide their identities, the general public is being deceived into thinking that corporations and the extremely wealthy are everyday individuals who have formed a grassroots movement. Often, by the time anyone finds out they have been tricked, the election is over. Digital advertising is particularly adept at achieving this deception and has even allowed foreign entities to produce political advertising related to U.S. elections. Additionally, groups, specifically dark money groups, are using negative and attack ads at higher rates. This is likely because they do not fear backlash effects against their preferred candidates. Finally, although much more research is needed, there seems to be mounting evidence that ads by unknown groups are at least marginally more effective and may possess more potential to affect election outcomes.

KEY TERMS

astroturfing   143

attack ads   151

backlash effect   145

contrast ads   151

demobilization hypothesis   151

digital astroturfing   143

disclaimer notice   146

earned media   159

effects decay   158

free media value   159

microtargeting   148

narrowcasting   148

native ads   147

negative ads   151

positive ads   150

sock puppets   149

trolling   149

truth-in-advertising   147

DISCUSSION QUESTIONS

1. How large of a role do you think advertising plays in election outcomes?
2. Do you believe that negative ads affect the political atmosphere in the United States? How so? What about attack ads more specifically?
3. Do you think ads by groups who can disguise themselves as ordinary citizens and who are not required to disclose donors are able to have a greater impact than ads that must reveal a candidate as "approving the message"? Explain your reasoning.
4. Do you think social media companies have a responsibility to make it clear if a "posting" is a paid-for political advertisement? Why or why not?

5. Do you think voters have a right to know who the largest donors of political advertisements are? Why or why not? Explain your reasoning.
6. Do you believe the news media should be more reflective about when and how it provides "free media" to political candidates? Why or why not?

ADDITIONAL READINGS

Brooks, Deborah Jordan and Michael Murov. "Assessing Accountability in a Post-*Citizens United* Era: The Effects of Attack Ad Sponsorship by Unknown Independent Groups." *American Politics Research* 40, no. 3 (May 2012): 383–418.

Dowling, Conor M., and Michael G. Miller. *Super PAC! Money, Elections and Voters after* Citizens United. New York: Routledge, 2014.

Franz, Michael, Erika Franklin Fowler, and Travis N. Ridout. "Loose Cannons or Loyal Foot Soldiers? Towards a More Complex Theory of Interest Group Advertising Strategies." *American Journal of Political Science* 60, no. 3 (July 2016): 738–51.

Geer, John G. *In Defense of Negativity: Attack Ads in Presidential Campaigns.* Chicago: University of Chicago Press, 2006.

Kovic, Marko, Adrian Rauchfleisch, Marc Sele, and Christian Caspar. "Digital Astroturfing in Politics: Definition, Typology, and Countermeasures." *Studies in Communication Science* 18, no. 1 (December 2018): 69–85.

7

Reform Ideas

* * *

MEGADONORS AND POLITICIANS RARELY ADMIT that there is an expectation of favors for donations, which is why some were surprised when in 2015 then Republican primary candidate Donald Trump said the following during a debate televised on Fox News: "I will tell you that our system is broken. I gave to many people before this—before two months ago I was a businessman. I give to everybody. When they call, I give. And you know what, when I need something from them two years later, three years later, I call them. They are there for me. That's a broken system."[1]

Earlier in the same debate, Republican Senator Rand Paul attacked Trump for refusing to make a pledge to support the eventual nominee and failing to promise not to run as an independent. Paul remarked that Trump was "hedging his bets" and that he "buys and sells politicians of all stripes," even pointing out that Trump had donated money to the Clintons in the past. Trump did not dispute this and, with a smug expression, shrugged as Paul made the accusations as though to communicate nonverbally, "Isn't it smart to donate to both sides, though?"

Those nonverbals during Paul's attack seem to line up with what Trump said at a rally in New Hampshire a month earlier when he attacked Jeb Bush's Super political action committee (PAC), which raised more than $100 million in a short time: "He [Bush] raises $100 million, so what does $100 million mean? $100 million means he's doing favors for so many people, it means lobbyists, it means special interests, it means donors. Who knows it better than me? I give to everybody. They do whatever I want. It's true."[2]

Critics of the current campaign finance system agree with Trump and Paul: there is an expectation of a "favor" of some kind. Perhaps the agreement is not a formal one like a direct bribe, but certainly many donors expect, at a minimum, access to the politicians to whom they donate large sums of money. This supports the argument that money is more than just speech: it is access to be heard in the first place. We all have "free speech" rights, but that does not necessarily mean that anyone—in this case, not even our own elected officials—truly hears us.

* * *

Our discussion of reform ideas begins with two major assumptions. The first is that the U.S. Supreme Court is unlikely to reverse major rulings such as *Citizens United* or *SpeechNow* any time soon; therefore, ideas such as overturning *Citizens United* are not discussed. Second, a constitutional amendment is also unlikely and therefore not a focus of this chapter. Instead, this chapter focuses on reforms that should be possible within the current legal framework. Indeed, many of the ideas that are explained already are in effect in some states, counties, and municipalities. This is not to conclude that the Court could not devise new rationales to strike down some of these programs but instead that the following reforms are either the most likely to survive, or would be immune from, legal challenges.

This chapter discusses six categories of reform:

- Hard money contribution limit increases
- Public election funding options
- Super PAC "insurance"
- Legislative recusal rules
- Enhanced disclosure and disclaimer laws
- Federal Election Commission (FEC) reform

INCREASE "HARD MONEY" CONTRIBUTION LIMITS

One school of thought on campaign finance reform is that contribution limits to candidates, parties, and/or PACs need to be increased or even eliminated. Advocates of this position offer several reasons. First, the limits today make running a successful campaign for federal office difficult without substantial spending from outside groups considering how much campaigns cost. More specifically, contribution limits make it that much harder for challengers to unseat incumbents who possess advantages that were discussed in previous chapters.[3]

Second, a theoretical objection is that contribution limits are based on a faulty assumption, namely, that "since money corrupts . . . more money corrupts more."[4] Some scholars argue that limiting the amount individuals can contribute to candidates increases—not decreases—the likelihood of corruption.[5] Although counterintuitive, the argument is that, because a viable campaign is always expensive, candidates will never be able to raise enough money via direct campaign contributions if limits are too low. Therefore, candidates must accept other forms of financial support because "[m]oney, like water, will always find an outlet."[6]

One of the ways money has found an outlet is via **bundled contributions**. A bundled contribution is when an individual or small group of people fundraise on behalf of a candidate to pool together contributions and then deliver one lump sum to the campaign. Candidates are only required to disclose these contributors if the bundler is officially registered as a lobbyist. In 2016, the Hillary Clinton campaign voluntarily disclosed bundlers' information if they raised over $100,000; the Trump campaign released no information.[7] There is evidence that bundled donations corrupt, if corruption means rewarding the biggest donors with important jobs once elected. For example, according to the Center for Responsive Politics, many of the biggest bundlers to Obama's 2008 and 2012 campaigns were given ambassadorships.[8]

Variation: Allow Parties and PACs but Not Candidates to Receive Increased Donations

A variation on this solution would be to allow much greater contributions by individuals to the political parties and PACs but not to individual candidates. The rationale for such a proposal is that donors tend to be more politically extreme than the general public. In turn, senators and members of the House of Representatives also are more extreme. Even if congressional districts flip from "blue" to "red" and vice versa, the new representatives are equally likely to be more extreme than their constituents. Bufami and Herron refer to this process as **leapfrog representation**, meaning that no matter which party is in power in a given district, moderate and centrist voters—a majority in most districts—still are not represented because their elected officials are more extreme ideologically.[9]

This version of increasing contribution limits is specifically designed to increase **alignment**. Alignment means that legislators' views and policies more closely match, or "align," with their constituents' views as opposed to the big donors' views. According to

Nicholas Stephanopoulos, who advocates for alignment as a principle in campaign finance reform, "both parties and PACs are relatively moderate in their giving patterns."[10] Thus, increasing limits to parties and PACs but not to candidates is potentially effective as an alignment strategy.

Problems Hard Money Contribution Increases Can Reduce

This solution alleges to solve, at least in part, the problem of a lack of election funding transparency. Advocates of eliminating contribution limits make the case that, under the current system, "money has been pushed away from politically accountable parties and candidates and toward unelected advocacy groups, leading to a warping in political competition."[11] Simply put, if individuals are allowed to donate more money directly to a candidate, then the public will have a much clearer picture of who is giving to whom because hard money can be accounted for more easily and reported to the public. In turn, the voters would have more of the information they need to hold elected officials accountable.

Additionally, giving directly to a candidate is generally believed to be more effective than giving to a nonprofit, which typically has other operating costs. For example, if someone gives $100 to a candidate, the candidate can use nearly all of that on campaigning. If someone gives $100 to a 501(c)(4), on average less than half of that can be spent on express advocacy advertising. Moreover, candidates get a steep discount on TV advertising. In most cases, nonprofits are charged at least twice as much as campaigns, but in some instances they are charged 600 to 800 percent more.[12] In the final analysis, persons seeking a better return on investment would likely choose to give directly to a candidate because the money has more potential to matter.

Of course, such arguments may be idealistic. Some large donors may opt to donate to dark money groups to remain anonymous. The potential for backlash in a full-disclosure system may reduce the donors' perceived return on investment, and therefore donating to a nondisclosing entity may still be the preferred choice.

PUBLIC FUNDING

Public funding ideas can take one of five possible forms: full funding, matching funds, partial funding, tax incentives, and vouchers. These are examined next.

Fully Funded Public Elections

A **full public funding** plan means that the government funds all the expenses of a qualifying candidate in exchange for an agreement that he or she cannot seek additional funding from outside donors. Such a program exists for the presidential election, but the limit is now too restrictive ($96.14 million for the general election in 2016) to run a successful presidential campaign.[13] Almost all presidential candidates turn down public funding.[14] The last major party nominee to accept public financing was Republican John McCain in 2008. Substantially raising this amount would likely be the only way to make it viable again at the presidential level.

Some states, namely, Arizona, Connecticut, and Maine, have full funding programs. These have often been called **clean elections** because, once utilized, no outside money from special interests can be accepted. In Arizona, a candidate for statewide office is required to raise $5 contributions from at least two hundred individuals to qualify for public funding. Each office sought has a different amount of public money made available. Qualifying gubernatorial candidates, for instance, receive approximately $1.1 million in public funds. The main idea behind full public funding for elections is that candidates accept public funding in exchange for rejecting donations from special interests that may—or are perceived to—have a corrupting influence.

Matching Funds

Several state governments provide **matching funds** at a certain ratio—anywhere from 5:1 up to 8:1—to increase campaign contributions up to a certain amount. Establishing programs with lower matching funds ratios, such as 1:1 or 3:1, is certainly possible. Generally, such programs require certain thresholds for eligibility, such as a minimum dollar amount raised, a minimum number of donations, or some combination thereof.

Currently, New York City has one of the most robust programs in place. The ratio is 8:1 (earlier 6:1), with a maximum contribution limit of $2,000 in public funds per contributor.[15] In New York City, the candidate must acquire a certain number of donations and a minimum dollar amount that differs per office sought. For example, city council candidates must acquire a minimum of seventy-five donations, each of at least $10, and a total of at least $5,000, to qualify for matching funds.[16] Strings are attached to the money as well. Donors must be disclosed. All expenses must be used on specifically defined campaign activities.[17] Candidates are required to participate in debates.[18]

Typically, candidates who accept the matching funds are prohibited from taking money from other sources, such as an outside group.

A proposal called the Empowering Citizens Act has been introduced in the U.S. House of Representatives but has never reached the floor for a vote. The proposed legislation would provide matching funds at a ratio of 6:1 for donations up to $200 for the presidential election.[19] The goal of this Act is to "amplify the voices of small donors."[20]

Partial Public Funding

Compared to fully funded elections and many of the more robust matching funds, partial funding is relatively modest. At most, a few states, such as Massachusetts and Minnesota, not only provide up to half of the campaign expenses but also require spending limit conditions.[21] As a result, these proposals are unlikely to have a significant impact on campaigns and elections, although they may provide just enough assistance to help a few candidates run legitimate campaigns who otherwise may not have made the attempt.

Tax Incentives

Tax incentive programs are designed to help donors rather than candidates. The few existing programs focus on small donations, typically $100 or less. These programs provide some form of incentive to help reduce a citizen's tax burden if they donate to a political candidate or party. Tax incentives can take two forms: credits and deductions.

A **tax credit** means that an individual gets a refund from the state's revenue system. For example, in Minnesota, donors send a receipt proving they donated to an eligible recipient, and the Department of Revenue sends a refund within six weeks. Like matching funds, these tax credits can be dollar for dollar, like Minnesota's, or partial, like a program that Virginia had at 50 percent. The Brennan Center for Justice advocates for a tax credit of $50 at the federal level.[22]

A **tax deduction** reduces a person's *taxable income*. For example, Montana residents can deduct up to $100 of taxable income for donations to candidates, parties, or PACs at the federal, state, or local level.[23] Tax deductions have proved much less effective at garnering participation because making the contribution still costs the donor money.[24] If a state's income tax rate is 5 percent, for example, $50 donations would still mean that donors spent $47.50 of their own money. For most would-be small donors, such small savings are rarely incentive enough to participate.

Vouchers

Tax incentive programs have two primary drawbacks: citizens still need to have the money upfront, and the programs can skew toward benefiting those who have something to gain by reducing their tax burden. Vouchers eliminate both of those concerns. Rather than individuals first coming up with the money, government **vouchers** worth a certain value are provided to registered and/or eligible voters. These vouchers, whether on paper or in some electronic form (an identification code, etc.), represent a certain dollar amount, which can then be donated to candidates, parties, or PACs. Like the other forms of public funding, advocates of voucher programs argue that an overall spending limit also needs to be implemented.[25]

In 2015, the city of Seattle began a "democracy voucher" program. Each election cycle, registered voters and eligible voters who sign up for the program are sent four vouchers in the mail, each worth $25. The vouchers can then be assigned and sent to chosen candidates, just like a check is written out to make a bill payment. In Seattle, the program is funded by property taxes, but each city, county, state, or the federal government, could choose to fund vouchers differently via income tax, property tax, sales tax, or some combination thereof.[26] Only one jurisdiction currently has a voucher plan, but advocates of the idea would like to see voucher programs expanded, including for federal elections.[27]

Drawbacks of Public Funding

Many of these programs have not kept pace with—or simply cannot afford—the overall spending necessary to win many elections, so, like the presidential public funding program, many of them are experiencing decreasing use. For example, the Arizona gubernatorial public funding program experienced the same destiny as the U.S. presidential public funding program. The cost to win the governor's office is greater than the allotted $1.1 million, which is why Arizona governor Doug Ducey turned down the money and raised more than double the publicly available funds, $2.4 million, for his 2014 campaign.[28] Unless and until there are ways to make the programs worthwhile, many candidates will continue to opt out, and the programs will be discontinued. This is particularly true if government leaders perceive there is no point in providing funding if no one will accept the money. Additionally, of course, some form of publicly generated revenue is required, an idea that will always receive pushback from those against spending taxpayer money.

Benefits of Public Funding Options

These programs have the potential to get more people involved in elections and the political process more broadly. For modest sums of money, or due to a belief or perception that tax dollars are working toward "cleaner" elections, average people can make a difference. When they believe their donations matter or that their tax dollars are being put to good use, they pay attention more closely to the electoral process and to the accomplishments (or lack of accomplishments) of their elected officials. They also follow politics more closely so they can hold elected officials accountable, either by supporting the same candidate or by switching support. Research has found that some versions of public election funding can encourage a more diverse pool of citizens to participate in the political process.[29]

Additionally, matching funds might enable a wider range of candidates to run for public office, especially in races that otherwise would have been uncontested or in which there was a candidate favored strongly enough to deter opposition.[30] Advocates contend that elections with some aspect of public funding in place have "put more, and more diverse, candidates on the ballot." The advocacy group Common Cause claims that the diversity of candidates has "doubled" in Arizona with the advent of clean elections. In Maine, the number of female candidates and legislators has increased 18 percent.[31] Michael Malbin of the Campaign Finance Institute points out, however, that there is no peer-reviewed research yet on the effects of clean elections and diversity of candidates.[32] Such results could be correlational but not causal. Nevertheless, public financing in its various forms possesses the potential to allow candidates to run for office who otherwise could not afford to do so. Starting a campaign is always difficult—even for an office as "low level" as a city council seat—but without either having enough personal resources or knowing enough individuals who can provide those resources, public funding can offer an open door for some who want to run for public office.

Finally, public financing of electoral campaigns has the potential to hold candidates more accountable. Small donor matching funds have the potential to "increase the proportional importance of small donors to candidates."[33] This would happen for two reasons. First, candidates need to appeal to a broader range of would-be supporters in the hopes of gaining donors or securing vouchers. Second, of course, such programs either entirely create or at least multiply donations, which makes small donations that much more valuable.

SUPER PAC AND INDEPENDENT
EXPENDITURE INSURANCE

Unlike reforms that rely on public funding, the idea of **Super PAC insurance**[34] is a private-sector plan designed to deter outside spending.[35] Insurance functions on the concepts of pooled resources and shared risks. Automobile insurance, for example, collects money from thousands (or millions) of individuals and puts that money into one large pot. If a person gets into an accident, the pooled resources pay for the damages. If too many people get into too many accidents, insurance costs increase for everyone. If fewer people get into accidents, then the insurance company profits more, and, hopefully, insurance premiums do not rise or may even come down. Everyone, one would hope, tries to avoid getting into accidents, which helps keep premiums lower.

Super PAC insurance works on similar principles but with a few twists. To illustrate how Super PAC insurance would work, imagine a candidate running for the House of Representatives in a competitive district. There is a high probability that outside groups will spend millions of dollars against this candidate. Let us assume she does not have the resources to counter that much spending if those groups flood the airwaves with oppositional advertisements. So she takes out an insurance policy, funded by her supporters, that protects her against the outside spending. Now imagine that a Super PAC spends $5 million in attack ads against her. This spending would trigger the candidate's insurance policy, just like if she got into a car accident, except the Super PAC insurance would pay out double or triple what the oppositional Super PAC spent. This means that an outside group caused the candidate they are against to receive a huge financial windfall. It would be as if the outside group just handed its opposition $10 or $15 million, two or three times more than it was able to spend initially.

Further imagine in the future that all or most candidates carry a Super PAC insurance policy. Outside groups would quickly realize that every dollar they spend is generating even more resources for the candidate they want to see defeated. The idea is not dissimilar from the Cold War doctrine of "mutually assured destruction."[36] If one side launches a nuclear strike, the other side will return with at least equal force, and the combined attacks escalate so rapidly that no one would "win." Thus, at least in a rational world, Super PACs and other outside groups would not risk helping their opponents more than they can help themselves.

Drawbacks of Super PAC Insurance
There are two potential drawbacks to this proposal. First, like any insurance, it requires a minimum threshold of participation to generate enough pooled resources to cover any triggered payouts. A critical mass of candidates would need to perceive the insurance as a wise use of campaign resources. Second, there is no guarantee that Super PACs and outside groups will refrain from spending. There is still the possibility that outside groups choose to spend large sums of money against candidates they want to defeat.

Benefits of Super PAC Insurance
As a for-profit, private venture, this solution requires no action from Congress and no public funding. In fact, Super PAC insurance has the potential to be an investment opportunity for small donors who desire not only to earn a profit but also to contribute to a solution that solves a problem in U.S. elections.[37] Additionally, because it involves only voluntary participation and contracts between private entities, it should be immune from legal challenges or being struck down as unconstitutional.[38]

In the past, nonstate actors have been able to deter outside spending. In 2012, Senators Elizabeth Warren and Scott Brown agreed to abide by the **People's Pledge** during their campaigns in Massachusetts. The People's Pledge required candidates to pay a penalty should outside groups spend on behalf of their campaign. The candidates appealed to outside groups to not spend money to help them or attack the opposition. They agreed to pay a penalty equal to half the amount of any outside expenditure for advertising from their campaign account to a charity of the opponent's choice. A postelection study concluded that the pledge dramatically reduced the level of both outside spending and negative advertising in that race compared to other contested races across the country.[39]

LEGISLATIVE RECUSAL

Nearly every legislative reform effort that has attempted to rein in campaign spending has met its demise in the U.S. Supreme Court, as chapter 2 recounted. This has led many to seek different avenues of reform to lessen the problems that are believed to be the result of such spending rather than to worry about the sources or amounts of the money. One such idea is **legislative recusal** policies that would prohibit decision makers from voting or sometimes even from participating in the process of creating and deliberating legislation if a conflict of interest or an inability to be impartial is present. Rather than attempting to legislate "inputs," such as contributions and expenditures, legislative recusal laws would attempt to control "outputs," in this case the policies and laws written and voted upon. The goal of recusal rules is to mitigate the effects of outside spending, assuming the concern is that legislators vote for laws and policies that benefit their largest donors.

Recusal rules are common in both the judicial system and most U.S. state legislatures. The U.S. justice system has long had judicial recusal rules. Judges are required to understand when they should not oversee a case because of a conflict of interest or an inability to be impartial. There is a long list of would-be disqualifying conditions, but most relevant to this discussion is that judges are required to recuse themselves when they have a financial interest or "any other interest" in the outcome of a case.[40] Additionally, only two state legislatures (Arkansas and Georgia) do not have legislative recusal laws. The forty-eight other states require recusal if there is a conflict of interest or a "personal" interest. Maryland, Massachusetts, Alaska, Missouri, New Mexico, and New York have recusal rules that expressly prohibit legislators from voting if they have a financial interest.[41]

Drawbacks of Recusal Rules

Judicial recusal relies on the judges deciding whether they should recuse themselves. This method poses some problems and has been recognized as potentially ineffective, for obvious reasons.[42] Relying on self-enforcement alone is unlikely to have the desired results. Equally problematic would be requiring other senators or other House members to decide who among them should be allowed to vote. Decisions would be either partisan or personal, and in either case defeat the purpose of integrity in the process. Therefore, law professor Eugene D. Mazo recommends that a neutral third party would need to decide who would be disallowed to vote.[43]

An additional concern is that we lack a consistently reliable set of practices to discover the sources of all money spent on behalf of candidates. Although some disclosure requirements are in place for independent expenditures and electioneering communications, as chapter 3 illustrated, the public is still in the dark about many of the sources of funding that are spent on behalf of candidates. For any such reform to work to full effect, more effective disclosure laws than what the FEC currently enforces would also be needed. These two reform areas are considered in the following sections: disclosure and enforcement.

Benefits of Recusal Rules

Most likely recusal rules in a legislative body would be enforced through some variation of ethics rules. If that were the case, there is some evidence to suggest that recusal rules could have an impact on accountability. Several studies have found that incumbents embroiled in ethics scandals and investigations suffer at the polls. One study concluded that scandals negatively impact incumbents and even have long-lasting effects past the initial election cycle.[44] Another study analyzed Senate elections from 1972 to 2016 and found that candidates who were involved in a scandal lost about 4 percent of the popular vote, enough in some states to cost them the election.[45] In other words, there is evidence to suggest that politicians who violate ethics rules are held accountable, at least often enough to act as a partial deterrent.

DISCLOSURE REFORM

Michael Malbin and Thomas Gais have suggested that campaign finance disclosure reform would be effective only if

> (1) Most candidates and political organizations report what they do accurately; (2) Such reports in fact comprise most of the activities and relationships important to voters; (3) Such reports are available in a useful format, and at an accessible location; (4) Interested, knowledgeable people read and interpret the reports and then make useful information available in a timely way to voters; (5) Voters are able and willing to use the information as a basis for making an election decision.[46]

Disclosure reform advocates have kept this in mind as they have proposed ideas. There are three main areas of concern regarding disclosure: reporting and collecting of donors and expenditures, dissemination of information, and disclaimer rules.[47]

Reporting and Collecting Donor and Expenditure Information

First, advocates of more robust disclosure laws argue that more types of organizations that engage in political campaign activities and election spending should be required to disclose donors. Dark money 501(c) groups currently are not required to do so to the public, but these social welfare organizations are required to disclose donations of more than

$5,000 to the Internal Revenue Service (IRS). The data are already collected, but the IRS could also be required to make it publicly available.[48]

Second, there is an "under-inclusiveness" of reporting. Super PACs are required to report detailed information to the FEC, but 501(c)s are not. Because 501(c)s are not required to disclose donors, Super PACs who receive money from them are only partially disclosing their donors. This has been called **gray money**.[49] Gray money "obscures the true sources of election spending."[50] Some legal scholars argue that the Federal Communications Commission currently has the authority to require "third-party purchasers of airtime for political and advocacy advertising to disclose their major direct and indirect funding sources," which would increase transparency.[51]

Third, even hard money disclosure, critics say, "falls short of meeting basic goals of transparency."[52] Sociologist Jennifer Heerwig points out several significant areas where disclosure laws fail to provide the public with an accurate picture of hard money donors. To provide a few examples, the current processes of filing to the FEC make several basic facts impossible to discover: how much is given in total by particular industries and how many unique individuals gave to candidates.[53] As a simple reform idea, Heerwig recommends that the FEC use a standardized form for collecting basic donor information. In particular, the form would gather data more consistently if it had predetermined options (or drop-down menus for an online version) for information such as "occupation." Currently, donors can write in anything (or even leave it blank), and much of it is information of little value, such as "self-employed" or "retired." Additionally, each donor could be assigned a unique identification number, much like college students or library patrons are assigned IDs. This way, more accurate and useful data could be collected.[54]

A Disclosure Plan for Better Dissemination
The previous three ideas would be positive steps but would not be ideal for disseminating the information to the public. A more comprehensive plan would bring "all entities that engage in election-related spending under one regime." This could be done by creating a new entity, but the FEC, with the correct reforms and improvements, could be tasked with more comprehensive record-keeping, disclosure, and dissemination duties.[55] Just as many other governmental agencies allow database access to researchers, scholars, and the public, the FEC would be required to maintain and publicize a more user-friendly database of electoral contributors.

Disclaimers

Citizens United upheld the requirement for disclaimers in independent expenditures, which is why all TV and radio ads include a phrase such as "[group's name] is responsible for the content of this message." Yet, as illustrated in chapter 6, the names of most groups at best tell voters almost nothing and at worst deceive them. Law professor Justin Levitt has suggested requiring the display of a **"Democracy Facts"** label on political advertisements.[56] The label would mimic the style of nutrition labels on foods (see table 7.1). It would contain basic information in a standardized format that, much like nutrition labels, would be instantly recognizable and quickly interpretable. These "Democracy Facts" would need to contain the information voters need as well. The labels would contain a "paid by" line that would contain the group's name. Below that, additional information, each on its own line, would include the total number of its financial supporters (to determine if the group is truly a grassroots organization composed of thousands of real people or an astroturf group with three corporate members, such as Citizens for Fire Safety), the percentage of money from the top five largest donors, and the identities of the top five donors.

Digital Ad Disclaimers

Digital ads have thus far evaded disclaimer requirements. Although the FEC issued an "advisory opinion" on December 15, 2017, stating that Take Back Action Fund, a 501(c)(4), must include disclaimers on its paid Facebook ads,[57] the FEC has not yet developed a

Table 7.1   Hypothetical Example of Funding Source Disclosure Label, Modeled on Familiar "Nutrition Facts" Labels on Packaged Foods

DEMOCRACY FACTS	
Paid by	Americans for America
Supporters	8,234
Percentage from Top 5 Contributors	78%
Top 5 Contributors	Bob Jones
	U.S. Company, Inc.
	The Business League, Inc.
	Susan Smith
	Attorneys United
Candidate Authorized	No

Source: Original idea by Justin Levitt, http://electionlawblog.org/archives/017415.html.

comprehensive, enforceable policy that requires digital ad disclaimers.[58] The original rationale for exclusion[59] was that digital ads did not have the space needed where disclaimers could be "conveniently printed." The frequent comparison was that digital ads were akin to "pens, bumper stickers, campaign pins, campaign buttons, and similar small items." If size was not the issue, the other rationale was based on this exemption: "its display was not practicable (for example, wearing apparel, water towers, and skywriting)."[60]

Perhaps in the days of rudimentary banner ads, these exemptions made sense, but there is no reason that disclaimers on digital ads are still impractical. Current Internet technology has many workarounds for both size and feasibility concerns. Printing a disclaimer, something like the previously mentioned "Democracy Label," on a pen or bumper sticker might be impossible, but somewhere on a digital ad could be the words "Paid Political Ad," and the words could function as a "hover over" icon that activates and displays a larger disclaimer. Alternatively, clicking on the "paid by" words takes the viewer to another page containing the detailed information.[61]

Drawbacks of Enhanced Disclosure and a Compromise

Critics of required disclosure argue that donors have a right to privacy.[62] Mandatory disclosure laws, they argue, have a chilling effect on speech. Moreover, they point to instances where donors were harassed and intimidated after the public found out about their political support. For example, supporters of California's "Proposition 8," which would have banned same-sex marriage in the state, were harassed and threatened by gay rights activists.[63]

A compromise could be **semi-disclosure** laws. Semi-disclosure would release nonpersonal information, which is not particularly valuable for informing voters, but would release information that has been demonstrated to fulfill the informational interest function that the courts have consistently upheld as both valuable and constitutional, such as the occupation, affiliation, or socioeconomic status of donors. This compromise could make both sides happy: individuals' privacy remains protected and useful information about how elections are funded would be made public.

Benefits of Better Disclosure

Research demonstrates that disclosure matters and provides useful information to voters. Chapter 6 discussed a few of these findings, but one of the most comprehensive experiments revealed that information about the source of a message has significant effects on voter perception, especially accompanied by "partisan cues." A total of 2,860 subjects were shown an ad that discussed job creation but did not mention any party affiliation of the candidate. A control group of 411 participants saw the ad with no disclaimer message. Some of the participants (781) were shown a disclaimer from a fictional group, "Americans for Change," along with the ad, but no additional information was included. Another version of the ad contained additional information but in two different versions. One group of the study participants (815) was shown a disclaimer comprised of labor unions as the source of the ad; the other group (853) was shown corporate and business donors. The results revealed that Democrats were less likely to report support for the candidate when they were shown the corporate disclaimer; Republicans were less likely to show support when they were shown the labor union disclaimer.[64]

FEC REFORM

There is no shortage of insulting labels aimed at the FEC. In a report arguing that "FEC" stands for "Failure to Enforce Commission," the authors compiled a list of slurs that have been leveled at the institution: "toothless tiger, toothless dog, pussycat agency, watchdog without a bite, FECkless, and designed for impotence."[65] Conservatives and liberals alike have lambasted the agency, even writing a bipartisan letter to President Trump explaining that a dysfunctional FEC "hurts honest candidates who are trying to follow the letter of the law and robs the American people of an electoral process with integrity."[66] The Commission is not viewed this way only by outsiders either. On an episode of *The Daily Show*, Ann Ravel, an FEC commissioner at that time, said that the agency is "enormously dysfunctional" and comparable to "men's nipples" (which is to say, mostly useless).[67]

The FEC is (supposed to be) composed of six commissioners,[68] of whom no more than three can be from the same political party. An affirmative vote of four members is required for any action to take place. Many important cases end in a 3–3 vote, which means nothing happens. When cases end up with a 3–3 vote, no advisory opinion is released; thus, candidates or groups genuinely seeking advice on legal campaign matters are left hanging. On one hand, this deadlock is by design so that neither party can use the FEC to its advantage or to harm the other party; on the other hand, the FEC has become deadlocked on so many cases that it often fails not only to enforce the law but also to clarify disputes and disagreements over existing campaign rules. Even when a vote ends in a decision other than a tie, the FEC "lacks any real power to take significant enforcement actions on its own." On the worth of the FEC, Wertheimer and Simon conclude that we have "reached the point where we have the illusion of campaign finance laws because in reality, there is little or no enforcement of these laws."[69]

FEC ineffectiveness has led to several problems that are of importance in the post–*Citizens United* era. The first pertains to coordination between candidates and allegedly independent groups. Although Super PACs legally can make unlimited independent expenditures, they are prohibited from coordinating with candidates. According to one critic, the FEC largely fails to address coordination, which makes it "possible for Super PACs to spend billions working hand in glove with campaigns."[70]

Second, the FEC is widely acknowledged as responsible for the current ineffective disclosure procedures.[71] Despite *Citizens United* and other court rulings upholding disclosure laws, the FEC has interpreted the law differently, only requiring disclosure if the donor specifically designated the money for political advertising. Donors rarely, if ever, earmark donations to nonprofits with any specific instructions such as "use for political ads only," and thus, they remain anonymous.[72] In fact, at one point (it was later overturned in court), the FEC narrowed its interpretation even further, "to the point of absurdity," when it also said that disclosure requirements only applied if a donor specified that the money was for a *particular ad* (not just advertising in general).[73]

In sum, the FEC is universally recognized as dysfunctional at best and damaging to democracy at worst. Between 2008 and 2017, the number of deadlocks increased "more than fivefold,"[74] but even when the commissioners reach a decision with at least four affirmative votes, the commission lacks any real power to bring about change or to enforce existing law. For all intents and purposes, the FEC is impotent. Can it be fixed?

Structural Reform of the FEC

Most committees, agencies, boards of directors, student councils, appeals courts, and so on have an odd number of members. This is not accidental. Those organizations were created that way to prevent ties (and the resultant deadlock). Neither is it accidental, however, that the FEC may well have been "designed to promote deadlock."[75]

An odd number of members could make things worse by giving more power to one party or ideological position. Even if the intent was to place two Democrats, two Republicans, and one independent on the commission, the possibility still exists that the independent is nevertheless ideological and votes with one party all the time. For this reason, simply changing the composition of FEC members may solve few, or even create new, problems.[76]

The Brennan Center for Justice has constructed a report of FEC reform recommendations, and, in addition to adding an independent member to create an odd number of commissioners, they also recommend other changes:

- To assign a "real leader" to the FEC, one who is accountable to the president and who has more authority over the Commission
- Create a better, bipartisan process to "vet" nominees
- Enforcing term limits and disallowing "holdovers"
- Empower the FEC with real enforcement abilities that can function in a more timely manner

Daniel Welner concludes his report on FEC reform with this:

> Ultimately, what we should hope for from a functional FEC is not an agency that always opts for or against strong regulation, but one that enforces duly enacted laws in a timely manner with the utmost fairness and is capable of making hard regulatory choices pursuant to its delegated authority. Creating such a body will not solve all the problems with our campaign finance system, but there is no better place to start.[77]

Judicial Reform

Ellen Weintraub, the chair of the FEC, has stated that the Washington, D.C., Circuit Court of Appeals has given the FEC a new "superpower."[78] She makes this claim because once the FEC has deadlocked on any complaint or case, the D.C. Circuit Court has decided that the matter is "judicially unreviewable." This new "case-killing" superpower is known as **deadlock deference**.[79] Every time the FEC deadlocks, the D.C. Circuit court has refused to hear the case.

Constitutional law professor Daniel Tokaji argues that judicial reform, particularly ending deadlock deference, is the most effective way to solve the most pressing problems caused by the FEC's current inefficacy. Structural reforms such as those proposed by the Brennan Center for Justice may seem to solve some of the Commission's dysfunction but could also result in something worse: control by one party or ideological perspective. In other words, deadlock is not necessarily negative if the judicial system were to function as a tiebreaker if individuals or groups seek further clarity.[80]

Until the FEC functions properly, and/or until the D.C. Circuit Court is willing to hear cases on which the FEC deadlocks, few campaign finance reforms will have much effect. Most independent groups are aware they do not have to fear most disclosure and coordination rules because the likelihood of any action against them is minimal. Simply put, laws and rules are only as effective as the enforcement mechanisms that ensure compliance, and currently there is virtually no enforcement of campaign finance laws.

CONCLUSION

This chapter explained six areas of proposed campaign finance reform: increasing hard money contribution limits, public funding models, Super PAC/independent expenditure insurance, legislative recusal rules for U.S. Congress, enhancing and improving disclosure and disclaimer laws, and FEC reform.

Advocates of hard money donation increases make the case that current limits are outdated and far too restrictive for candidates to run legitimate and ultimately successful campaigns. Therefore, candidates must rely on outside spending. As a result, the public is left in the dark about who is financing significant portions of campaign spending. Increasing hard money limits, advocates argue, would decrease corruption and increase campaign transparency.

Many forms of public funding were explained. Full public funding seeks to reduce the influence of outside spending. Matching funds, in addition to limiting the influence of outside groups, also seek to amplify the voices of smaller donors. Candidates must be more responsive to everyday voters to secure their donations and maintain their confidence for future elections. Partial funding has limited effects but still possesses some potential to allow underfunded candidates to run legitimate campaigns. Tax incentives can take two forms: credits or deductions. Credits, often in the form of rebates, are more effective because they provide a dollar-for-dollar benefit to small donors. Tax deductions are less effective because the benefits to donors are much smaller. Vouchers are the newest idea and have thus far only been attempted in one city, Seattle. In a voucher system, candidates must be mindful of the entire electorate because they would be relying on registered and eligible voters to make decisions to send them vouchers.

Rather than courting several large donors to fund a campaign, candidates would need to appeal to a broader range of citizens.

Super PAC insurance, unlike public funding proposals, is a private-sector solution based on the idea of "mutually assured destruction" because outside spending would trigger a magnified response that would benefit the target of the spending. If enough candidates agree to purchase such insurance policies, there would be enough resources pooled for payouts, which could lead to a deterrent effect that would reduce outside spending. As an additional benefit, Super PAC insurance has the potential to be profitable for investors and the companies offering the insurance policies.

Legislative recusal rules are aimed at preventing legislators from writing and/or voting for policies favorable to their largest donors. Elected officials would be barred from voting on matters where they had a demonstrable conflict of interest, such as the potential for personal financial gain or giving a "favor" to a donor.

Enhanced disclosure and disclaimer laws reside in the one remaining legal area about campaign expenditures. The Court has struck down all independent spending limits but has nevertheless repeatedly affirmed the value and necessity of transparency in campaigns and elections. Still, loopholes exist that allow many donors and groups to obscure the sources of campaign funding. This is especially true regarding digital political advertising, which currently evades most disclaimer requirements. In addition to clarifying disclosure rules, better enforcement of such laws is also needed, which is why this set of reforms also rests on the next category: fixing the FEC.

The FEC is widely recognized as dysfunctional or worse. In fact, the FEC is becoming increasingly impotent, and at the time of this writing only has four members. Any hope for reforming campaign finance in a useful and effective manner rests on improving the efficacy either of the FEC itself, the judicial appeals process of allowing deadlocked FEC rulings to stand or both.

Although overturning *Citizens United* and other Court rulings would certainly undo some of the most significant concerns regarding electoral spending, the likelihood of such a reversal is minuscule, at least in the next decade. Likewise, although a constitutional amendment to, for example, ban unlimited outside spending, is possible, such a solution is also unlikely. This chapter has instead focused on solutions that are pragmatic, feasible, and likely to hold up in the courts; in some cases, these solutions are even being implemented now at non-federal levels of government and may have potential to be adopted more widely in other states or even at the federal level in the future.

KEY TERMS

alignment   165
bundled contributions   165
clean elections   167
deadlock deference   180
"Democracy Facts" label   176
full public funding   167
gray money   175
leapfrog representation   165
legislative recusal   172

matching funds   167
partial public funding   168
People's Pledge   172
tax credit   168
tax deduction   168
semi-disclosure   177
Super PAC insurance   171
vouchers   169

DISCUSSION QUESTIONS

1. What category of election reform, if any, do you prefer, and why? How does your preference line up with the theories of free speech from chapter 2?
2. Do you think increasing "hard money" can solve the problems its advocates claim? Why or why not?
3. Which method of public funding do you believe would be the most effective? Justify your answer.
4. Do you think private sector solutions like Super PAC insurance can work? Why or why not?
5. How would you balance concerns about transparency measures (disclosure and disclaimer) with privacy concerns?
6. Assuming the FEC remains the primary election "watchdog" agency, what FEC reforms do you think are needed to make it function better?

ADDITIONAL READING

Baker, Anne E. "The Fundraising Disadvantages Confronting American Political Parties." *The Forum* 13, no. 2 (August 2015): 223–44.

Dalye, Brendan, and Erik Snowberg. "Even if It Is Not Bribery: The Case for Campaign Finance Reform." *The Journal of Law, Economics, and Organization* 27, no. 2 (August 2011): 324–49.

La Raja, Raymond J., and Brian F. Schaffner. "The Future of Reform: Build Canals, Not Dams." In *Campaign Finance and Political Polarization: When Purists Prevail*, 134–60. Ann Arbor: University of Michigan Press, 2015.

Malbin, Michael J., Peter W. Brusoe, and Brendan Glavin. "Small Donors, Big Democracy: New York City's Matching Funds as a Model for the Nation and States." *Election Law Journal* 11, no. 1 (February 2012): 3–20.

Mazo, Eugene D. and Timothy H. Kuhner, eds. *Democracy by the People: Reforming Campaign Finance in America*. Cambridge: Cambridge University Press, 2018.

Nichols, Philip M. "The Perverse Effect of Campaign Contribution Limits: Reducing the Allowable Amount Increases the Likelihood of Corruption in the Federal Legislature." *American Business Law Journal* 48, no. 1 (October 2011): 77–118.

Sebold, Karen, and Andrew J. Dowdle. "Can 'Letting in Sunlight'" Lead to Accidental Sunburn? The Unintended Consequences of Campaign Finance Reform on the Financing of U.S. Presidential Candidates." *Election Law Journal* 17, no. 3 (2018): 209–20.

Notes

★ ★ ★

CHAPTER 1: SUPER PACS AND DARK MONEY AS GAME CHANGERS

1. "Total Outside Spending by Election Cycle, All Groups," Center for Responsive Politics, accessed May 25, 2019, https://www.opensecrets.org/outsidespending/cycle_tots.php?cycle=2018&view=A&chart=A#viewpt.com.

2. Francis E. Lee, *Insecure Majorities: Congress and the Perpetual Campaign* (Chicago: Chicago University Press, 2016).

3. Ray La Raja, "Why Super PACs: How the American Party System Outgrew the Campaign Finance System," *The Forum* 10, no. 4 (December 2012): 93.

4. Alan Abramowitz and Jennifer McCoy, "United States: Racial Resentment, Negative Partisanship, and Polarization in Trump's America," *The Annals of the American Academy of Political and Social Science* 681, no. 1 (January 2019): 137–56. doi:10.1177/0002716218811309.

5. "Qualifying as a Multicandidate Committee," Federal Election Commission, accessed June 6, 2019, https://www.fec.gov/help-candidates-and-committees/making-disbursements-pac/qualifying-multicandidate-committee-nonconnected-pac.

6. Lauren Daniel, "527s in a Post-Swift Boat Era: The Current and Future Role of Issue Advocacy Groups in Presidential Elections," *Northwestern Journal of Law and Social Policy* 5, no. 1 (Spring 2010): 149.

7. "Social Welfare Organizations," Internal Revenue Service, accessed May 27, 2019, https://www.irs.gov/charities-non-profits/other-non-profits/social-welfare-organizations.

8. "Making Independent Expenditures," Federal Election Commission, accessed June 6, 2019, https://www.fec.gov/help-candidates-and-committees/making-independent-expenditures.

9. Federal Election Commission, "Making Independent Expenditures."

10. "Glossary," Federal Election Commission, accessed May 27, 2019, https://www.fec.gov.

11. Michael Beckel and Amisa Ratliff, "All Expenses Still Paid. A Look at Leadership PACs' Latest Outlandish Spending," *Issue One*, May 22, 2019, https://www.issueone.org/wp-content/uploads/2019/05/All-Expenses-Still-Paid.pdf.

12. "2020 Campaign Contribution Limits," Center for Responsive Politics, accessed June 6, 2019, https://www.opensecrets.org/overview/limits.php.

13. Will Steakin and Rachel Scott, "Trump Campaign Doesn't Want This Pro-Trump Super PAC's Help, the Group Is Doing It Anyway," ABC News, May 17, 2019, https://abcnews.go.com/Politics/trump-campaign-pro-trump-super-pacs-group/story?id=63081874.

14. Steakin and Scott, "Trump Campaign Doesn't Want Help."

15. Steakin and Scott, "Trump Campaign Doesn't Want Help."

16. Steakin and Scott, "Trump Campaign Doesn't Want Help."

17. Tom Howell Jr., "Trump Super PAC Waiting for Right Time to Battle against 2020 Democratic Presidential Field," *Washington Times*, May 9, 2019, https://www.washingtontimes.com/news/2019/may/9/america-first-action-super-pac-waiting-for-right-t.

18. Steakin and Scott, "Trump Campaign Doesn't Want Help."

19. Maegan Vasquez and Fredreka Schouten, "Pro-Trump Group Shifts Focus after Trump Campaign Rebuke," CNN, May 22, 2019, https://www.cnn.com/2019/05/21/politics/trump-campaign-pressure-outside-groups/index.html.

20. Kaitlan Collins, Jeremy Diamond, and Sarah Westwood, "Trump 'Livid' after Report a Former Campaign Aide Misled on Fundraising," CNN, May 7, 2019, https://www.cnn.com/2019/05/07/politics/donald-trump-david-bossie-fundraising/index.html.

21. Maggie Christ and Brendan Fischer, *"Can I Count on You?" How the Presidential Coalition Has Capitalized on Its Leader's Ties to the President and Misled Donors* (Washington, DC: Campaign Legal Center, 2019), 7. https://campaignlegal.org/document/profiting-proximity-report-presidential-coalitions-misleading-fundraising-practices.

22. Alayna Treene, Jonathan Swan, Harry Stevens, "Scoop: Inside a Top Trump Adviser's Fundraising Mirage," *Axios*, May 5, 2019, https://www.axios.com/david-bossie-fundraising-presidential-coalition-3bf22829-8a89-4a10-84b7-7310e02c2ef2.html.

23. Treene, Swan, and Stevens, "Scoop."

24. Christ and Fischer, *"Can I Count on You?,"* 14.

25. Christ and Fischer, *"Can I Count on You?,"* 4.

26. Cory Manento, "Party Crashers: Interest Groups as a Latent Threat to Party Networks in Congressional Primaries," *Party Politics* (March 2019), doi:10.1177/1354068819834528.

27. Alan Abramowitz, Brad Alexander, and Matthew Gunning. "Incumbency, Redistricting, and the Decline of Competition in U.S. House Elections," *The Journal of Politics* 68, no. 1 (2006): 75–88.

28. Leandra Bernstein, "Trump's 2020 Campaign Will Spend at Least $1 Billion, Parscale Tells 'America This Week,'" ABC7 WJLA, April 24, 2019, https://wjla.com/news/nation-world/trumps-2020-campaign-will-spend-1-billion-at-least-parscale-tells-america-this-week.

29. "2016 Presidential Race," Center for Responsive Politics, accessed May 27, 2019. https://www.opensecrets.org/pres16.

30. "Cost of Elections and Outside Spending," Delaware Get Money Out, accessed May 28, 2019, http://degetmoneyout.org/cost-of-elections-outside-spending.

31. "Cost of Election," Center for Responsive Politics, accessed May 28, 2019, https://www.opensecrets.org/overview/cost.php.

32. Michelle Ye Hee Lee, "Eleven Donors Have Plowed $1 Billion into Super PACs since They Were Created," *Washington Post*, October 26, 2018, https://www.washingtonpost.com/politics/eleven-donors-plowed-1-billion-into-super-pacs-since-2010/2018/10/26/31a07510-d70a-11e8-aeb7-ddcad4a0a54e_story.html.

33. Ian Vandewalker, "Outside Spending and Dark Money in Toss-Up Senate Races: Post-Election Update," *Brennan Center for Justice*, November 10, 2014, https://www.brennancenter.org/analysis/outside-spending-and-dark-money-toss-senate-races-post-election-update.

34. Vandewalker, "Outside Spending and Dark Money."

35. Timothy Werner, "The Sound, the Fury, and the Non-Event: Business Power and the Market Reactions to the *Citizens United* Decision," *American Politics Research* 39, no. 1 (Spring 2011): 118–41.

36. Robert G. Boatright, Brendan Glavin, and Michael Malbin, "Independent Expenditures in Congressional Primaries after *Citizens United*: Implications for Interest Groups, Incumbents and Political Parties," *Interest Groups & Advocacy* 5, no. 2 (February 2016): 119–40.

37. Catherine Thompson, "Former Bush Strategist Rips GOPers for 'Kissing the Ring' of Sheldon Adelson," *Talking Points Memo*, March 31, 2014, https://talkingpointsmemo.com/livewire/matthew-dowd-chides-gopers-kissing-the-ring-sheldon-adelson.

38. Alex Leary, "Marco Rubio Is Trying to Win the 'Sheldon Adelson Primary,'" *Tampa Bay Times*, December 14, 2015, https://www.miamiherald.com/news/politics-government/election/marco-rubio/article49765670.html.

39. Jesse H. Rhodes, Brian F. Schaffner, and Raymond J. La Raja. "Detecting and Understanding Donor Strategies in Midterm Elections," *Political Research Quarterly* 71, no. 3 (September 2018): 503–16.

40. Matea Gold, "Now It's Even Easier for Candidates and Their Aides to Help Super PACs," *Washington Post*, https://www.washingtonpost.com/politics/now-its-even-easier-for-candidates-and-their-aides-to-help-super-pacs/2015/12/24/d8d1ff4a-a989–11e5–9b92-dea7cd4b1a4d_story.html.

41. Gold, "Now It's Even Easier."

42. Vasquez and Schouten, "Pro-Trump Group Shifts Focus."

43. Editorial Board, "The Power of Super PACs," *Washington Post*, January 9, 2012, https://www.washingtonpost.com/opinions/the-power-of-super-pacs/2012/01/09/gIQA51zbmP_story.html.

44. Adam Wollner and National Journal, "10 Ways Super PACs and Campaigns Coordinate, Even Though They're Not Allowed To," *Atlantic*, September 27, 2015, https://www.theatlantic.com/politics/archive/2015/09/10-ways-super-pacs-and-campaigns-coordinate-even-though-theyre-not-allowed-to/436866.

45. "Correct the Record," InfluenceWatch, accessed June 7, 2019, https://www.influencewatch.org/political-party/correct-the-record.

46. Emery P. Dalesio, "Online Video of GOP House Candidate May Target Super PACs," AP News, May 24, 2019, https://www.apnews.com/f2311854c72f4dafac944296f402dda3.

47. Dalesio, "Online Video of GOP House Candidate May Target Super PACs."

48. Paul Blumenthal, "Dark Money Group's #McConnelling Violates Campaign Laws: Watchdogs," *Huffington Post*, March 24, 2014, https://www.huffpost.com/entry/mcconnelling_n_5021419.

49. Wollner and National Campaign, "10 Ways Super PACs and Campaigns Coordinate."

50. Paul Blumenthal, "Pat Toomey's PAC May Have Broken FEC Rules by Donating to a Super PAC Run by His Former Aides," *Huffington Post*, July 2, 2015, https://www.huffpost.com/entry/pat-toomey-super-pac_n_7713794.

51. Blumenthal, "Pat Toomey's PAC."

52. Emma Roller and National Journal, "When a Super PAC Acts Like a Campaign," *Atlantic*, September 10, 2015, https://www.theatlantic.com/politics/archive/2015/09/when-a-super-pac-acts-like-a-campaign/455679.

53. Roller and National Journal, "Super PAC Acts Like a Campaign."

54. Roller and National Journal, "Super PAC Acts Like a Campaign."

55. Jeremy W. Peters, "Conservative 'Super PACs' Synchronize Their Messages," *The New York Times*, September 24, 2012, https://www.nytimes.com/2012/09/25/us/politics/conservative-super-pacs-sharpen-their-synchronized-message.html.

56. Peters, "Conservative 'Super PACs.'"

57. Peters, "Conservative 'Super PACs.'"

58. Peters, "Conservative 'Super PACs.'"

59. Peters, "Conservative 'Super PACs.'"

60. Phil Mattingly, "The Super PAC Workaround: How Candidates Quietly, Legally, Communicate," August 24, 2014, *Bloomberg Businessweek*, https://www.bloomberg.com/news/articles/2014-08-28/how-candidates-communicate-legally-with-super-pacs.

61. Mattingly, "The Super PAC Workaround."

62. Mattingly, "The Super PAC Workaround."

63. Mattingly, "The Super PAC Workaround."

64. "American Bridge 21st Century," Center for Responsive Politics, accessed May 31, 2019, https://www.opensecrets.org/outsidespending/contrib.php?cycle=2018&cmte=C00492140.

65. According to The Citizens Audit, David Brock, the founder of American Bridge 21st Century, has "7 non-profits, 3 Super PACs, one 527-committee, one LLC, one joint fundraising committee, and one unregistered solicitor in his office in Washington DC," https://www.bombthrowers.com/article/david-brocks-money-laundering-exposed/.

66. "Potential Candidates' Verbal Gymnastics Proves Lucrative," CBS News, June 12, 2015, https://www.cbsnews.com/news/why-potential-presidential-candidates-delay-official-announcement-unlimited-campaign-donations.

67. CBS News, "Verbal Gymnastics."

68. "Brandon Martin Responds to Super PAC Smear Campaign," uploaded May 23, 2018, YouTube, video, 3:11, https://www.youtube.com/watch?v=_9xgbDRVc_Q.

69. David Karol, *Party Position Change in American Politics: Coalition Management*, (Cambridge, UK: Cambridge University Press, 2009), 182–84.

70. Gregory Koger, Seth Masket, and Hans Noel, "Partisan Webs: Information Exchange and Party Networks," *British Journal of Political Science* 39, no. 3 (July 2009): 633–53.

71. Robin Kolodny and Diana Dwyre, "Convergence or Divergence? Do Parties and Outside Groups Spend on the Same Candidates, and Does It Matter?" *American Politics Research* 46, no. 3 (May 2018): 375–401.

72. Robin and Dwyre, "Convergence or Divergence?"

73. "Making Independent Expenditures," Federal Election Commission, accessed June 13, 2019, https://www.fec.gov/help-candidates-and-committees/making-independent-expenditures.

74. "Congressional Leadership Fund: Contributors, 2012 Cycle," Center for Responsive Politics, accessed June 13, 2019, https://www.opensecrets.org/pacs/pacgave2.php?cmte=C00504530&cycle=2012.

75. "Senate Leadership Fund: Spending by Cycle," Center for Responsive Politics, accessed June 13, 2019, https://www.opensecrets.org/pacs/lookup2.php?strID=C00571703.

76. "Senate Majority PAC: Spending by Cycle," Center for Responsive Politics, accessed June 13, 2019, https://www.opensecrets.org/pacs/lookup2.php?strID=C00484642&cycle=2018.

77. Our analysis is based on data from the Center for Responsive Politics.

78. "Political Nonprofits: Top Election Spenders," Center for Responsive Politics, accessed June 2, 2019, https://www.opensecrets.org/outsidespending/nonprof_elec.php?cycle=2018.

79. Anna Massoglia, "State of Money in Politics: Billion-Dollar 'Dark Money' Spending Is Just the Tip of the Iceberg," Center for Responsive Politics, February 21, 2019, https://www.opensecrets.org/news/2019/02/somp3-billion-dollar-dark-money-tip-of-the-iceberg.

80. "Dark Money Basics," Center for Responsive Politics, accessed June 2, 2019. https://www.opensecrets.org/dark-money/basics.

81. Scott Blackburn, "Money Doesn't Buy Elections, 'Dark Money' Keeps Falling, and Other Lessons from the 2018 Midterms," Institute for Free Speech, November 9, 2018, https://www.ifs.org/blog/money-doesnt-buy-elections-dark-money-keeps-falling-and-other-lessons-from-the-2018-midterms.

82. Karl Evers-Hillstrom, " 'Dark Money' Groups Funneled Millions to Powerful Super PACs During 2018 Midterms," Center for Responsive Politics, January 3, 2019, https://www.opensecrets.org/news/2019/01/dark-money.

83. Brice McKeever, "The Nonprofit Sector in Brief," National Center for Charitable Statistics, January 3, 2019, https://nccs.urban.org/project/nonprofit-sector-brief.

84. Michael Beckel, "Dark Money Illuminated," Issue One, September 2018, https://www.issueone.org/wp-content/uploads/2018/09/Dark-Money-Illuminated-Report.pdf.

85. Travis N. Ridout, Michael M. Franz, and Erika Franklin Fowler, "Sponsorship, Disclosure, and Donors: Limiting the Impact of Outside Group Ads," *Political Research Quarterly* 68, no. 1 (2015): 154–66, http://www.jstor.org/stable/24371979.

86. Conor M. Dowling and Amber Wichowsky, "Does It Matter Who's Behind the Curtain? Anonymity in Political Advertising and the Effects of Campaign Finance Disclosure," *American Politics Research* 41, no. 6 (November 2013): 965–96, doi:10.1177/1532673X13480828.

87. Kenneth M. Winneg, Bruce W. Hardy, Jeffrey A. Gottfried, and Kathleen Hall Jamieson. "Deception in Third Party Advertising in the 2012 Presidential Campaign," *American Behavioral Scientist* 58, no. 4 (April 2014): 524–35, doi:10.1177/0002764214524358.

88. Ridout, Franz, and Franklin Fowler, "Sponsorship, Disclosure, and Donors," 163.

89. There is no widely used definition of "issue advocacy." We therefore relied on the following source: Michelle Baker, "Charities and Issue Advocacy: Doing It Right—Part One," *Nonprofit Law Blog*, July 30, 2014, http://www.nonprofitlaw blog.com/charities-issue-advocacy-right-part-one.

90. *Buckley v. Valeo*, 424 U.S. 1, 42 (1976).

91. *Buckley v. Valeo*.

92. Drew Dimmery and Andrew Peterson, "Shining the Light on Dark Money: Political Spending by Nonprofits," *RSF: The Russell Sage Foundation Journal of the Social Sciences* 2, no. 7 (2016): 51–68, doi:10.7758/rsf.2016.2.7.04.

93. *Citizens United v. Federal Election Commission*, 558 U.S. 310 (2010).

94. Todd Donovan and Shaun Bowler, "To Know It Is to Loath It: Perceptions of Campaign Finance and Attitudes about Congress," *American Politics Research* 47, no. 5 (2019): 951–69. doi:10.1177/1532673X18820860.

95. Bramlett, Brittany H., James G. Gimpel, and Frances E. Lee, "The Political Ecology of Opinion in Big-Donor Neighborhoods," *Political Behavior* 33, no. 4 (2011): 565–600, http://www.jstor.org/stable/41488877.

96. Bramlett, Gimpel, and Lee, "The Political Ecology."

97. Kim Hart, "Exclusive Poll: Only Half of Americans Have Faith in Democracy," *Axios*, November 5, 2018, https://www.axios.com/poll-americans-faith-in-demo cracy-2e94a938-4365-4e80-9fb6-d9743d817710.html.

98. Craig Bannister, "Pelosi's San Francisco Boasts Most Billionaires per Capita of Any City in the World," *CNS News*, May 10, 2019, https://www.cnsnews.com/blog/ craig-bannister/pelosis-san-francisco-boasts-most-billionaires-capita-any-city-world.

99. "My Congressional District," United States Census Bureau, accessed June 4, 2019, https://www.census.gov/mycd/?st=36&cd=15.

100. U.S. Census Bureau, Real Median Household Income in the United States [MEHOINUSA672N], retrieved from FRED, Federal Reserve Bank of St. Louis, https://fred.stlouisfed.org/series/MEHOINUSA672N, June 4, 2019,

101. "Donor Demographics," Center for Responsive Politics, accessed June 4, 2019, https://www.opensecrets.org/overview/donordemographics.php.

102. Martin Gilens, *Affluence and Influence: Economic Inequality and Political Power in America* (Princeton, NJ: Princeton University Press, 2012): 2.

103. Stan Oklobdzija, "Closing Down and Cashing In: Extremism and Political Fundraising," *State Politics & Policy Quarterly* 17, no. 2 (June 2017): 201–24, doi:10.1177/1532440016679373.

104. Anne E. Baker, "Getting Short-Changed? The Impact of Outside Money on District Representation," *Social Science Quarterly* 97, no. 5 (November 2016): 1096–107, https://doi.org/10.1111/ssqu.12279.

105. Jesse H. Rhodes and Brian F. Schaffner, "Testing Models of Unequal Representation: Democratic Populists and Republican Oligarchs?," *Quarterly Journal of Political Science* 12, no. 2 (September 2017): 185–204, http://dx.doi. org/10.1561/100.00016077.

106. Ciara Torres-Spelliscy, "Republicans Are Candid about the True Price of the Tax Bill," Brennan Center for Justice, November 21, 2017, https://www.brennancen ter.org/blog/republicans-are-candid-about-true-price-tax-bill.

107. Rebecca Savransky, "Graham: 'Financial Contributions Will Stop' if GOP Doesn't Pass Tax Reform," *Hill*, November 9, 2017, https://thehill.com/policy/

finance/359606-graham-financial-contributions-will-stop-if-gop-doesnt-pass-tax-reform.

108. Daniel I. Weiner, "The Tax Overhaul Is Proof That Money in Politics Affects All of Us," *Brennan Center for Justice*, December 4, 2017, https://www.brennancenter.org/blog/tax-overhaul-proof-money-politics-affects-all-us.

CHAPTER 2: THE FIRST AMENDMENT AND LEGAL ISSUES

1. United States Senate, "The Election Case of William A. Clark of Montana (1900)," accessed June 3, 2019, https://www. Senate.gov/artandhistory/history/common/contested_elections/089William_Clark.htm.

2. This was required until the ratification of the Seventeenth Amendment in 1912, which changed the election of U.S. senators to a direct, statewide election.

3. Adjusting for inflation, this would be the equivalent of a nearly $2.8 million.

4. U.S. Senate, "The Election Case of William A. Clark."

5. U.S. Senate, "The Election Case of William A. Clark."

6. *Western Tradition Partnership v. Attorney General of the State of Montana*, MT 328 (2011).

7. *American Tradition Partnership v. Steve Bullock, Attorney General of Montana*, 567 U.S. 1 (2012).

8. *American Tradition Partnership v. Steve Bullock, Attorney General of Montana*, 567 U.S. 1–2 (2012) (Breyer, dissenting).

9. "*Citizens United* and States," National Conference of State Legislatures, accessed June 3, 2019, http://www.ncsl.org/research/elections-and-campaigns/citizens-united-and-the-states.aspx.

10. "*Citizens United* and States," National Conference of State Legislatures.

11. Jerome A. Barron and C. Thomas Dienes, *First Amendment Law in a Nutshell*, 5th ed. (St. Paul, MN: West Academic Publishing, 2018), 8.

12. *Abrams v. United States*, 250 U.S. 616 (1919).

13. Gary Francione, "Experimentation and the Marketplace Theory of the First Amendment," *University of Pennsylvania Law Review* 136 (1987): 422.

14. *Williams v. Rhodes*, 393 US 23, 32 (1968).

15. *FCC v. League of Women Voters*, 468 US 364, 377–78 (1984).

16. *Associated Press v. United States*, 326 US 1, 20 (1945).

17. *Adderley v. Florida*, 385 US 39, 49 (1966) (Douglas, J., dissenting).

18. *City Council v. Taxpayers for Vincent*, 466 US 789, 803 (1984).

19. Jerome A. Barron, "Access to the Press. A New First Amendment Right," *Harvard Law Review* 80, no. 8 (1967): 1641.

20. Jason Lynch, "Advertisers Spent $5.25 Billion on the Midterm Election, 17% More Than in 2016," *Adweek*, Nov. 15, 2018, https://www.adweek.com/tv-video/advertisers-spent-5-25-billion-on-the-midterm-election-17-more-than-in-2016/.

21. C. Edwin Baker, "Campaign Expenditures and Free Speech," *Harvard Law Review* 33, no. 1 (1998): 1–55.

22. Matthew Ingram, "Can Social Media Have a Positive Effect on Democracy?" *Columbia Journalism Review*, May 30, 2018, https://www.cjr.org/the_new_gate keepers/social-media-democracy.php.

23. Barron and Dienes, *First Amendment Law*, 8–10.

24. Brendan Nyhan and Jason Reifler, "When Corrections Fail: The Persistence of Political Misperceptions," *Political Behavior* 32, no. 2 (June 2010): 303–30.

25. Alexander Meiklejohn, *Free Speech and Its Relation to Self-Government* (New York: Harpers Brothers, 1948).

26. *The New York Times v. Sullivan*, 376 U.S. 254, 296–97 (1964).

27. *Central Hudson Gas & Electric Corp. v. Public Service Commission*, 447 US 557, 591 (1980) (Rehnquist, J., dissenting).

28. Barron and Dienes, *First Amendment Law*, 12–13. The authors argue that under the self-governance model, the "government is given 'reasonably broad power' to regulate speech which does not further democratic deliberation."

29. Barron and Dienes, *First Amendment Law*, 12–13. The authors add that "the calculus for determining what speech is in and what is out remains unclear."

30. C. Edwin Baker, *Human Liberty and Free Speech* (New York: Oxford University Press, 1989), 5.

31. Jaime Fuller, "From George Washington to Shaun McCutcheon: A Brief-ish History of Campaign Finance Reform," *The Washington Post*, April 3, 2014, https://www.washingtonpost.com/news/the-fix/wp/2014/04/03/a-history-of-campaign-finance-reform-from-george-washington-to-shaun-mccutcheon/.

32. Brennan Center for Justice, "Unregulated Soft Money Now Pays for Most Party Electioneering Ads," March 28, 2001, https://www.brennancenter.org/press-release/unregulated-soft-money-now-pays-most-party-electioneering-ads.

33. The text of the ads can be read in the endnotes 3 through 5 of the district court case text for *Wisconsin Right to Life v. FEC*, 466 F. Supp. 2d 195 (D.D.C. 2006), accessed June 4, 2019, https://www.courtlistener.com/opinion/2403174/wisconsin-right-to-life-v-federal-elec-comn/.

34. *Hillary: The Movie*, DVD, directed by Alan Peterson (Washington, DC: Citizens United Production, 2008).

35. "Contribution Limits for 2013–2014," Federal Election Commission, https://www.fec.gov/updates/contribution-limits-2013-2014/.

36. Brief for the Appellee at 37, *McCutcheon*, 134 S. Ct. 1434 (No. 12–536)

37. Trevor Timm, "It's Time to Stop Using the 'Fire in a Crowded Theater' Quote," *The Atlantic*, November 12, 2012, https://www.theatlantic.com/national/archive/2012/11/its-time-to-stop-using-the-fire-in-a-crowded-theater-quote/264449/.

38. *Schenck v. United States*, 249 U.S. 47 (1919).

39. We should note that advocates of the liberty model recognize that "balancing" is "possibly the most universally accepted tenet of First Amendment doctrine," even though they largely disagree with it. Baker, *Human Liberty*, 125.

40. *Buckley v. Valeo*, 424 U.S. 1, 25 (1976), 48–49.

41. Yasmin Dawood, "Equal Participation and Campaign Finance," in *Democracy by the People: Reforming Campaign Finance in America*, ed. Eugene D. Mazo and Timothy H. Kuhner (Cambridge, MA: Cambridge University Press, 2018), 426–27.

42. 501(c)(3)s are limited to "insubstantial" lobbying efforts, which the Internal Revenue Service defines as less than 10 percent of its operating budget. Internal Revenue Service, "Applying for 501(c)(3) Tax-Exempt Status, pub. no. 4220" (revised March 2018), 3, accessed November 5, 2019, https://www.irs.gov/pub/irs-pdf/p4220.pdf.

43. *Federal Election Commission v. Massachusetts Citizens for Life* 479 U.S. 238 (1986).

44. C. Edwin Baker, "The Independent Significance of the Press Clause under Existing Law," *Hofstra Law Review* 35, no. 3 (2007), https://scholarlycommons. law.hofstra.edu/ cgi/viewcontent.cgi?article=2264&context=hlr. See also Robert C. Post, *Citizens Divided: Campaign Finance Reform and the Constitution* (Cambridge, MA: Harvard University Press, 2014), 70–73.

45. Potter Stewart, "Or of the Press," *Hastings Law Journal* 26, no. 3 (1975): 633.

46. *Citizens United*, 431, n. 57.

47. *First National Bank of Boston v. Bellotti*, 435 U.S. 765, 782 (1978).

48. Michael W. McConnell, "Reconsidering *Citizens United* as a Press Clause Case," *Yale Law Journal* 123, no. 2 (November 2013): 438.

49. Richard Hasen, *Plutocrats United: Campaign Money, the Supreme Court, and the Distortion of American Elections* (New Haven, CT: Yale University Press, 2016), 126.

50. Sonja R. West, "The Media Exemption Puzzle of Campaign Finance Laws," *University of Pennsylvania Law Review Online* 164, no. 2 (2016), https://scholarship. law.upenn.edu/cgi/viewcontent.cgi?article=1178&context=penn_law_review_ online.

51. Bradley Jones, "Most Americans Want to Limit Campaign Spending, Say Big Donors Have Greater Political Influence," Pew Research Center, May 8, 2018, https://www.pewresearch.org/fact-tank/2018/05/08/most-americans-want-to-limit-campaign-spending-say-big-donors-have-greater-political-influence/.

52. Federal Election Commission, "Contribution Limits," https://www.fec.gov/ help-candidates-and-committees/candidate-taking-receipts/contribution-limits/.

53. *Federalist Papers 57*, accessed November 5, 2019, https://avalon.law.yale. edu/18th_century/fed57.asp.

54. Constitution Society, "Essays of Brutus, #3," accessed June 13, 2019, https:// www.constitution.org/afp/brutus03.htm.

55. Constitution Society, "Essays of Brutus, #4," accessed June 13, 2019, https:// www.constitution.org/afp/brutus04.htm.

56. *Buckley*, 26–27.

57. *McConnell v. FEC* 540 U.S. 93, 34 (2003); the quoted portions reference prior rulings.

58. *McCutcheon*, 19.

59. Adam Lioz, "Raising All of Our Voices for Democracy: A Hybrid Public Funding Proposal," in *Democracy by the People: Reforming Campaign Finance in America*, ed. Eugene D. Mazo and Timothy H. Kuhner (Cambridge: Cambridge University Press, 2018), 128.

60. *McCutcheon v. FEC*, 3.

61. Deborah Hellman, "Liberty, Equality, Bribery, and Self-government: Reframing the Campaign Finance Debate," in *Democracy by the People: Reforming Campaign Finance in America*, ed. Eugene D. Mazo and Timothy H. Kuhner (Cambridge: Cambridge University Press, 2018), 58–73.

62. There could perhaps be a few more if someone owns properties in multiple states.

63. Campaign Legal Center, "The Court's Changing Conception of Corruption," May 7, 2015, https://campaignlegal.org/update/courts-changing-conception-corruption.

64. Congress.gov, "S.3295 DISCLOSE Act," accessed July 13, 2019, https://www.congress.gov/bill/111th-congress/ Senate-bill/3295/text.

65. David M. Herszenhorn, "Campaign Finance Bill Is Set Aside, *The New York Times*, July 27, 2010, https://www.nytimes.com/2010/07/28/us/politics/28 donate.html.

66. From most recent to oldest, the DISCLOSE Act has been introduced as the following piece of legislation: H.R. 2977 (116th Congress), S. 1147 (116th Congress), H.R. 6239 (115th Congress), S. 3150 (115th Congress), S. 1585 (115th Congress), S. 229 (114th Congress), S. 3369 (112th Congress), S. 2219 (112th Congress), S. 3628 (111th Congress), and its original version as H.R. 5175 (111th Congress). All can be found at Congress.gov by searching "DISCLOSE Act," https://www.congress.gov/search.

67. In addition to the "informational interest," the Supreme Court has also identified an anticorruption interest and an enforcement interest. The corruption argument has been explored already, and the enforcement interest is covered elsewhere in this book, so the focus in this section is on the informational interest argument. See Jennifer A. Heerwig and Katherine Shaw, "Through a Glass, Darkly: The Rhetoric and Reality of Campaign Finance Disclosure," *Georgetown Law Journal* 102 (2014): 1465.

68. *Buckley*, 67.

69. Lear Jiang, "Disclosure's Last Stand? The Need to Clarify the 'Informational Interest' Advanced by Campaign Finance Disclosure," *Columbia Law Review* 119 (2019): 496–498.

70. *Wieman v. Updegraff* 344 U.S. 183, 195 (1952) (Frankfurter, F. concurring).

71. David M. Primo, "Full Disclosure: How Campaign Finance Disclosure Laws Fail to Inform the Public and Stifle Public Debate," *Institute for Justice*, October 2011, 4.

We feel compelled to disclose that many of these foundations and institutes making the case against disclosure laws are themselves funded by wealthy individuals who wish may wish to remain unknown to the general public. The Koch brothers provided the seed money for the "Institute for Justice" (IJ) and have been the primary donors. According to SourceWatch, "a statement on IJ's website, 'Charles Koch provided the initial seed funding that made it possible to launch the Institute in 1991. David Koch has been a generous benefactor each year of IJ's first decade.' Since its founding, IJ has received donations from a number of groups with links to the Koch brothers, including a donation of $15,000 from the Charles G. Koch Foundation in 2001 and two donations of $250,000 each from the David H. Koch Foundation in 1999 and 2001. IJ also received $716,800 from DonorsTrust and the Donors Capital Fund between 2010 and 2012." See "Institute for Justice," The Center for Media and Democracy, accessed June 22, 2019, https://www.sourcewatch.org/index.php/Institute_for_Justice.

72. Omri Ben-Shahar and Carl E. Schneider, "The Failure of Mandated Disclosure," *University of Pennsylvania Law Review* 159 (2011): 687.

73. After the Supreme Court decision in *Western Tradition*, Montana passed disclosure laws that have thus far been upheld. See Martin Kidston, "9th Circuit Upholds Montana's Disclosure Laws against Dark Money Challenge," *Missoula Current*, May 24, 2018, https://www.missoulacurrent.com/government/2018/05/9th-circuit-dark-money/.

74. Michael S. Kang, "The End of Campaign Finance Law," *Virginia Law Review* 98, no. 1 (March 2012): 49.

75. *Citizens United v. FEC* (2010).

CHAPTER 3: DONORS, EXPENDITURES, AND REPRESENTATION

1. Nicholas Confessore, Sarah Cohen, and Karen Yourish, "The Families Financing the 2016 Presidential Election," *The New York Times*, October 15, 2015, https://www.nytimes.com/interactive/2015/10/11/us/politics/2016-presidential-election-super-pac-donors.html.

2. Eric Lichtblau and Nicholas Confessore, "From Fracking to Finance, A Torrent of Campaign Cash," *The New York Times*, October 10, 2015, https://www.nytimes.com/2015/10/11/us/politics/wealthy-families-presidential-candidates.html#donors-list.

3. Nicholas Confessore, Sarah Cohen, and Karen Yourish, "Small Pool of Rich Donors Dominates Election Giving," *The New York Times*, August 1, 2015, https://www.nytimes.com/2015/08/02/us/small-pool-of-rich-donors-dominates-election-giving.html.

4. Confessore, Cohen, and Yourish, "The Families."

5. Nadja Popovich, Livia Albeck-Ripka, and Kendra Pierre-Louis, "84 Environmental Rules Being Rolled Back Under Trump," *The New York Times*, August 29, 2019, https://www.nytimes.com/interactive/2019/climate/trump-environment-rollbacks.html.

6. Popovich, Albeck-Ripka, and Pierre-Louis, "84 Environmental Rules."

7. Mike Allen, "Sheldon Adelson: Inside the Mind of the MegaDonor," *Politico*, September 23, 2012, https://www.politico.com/story/2012/09/sheldon-adelson-inside-the-mind-of-the-mega-donor-081588?o=3.

8. Brittany H. Bramlett, James G. Gimpel, and Frances E. Lee, "The Political Ecology of Opinion in Big-Donor Neighborhoods," *Political Behavior* 33, no. 4 (2011): 565, http://www.jstor.org/stable/41488877.

9. Bramlett, Gimpel, and Lee, "The Political Ecology," 565.

10. John J. Dowling, III, "How Citizens United vs FEC Impacted the Quality of Democracy" (undergraduate honors college theses, Long Island University, 2017), https://digitalcommons.liu.edu/post_honors_theses/6.

11. Abdul-Razzak Nour, Carlo Prato, and Stephane Wolton, "After Citizens United: How Outside Spending Shapes American Democracy," March 2019, https://ssrn.com/abstract=2823778.

12. Stan Oklobdzija, "Closing Down and Cashing In: Extremism and Political Fundraising," *State Politics & Policy Quarterly* 17, no. 2 (June 2017): 201, doi:10.1177/1532440016679373.

13. Michelle Ye Hee Lee, "Eleven Donors have Plowed $1 Billion into Super PACs since They Were Created," *The Washington Post*, October 26, 2018, https://www.washingtonpost.com/politics/eleven-donors-plowed-1-billion-into-super-pacs-since-2010/2018/10/26/31a07510-d70a-11e8-aeb7-ddcad4a0a54e_story.html.

14. These statistics are from our analysis of data by the Center for Responsive Politics.

15. "Top Individual Donors to Super PACs," Center for Responsive Politics, accessed August 24, 2019, https://www.opensecrets.org/overview/topindivs.php.

16. Dan Eggen, "Super PACs Dominate Republican Primary Spending," *Washington Post*, January 16, 2012, https://www.washingtonpost.com/politics/super-pacs-dominate-republican-primary-spending/2012/01/11/gIQAdcoq3P_story.html.

17. "Outside Spending, by Super PAC," Center for Responsive Politics, accessed August 25, 2019, https://www.opensecrets.org/outsidespending/summ.php?chrt=V&type=S.

18. Center for Responsive Politics, "Outside Spending, by Super PAC."

19. "Outside Spending by Single-Candidate Super PACs," Center for Responsive Politics, accessed August 25, 2019, https://www.opensecrets.org/outsidespending/summ.php.

20. "Fix Democracy First," Issue One, accessed August 25, 2019, https://www.issueone.org/.

21. "Dark Money Illuminated," Issue One, accessed August 25, 2019, https://www.issueone.org/wp-content/uploads/2018/09/Dark-Money-Illuminated-Report.pdf.

22. All these findings come directly from Issue One's "Dark Money Illuminated." The corresponding database can be accessed at https://www.issueone.org/dark-money/.

23. "Dark Money Process," Center for Responsive Politics, accessed August 25, 2019, https://www.opensecrets.org/dark-money/process.

24. Issue One, "Dark Money Illuminated," 5–7.

25. "About Us," American Future Fund, accessed August 29, 2019, https://americanfuturefund.com/about-us/.

26. Maggie Haberman, "Ad by Pro-Trump Group Attacks the Club for Growth," *The New York Times*, April 18, 2017, https://www.nytimes.com/2017/04/18/us/politics/attack-ad-sheldon-adelson-club-for-growth.html.

27. "Patriot Majority Action Plan," Patriot Majority, accessed August 25, 2019, https://www.patriotmajority.org/action-plan.

28. Conor M. Dowling and Michael G. Miller, *Super PAC! Money, Elections, and Voters after* Citizens United (New York: Routledge, 2014), 70–71.

29. Anna Massoglia, "State of Money in Politics: Billion-Dollar 'Dark Money,'" Center for Responsive Politics, February 21, 2019, https://www.opensecrets.org/news/2019/02/somp3-billion-dollar-dark-money-tip-of-the-iceberg/.

30. B. Holley Schadler, *The Connection. Strategies for Creating and Operating 501(C)3s, 501(C)4s, and Political Organizations*, 4th ed. (Washington, DC: Alliance for Justice, 2018), 16.

31. Schadler, *The Connection*, 23.

32. Schadler, *The Connection*, 17.

33. Schadler, *The Connection*, 17.

34. Robert Maguire, "A New Low in Campaign Finance," *New York Times*, October 27, 2015, https://www.nytimes.com/2015/10/27/opinion/a-new-low-in-campaign-finance.html.

35. Maguire, "A New Low."

36. John Francis Reilly, Carter C. Hull, and Barbara A. Braig Allen, "IRC 501(c)4 Organizations," Internal Revenue Service, 2003, https://www.irs.gov/pub/irs-tege/eotopici03.pdf.

37. Issue One, "Dark Money Illuminated," 12.

38. Lee Aitken, "There Is No Way to Follow the Money," *Atlantic*, December 16, 2013, https://www.theatlantic.com/politics/archive/2013/12/theres-no-way-to-follow-the-money/282394/.

39. Zachary G. Parks, "Federal Court Decision Puts Brakes on Issue Ads," *Covington*, March 21, 2018, https://www.insidepoliticallaw.com/2018/03/21/federal-court-decision-puts-brakes-issue-ads/.

40. "*Crew v. FEC* (16–2255/18–5136)," Federal Election Commission, accessed September 1, 2019, https://transition.fec.gov/law/litigation/CREW_162255.shtml#ac.

41. Paul Farhi, "Four Years Later, the IRS Tea Party Scandal Looks Very Different. It May Not Even Be a Scandal," *The Washington Post*, October 5, 2017, https://www.washingtonpost.com/lifestyle/style/four-years-later-the-irs-tea-party-scandal-looks-very-different-it-may-not-even-be-a-scandal/2017/10/05/4e90c7ec-a9f7-11e7-850e-2bdd1236be5d_story.html.

42. "IRS: Agency to Consider Changes to 501(c)(4) Eligibility Rules as Requested by Campaign Legal Center and Democracy 21," Campaign Legal Center, accessed March 30, 2019, https://campaignlegal.org/index.php/press-releases/irs-agency-consider-changes-501c4-eligibility-rules-requested-campaign-legal-center.

43. Libby Watson, "A Glossary of Campaign Finance in the U.S.," Sunlight Foundation, February 17, 2016, https://sunlightfoundation.com/2016/02/17/a-glossary-of-campaign-finance-in-the-u-s/.

44. Aitken, "No Way to Follow the Money."

45. Phil Drake, "Governor Bullock's Order Targets Dark Money Spending," *Great Falls Tribune*, June 8, 2018, https://www.greatfallstribune.com/story/news/2018/06/08/montana-governors-executive-order-reveals-dark-money/685517002/.

46. Michael Becker, "Super PACs and Dark Money Groups Combined to Outspend Candidates in a Record Number of Races in 2018," Issue One, December 18, 2018, https://www.issueone.org/super-pacs-and-dark-money-groups-combined-to-outspend-candidates-in-a-record-number-of-races-in-2018/.

47. Becker, "Super PACs and Dark Money Groups."

48. "Races in Which Outside Spending Exceeds Candidate Spending," Center for Responsive Politics, accessed August 25, 2019, https://www.opensecrets.org/outsidespending/outvscand.php?cycle=2018.

49. Becker, "Super PACs and Dark Money Groups."

50. "Republican Party of Dallas County," Center for Responsive Politics, accessed August 26, 2019, https://www.opensecrets.org/pacs/pacgave2.php?sort=A&cmte=C00342857&cycle=2018&Page=4.

51. Paul Blumenthal, "Republicans Admit that CEOs and Donors Really Need the Tax Cut Bill to Pass—or Else," *HuffPost*, November 9, 2017, https://www.huffpost.com/entry/gary-cohn-tax-cut-ceos-donors_n_5a049571e4b0f76b05c4249e.

52. Megan Brenan, "More Still Disapprove than Approve of 2017 Tax Cut," Gallup, October 10, 2018, https://news.gallup.com/poll/243611/disapprove-approve-2017-tax-cuts.aspx.

53. Angie Drobnic Holan, "Obama Abandons Cap and Trade as Republicans Take Over the House," Politifact, November 8, 2010, https://www.politifact.com/truth-o-meter/promises/obameter/promise/456/create-cap-and-trade-system-with-interim-goals-to-/.

54. Clare O'Connor, "As Obama Pushes for Minimum Wage Increase, Billionaire Charles Koch Rails against It with Media Campaign," *Forbes*, August 8, 2013, https://www.forbes.com/sites/clareoconnor/2013/08/08/as-obama-pushes-for-minimum-wage-increase-billionaire-charles-koch-rails-against-it-with-media-campaign/#7a8033ea56f5.

55. Annie Snider, "Former Koch Official Runs EPA Chemical Research," *Politico*, February 4, 2019, https://www.politico.com/story/2019/02/04/former-koch-official-runs-epa-chemical-research-1136230.

56. Karl Evers-Hillstrom, "Secretive Front Group Targets Vulnerable Senators with $2.3 Million Ad Blitz over Surprise Medical Bills Fight," Center for Responsive Politics, August 6, 2019, https://www.opensecrets.org/news/2019/08/secretive-front-group-targets-vulnerable-senators-with-2-3-million-ad-blitz-over-surprise-medical-bills-fight/.

57. Sandra Fish, "August 2, 2019," uploaded August 2, 2019, YouTube video, accessed August 27, 2019, https://www.youtube.com/watch?v=JkvaCtf0_Rc.

58. Evers-Hillstrom, "Secretive Front Group."

59. Dan Eggen, "Chevron Donates $2.5 Million to GOP Super PAC," *The Washington Post*, October 26, 2012, https://www.washingtonpost.com/news/post-politics/wp/2012/10/26/chevron-donates-2-5-million-to-gop-super-pac/.

60. Ciara Torres-Spelliscy, "The Looming Pay-to-Play Problem," Brennan Center for Justice, April 15, 2015, https://www.brennancenter.org/blog/looming-pay-play-problem.

61. Patrick Caldwell, "Critics Say Chevron Flouted Pay-to-Play Law. FEC Says It's All Good," *MotherJones*, March 24, 2014, https://www.motherjones.com/politics/2014/03/chevron-super-pac-fec-pay-play/.

62. Brian Schwartz, "Wealthy Former Hillary Clinton Donor Stephen Rosenberg Is Using Secret Shell Company to Back Trump," CNBC, August 28, 2019, https://www.cnbc.com/2019/08/28/former-clinton-donor-stephen-rosenberg-uses-shell-company-for-trump.html.

63. Karl Evers-Hillstrom and Kietryn Zychal, "Dark Money: Coming from a Shell Company Near You," Center for Responsive Politics, January 29, 2019, https://www.opensecrets.org/news/2019/01/dark-money-coming-from-a-shell-company-near-you/.

64. Vicky Ward, "Pro-Trump Super PAC Paid Thousands to Firm Owned by Trump's Campaign Manager," CNN, August 30, 2019, https://www.cnn.com/2019/08/30/politics/pro-trump-super-pac-paid-thousands-to-firm-owned-by-brad-parscales-wife/index.html.

65. Ward, "Pro-Trump Super PAC."

66. Sarah Childress, "James Bopp: What Citizens United Means for Campaign Finance," PBS, October 30, 2012, https://www.pbs.org/wgbh/frontline/article/james-bopp-what-citizens-united-means-for-campaign-finance/.

67. Todd Donovan and Shaun Bowler, "To Know It Is to Loath It: Perceptions of Campaign Finance and Attitudes About Congress," *American Politics Research* 47, no. 5 (September 2019): 964–65, doi:10.1177/1532673X18820860.

68. Jesse H. Rhodes and Brian F. Schaffner, "Testing Models of Unequal Representation: Democratic Populists and Republican Oligarchs?," *Quarterly Journal of Political Science* 12, no. 2 (September 2017): 185–204, http://dx.doi.org/10.1561/100.0001607.

69. Anne E. Baker, Baker, "Getting Short-changed? The Impact of Outside Money on District Representation," *Social Science Quarterly* 97, no. 5 (2017): 1096, doi:10.1111/ssqu.12279.

70. Liz Essley Whyte, "Groups Decrying Dark Money Use Shadowy Money Themselves," The Center for Public Integrity, January 20, 2016, https://publicintegrity.org/state-politics/groups-decrying-dark-money-use-shadowy-money-themselves/.

CHAPTER 4: NEW TRENDS IN PRESIDENTIAL CAMPAIGNS

1. Dan Eggen and T. W. Farnam, "New 'Super PACs' Bringing Millions into Campaigns," *Washington Post*, September 27, 2010, http://www.washingtonpost.com/wp-dyn/content/article/2010/09/27/AR2010092706500.html.

2. Gideon Resnick, "Campaign Finance Group to 2020 Dems: Disavow and Shut Down All Super PACs," *The Daily Beast*, March 8, 2019, https://www.thedailybeast.com/campaign-finance-group-to-2020-dems-disavow-and-shut-down-all-Super-pacs.

3. Elena Schneider and Nick Niedzwiadek, "Gillibrand Rejects Super PAC support," *Politico*, January 16, 2019, https://www.politico.com/story/2019/01/16/gillibrand-rejects-Super-pac-support-1104551.

4. Kevin Robillard, "Joe Biden Rejects Help from New Super PAC," *HuffPost*, April 27, 2019, https://www.huffpost.com/entry/joe-biden-rejects-help-from-new-Super-pac_n_5cc47617e4b08e4e3482b2b1.

5. Resnick, "Campaign Finance Group."

6. Emily Larsen, "Democratic 2020 Hopefuls' Feel-Good, Anti-PAC Pledges Leave Plenty of Room for Huge PAC Benefits," *Washington Examiner*, April 10, 2019, https://www.washingtonexaminer.com/news/democratic-2020-hopefuls-feel-good-anti-pac-pledges-leave-plenty-of-room-for-huge-pac-benefits.

7. Fredreka Schouten and Dan Merica, "Democrats Are Denouncing Big Money. But They Are Powerless to Stop It in 2020," CNN, January 11, 2019, https://www.cnn.com/2019/01/11/politics/2020-candidates-and-super-pacs/index.html.

8. Resnick, "Campaign Finance Group."

9. Michael Warren and Fredreka Schouten, " 'It's Been a Disaster.' Inside the Trump Super PAC Struggles," CNN, June 8, 2019, https://www.cnn.com/2019/06/07/politics/trump-Super-pac-america-first/index.html.

10. Warren and Schouten, "Inside the Trump Super PAC Struggles."

11. Betsy Klein, "Pro-Trump Group Launching Ads Supporting Meadows, Jordan," CNN, March 19, 2019, https://www.cnn.com/2019/03/19/politics/america-first-policies-mark-meadows-jim-jordan/index.html.

12. Warren and Schouten, "Inside the Trump Super PAC Struggles."

13. David M. Drucker, "Trump Allies Fear His Mission-Critical Super PAC Is Not Ready for Prime Time," *Washington Examiner*, June 3, 2019, https://www.washingtonexaminer.com/news/campaigns/trump-allies-fear-his-mission-critical-Super-pac-is-not-ready-for-prime-time.

14. Shane Goldmacher, "2020 Democrats Face a Vexing Issue: Big Money from the Rich," *The New York Times*, December 11, 2018, https://www.nytimes.com/2018/12/11/us/politics/democrats-2020-super-pac.html.

15. Goldmacher, "2020 Democrats."

16. Goldmacher, "2020 Democrats."

17. Alexander Burns and Jonathan Martin, "Joe Biden Announces 2020 Run for President, after Months of Hesitation," *New York Times*, April 25, 2019, https://www.nytimes.com/2019/04/25/us/politics/joe-biden-2020-announcement.html.

18. Associated Press, "Here's Why Joe Biden Is Still Waiting to Make His 2020 Announcement," *MarketWatch*, February 11, 2019, https://www.marketwatch.com/story/why-joe-biden-is-still-waiting-on-the-2020-sidelines-2019-02-11.

19. Nick Gass, "Jeb Bush to Announce 2016 Bid on June 15," *Politico*, June 4, 2015, https://www.politico.com/story/2015/06/jeb-bush-to-announce-2016-intentions-on-june-15-118626.

20. Paul Blumenthal, "Jeb Bush Messes Up Charade of Not Running for President," *HuffPost*, May 13, 2015, https://www.huffpost.com/entry/jeb-bush-president_n_7278624.

21. Joseph Tanfani and Seema Mehta, "Super PACs Stretch the Rules that Prohibit Coordination with Presidential Campaigns," *Los Angeles Times*, October 7, 2015, https://www.latimes.com/nation/la-na-politics-Superpacs-impact-20151005-story.html.

22. Nicholas Confessore and Eric Lichtblau, "'Campaigns' Aren't Necessarily Campaigns in the Age of 'Super PACs,'" *The New York Times*, May 17, 2015, https://www.nytimes.com/2015/05/18/us/politics/Super-pacs-are-remaking-16-campaigns-official-or-not.html?_r=0.

23. Bob Biersack, Viveca Novak, and Will Tucker, "A Few New Faces—But Not Many—among Megadonors to Presidential Super PACs," Center for Responsive Politics, August 1, 2015, https://www.opensecrets.org/news/2015/08/a-few-new-faces-but-not-many-among-megadonors-to-presidential-Super-pacs/.

24. Jenna Johnson, "Carly Fiorina Begins Presidential Bid," *The Washington Post*, May 4, 2015, https://www.washingtonpost.com/news/post-politics/wp/2015/05/04/carly-fiorina-expected-to-announce-run-for-president-monday/.

25. Robert Maguire and Will Tucker, "How Carly Fiorina's Super PAC Mirrors Her Campaign," *Time*, November 19, 2015, https://time.com/4120431/carly-fiorina-Super-pac/.

26. Chris Moody, "With Eye on a Presidential Bid, Carly Fiorina Hires Republican Party Spokeswoman," CNN, January 2, 2015, https://www.cnn.com/2015/01/02/politics/carly-fiorina-hires-republican-party-spokeswoman/.

27. Paul S. Ryan, "'Testing the Waters' and the Big Lie: How Prospective Presidential Candidates Evade Candidate Contribution Limits while the FEC Looks the Other Way," Campaign Legal Center, 2015, http://www.campaignlegalcenter.org/sites/default/files/Testing_the_Waters_and_the_Big_Lie_2.19.15.pdf.

28. Ryan, " 'Testing the Waters,' " 1–2.

29. Matea Gold, Tom Hamburger, and Jenna Johnson, "The Inside Story of Trump Campaign's Connections to a Big-Money Super PAC," *The Washington Post*, October 18, 2015, https://www.washingtonpost.com/politics/the-inside-story-of-donald-trumps-connections-to-a-big-money-super-pac/2015/10/18/532b61d4-72b5-11e5-8248-98e0f5a2e830_story.html.

30. Federal Election Commission, C.F.R. §109.21(d)(4),(5), https://www.fec.gov/regulations/109-21/2019-annual-109#109-21-d-4.

31. "Revolving Door Prohibitions," National Conference of State Legislatures, accessed June 19, 2019, http://www.ncsl.org/research/ethics/50-state-table-revolving-door-prohibitions.aspx.

32. Ruby Cramer, "Clinton Super PAC Executive Director Exits amid Shake-Up," *BuzzFeed*, May 20, 2015, https://www.buzzfeednews.com/article/rubycramer/priorities-wicks#.gnoVlExgl.

33. "Hillary for California Announces Leadership Team," Democracy in Action, April 22, 2016, http://www.p2016.org/clinton/clinton042216prca.html.

34. Tanfani and Mehta, "Super PACs Stretch the Rules."

35. Michael J. Goff, *The Money Primary: The New Politics of the Early Presidential Nomination Process* (Lanham, MD: Rowman & Littlefield, 2004).

36. Ashley Parker, " 'Koch Primary' Tests Hopefuls in the G.O.P.," *The New York Times*, January 20, 2015, https://www.nytimes.com/2015/01/21/us/koch-seminar-is-early-proving-ground-for-gop-hopefuls.html.

37. Girish J. Gulati, "Super PACs and Financing the 2012 Presidential Election," *Society* 49, no. 5 (September 2012): 409–17, https://doi.org/10.1007/s12115-012-9575-3.

38. "Independent Expenditure 15-Month Data Summaries 1/1/15–3/31/16," Federal Election Commission, accessed June 30, 2019, https://transition.fec.gov/press/summaries/2016/ElectionCycle/15m_IE_EC.shtml.

39. Barry Wynn, "Super PACs Are a Game Changer," interview by Cheryl Casone, *Fox Business*, January 26, 2012, video, https://video.foxbusiness.com/v/1416114798001/#sp=show-clips.

40. "Also-Rans: 2016 Presidential Race," Center for Responsive Politics, accessed June 27, 2019, https://www.opensecrets.org/pres16/also-rans.

41. Matea Gold and Anu Narayanswamy, "2016 Fundraising Shows Power Tilting to Groups Backed by Wealthy Elite," *The Washington Post*, July 15, 2015, https://www.washingtonpost.com/politics/2016-fundraising-shows-power-tilting-to-groups-backed-by-wealthy-elite/2015/07/15/4c915a74-2b05-11e5-a250-42bd812efc09_story.html.

42. Gold and Narayanswamy, "2016 Fundraising."

43. Adam Lioz, Juhem Navarro-Rivera, and Sean McElwee, "Court Cash: 2016 Election Money Resulting Directly from Supreme Court Rulings," Demos, March 14, 2017, https://www.demos.org/research/court-cash-2016-election-money-resulting-directly-supreme-court-rulings.

44. This is from our analysis, with the data coming from the Center for Responsive Politics.

45. These statistics come from our own analysis based on Center for Responsive Politics data.

46. Michael Malbin, "Obama and Romney Each Have Their Best Months so Far, Gearing Up for the General Election," Campaign Finance Institute, April 24, 2012, http://www.cfinst.org/pdf/federal/president/2012/Pres12_M4_Table6.pdf.

47. Malbin, "Obama and Romney Each Have Their Best Months," http://www.cfinst.org/pdf/federal/president/2012/Pres12_M4_Table1.pdf.

48. "Independent Spending Totals," *The New York Times*, accessed June 15, 2019, https://www.nytimes.com/elections/2012/campaign-finance/independent-expendi tures/totals.html.

49. Nathaniel Persily, "The Law of American Party Finance," in *Party Funding and Campaign Financing in International Perspective*, ed. K. D. Ewing and Samuel Issacharoff (Portland, OR: Hart Publishing, 2006), 221.

50. "Washington's Open Secret: Profitable PACs," CBS News, last modified October 21, 2013, https://www.cbsnews.com/news/washingtons-open-secret-profitable-pacs/.

51. Heather Haddon and Reid J. Epstein, "Chris Christie Joins Crowded GOP Fight for Donors," *Wall Street Journal*, January 26, 2015, https://www.wsj.com/articles/chris-christie-joins-crowded-gop-fight-for-donors-1422248464.

52. Lucy McCalmont, "Christie Launches Leadership PAC," *Politico*, January 26, 2015, https://www.politico.com/story/2015/01/chris-christie-leadership-pac-114591.

53. "Leadership for America, Expenditures," Center for Responsive Politics, accessed June 27, 2019, https://www.opensecrets.org/pacs/expenditures.php?cycle=2016&cmte=C00571778.

54. "Leadership for America, Summary," Center for Responsive Politics, accessed June 27, 2019, https://www.opensecrets.org/pacs/lookup2.php?cycle=2016&strID=C00571778.

55. "Reclaim America PAC, Expenditures, 2016 Cycle," Center for Responsive Politics, accessed June 27, 2019, https://www.opensecrets.org/pacs/expenditures.php?cycle=2016&cmte=C00500025.

56. Kurtis Lee, "Campaign Cash: 'Leadership PACs' Becoming Vehicle of Choice for Presidential Candidates," *Los Angeles Times*, March 11, 2015, https://www.latimes.com/nation/politics/la-na-presidential-pacs-2016-20150311-story.html.

57. Lee, "Campaign Cash."

58. Lee, "Campaign Cash."

59. Maggie Severns and Christopher Catelago, "Biden Uses Midterms Haul to Bolster his 2020 Chances," *Politico*, January 8, 2019, https://www.politico.com/story/2019/01/08/joe-biden-2020-election-pac-1086016.

60. Severns and Catelago, "Biden Uses Midterms."

61. "Joint Fundraising Committees," Center for Responsive Politics, accessed July 5, 2019, https://www.opensecrets.org/jfc/.

62. Center for Responsive Politics, "Joint Fundraising Committees."

63. Carrie Levine, "Soft Money Is Back—and Both Parties Are Cashing In," *Politico*, August 4, 2017, https://www.politico.com/magazine/story/2017/08/04/soft-money-is-backand-both-parties-are-cashing-in-215456.

64. Levine, "Soft Money Is Back."

65. "Contribution Limits for 2013–14," Federal Election Commission, last modified February 12, 2013, https://www.fec.gov/updates/contribution-limits-2013-2014/.

66. Camille Erickson, "A Lag in Fundraising Casts Doubt on DNC's 2020 Influence," Center for Responsive Politics, May 7, 2019, https://www.opensecrets.org/news/2019/05/a-lag-in-fundraising-casts-doubt-on-dncs-2020-influence/.

67. "Coordinated Communications," Federal Election Commission, accessed July 6, 2019, https://www.fec.gov/help-candidates-and-committees/candidate-taking-receipts/coordinated-communications/.

68. Brendan O'Connor, "Trump Accuses Cruz and Rubio of Talking to Their Super PACs," *Gawker*, March 8, 2016, https://gawker.com/trump-accuses-cruz-and-rubio-of-talking-to-their-super-1763703945.

69. Nick Corasaniti and Matt Flegenheimer, "As TV Ad Rates Soar, 'Super PACs' Pivot to Core Campaign Work," *The New York Times*, December 22, 2015, https://www.nytimes.com/2015/12/23/us/politics/as-tv-ad-rates-soar-super-pacs-pivot-to-core-campaign-work.html.

70. Eric Lichtblau, "F.E.C. Can't Curb 2016 Election Abuse, Commission Chief Says," *The New York Times*, May 2, 2015, https://www.nytimes.com/2015/05/03/us/politics/fec-cant-curb-2016-election-abuse-commission-chief-says.html.

71. Corasaniti and Flegenheimer, "As TV Ad Rates Soar."

72. Joseph Tanfani and Seema Mehta, "Super PACs Stretch the Rules That Prohibit Coordination with Presidential Campaigns," *Los Angeles Times*, October 6, 2015, https://www.latimes.com/nation/la-na-politics-superpacs-impact-20151005-story.html.

73. Tanfani and Mehta, "Super PACs Stretch the Rules."

74. Brad Parscale, "CNN Gets Rare Look into Trump's Re-Election Campaign," interview by Dana Bash, CNN, March 19, 2019, video, https://www.cnn.com/videos/politics/2019/03/19/brad-parscale-trump-re-election-effort-bash-dnt-lead-vpx.cnn.

75. T. W. Farnam, "GOP Candidates' Ad Spending Down, but Anti-Obama Groups Take to Airwaves Early," *Washington Post*, December 28, 2011, https://www.washingtonpost.com/politics/gop-candidates-ad-spending-down-but-anti-obama-groups-take-to-airwaves-early/2011/12/28/gIQAIRwANP_story.html.

76. Samuel L. Popkin, *The Candidate: What It Takes to Win—and Hold—the White House* (New York: Oxford University Press, 2013), 3–8.

77. Tom McCarthy, "Is This Guy Serious? Could Republican Frontrunner Trump Actually Win?," *The Guardian*, July 19, 2015, https://www.theguardian.com/us-news/2015/jul/19/is-this-guy-serious-could-republican-frontrunner-donald-trump-actually-win.

78. McCarthy, "Is This Guy Serious?"

79. David Catanese, "McCain 'Concerned' about November," *Politico*, February 19, 2012, https://www.politico.com/blogs/politico-now/2012/02/mccain-concerned-about-november-114942.

80. Jim Arkedis, "The GOP Primary Is Badly Wounding Mitt Romney," *The Atlantic*, February 13, 2012, https://www.theatlantic.com/politics/archive/2012/02/the-gop-primary-is-badly-wounding-mitt-romney/252929/.

81. Brian C. Mooney, "Super PACs Fueling GOP Attack Ads. Eventual Nominee Could Pay a Price," *The Boston Globe*, February 2, 2012, http://archive.boston.com/news/politics/articles/2012/02/02/damage_from_super_pac_ads_is_hurting_gop_presidential_candidates/.

82. "Coordinated Party Expenditures," Federal Election Commission, accessed July 3, 2019, https://www.fec.gov/help-candidates-and-committees/making-disbursements-political-party/coordinated-party-expenditures/.

83. Gary C. Jacobson, "A Collective Dilemma Solved: The Distribution of Party Campaign Resources in the 2006 and 2008 Congressional Elections," *Election Law Journal* 9, no. 4 (2010): 381–97.

84. Diana Dwyre, "Political Parties and Campaign Finance: What Role Do the National Parties Play?" (paper presented at the Campaign Finance Task Force Conference, Bipartisan Policy Center, Washington, DC, April 21, 2017), 33.

85. Paul Blumenthal, "Hillary Clinton Has a Big Cash Advantage for the Campaign's Final Weeks," *HuffPost*, October 28, 2016, https://www.huffpost.com/entry/hillary-clinton-donald-trump_n_5812c76be4b0990edc304112.

86. "Republican National Committee," Center for Responsive Politics, accessed July 7, 2019, https://www.opensecrets.org/parties/indexp.php?cycle=2016&cmte=RNC.

87. Brakkton Booker, "Supplement Trump's Lacking Ground Game in Critical States," NPR, September 2, 2016, https://www.npr.org/2016/09/02/492434914/rnc-hires-staff-to-supplement-trumps-lacking-ground-game-in-critical-states.

88. Joshua P. Darr and Matthew S. Levendusky, "Relying on the Ground Game: The Placement and Effect of Campaign Field Offices," *American Politics Research* 42, no. 3 (May 2014): 529, doi:10.1177/1532673X13500520.

89. Steven Lemongello, "How Did Trump Win Florida? A GOP Ground Game Years in the Making," *Orlando Sentinel*, November 16, 2016, https://www.orlandosentinel.com/politics/os-how-did-trump-win-florida-a-gop-ground-game-years-in-the-making-20161116-story.html.

90. Lemongello, "How Did Trump Win Florida."

91. Erich Lach, "Why Famous, Powerful Presidential Candidates Are Begging You for Five Dollars," *The New Yorker*, June 10, 2019, https://www.newyorker.com/news/news-desk/why-famous-powerful-presidential-candidates-are-begging-you-for-five-dollars.

92. Carrie Levine, "Why Democrats Are Falling Over Themselves to Find Small-Dollar Donors," Center for Public Integrity and *FiveThirtyEight*, April 17, 2019, https://publicintegrity.org/federal-politics/elections/democrats-small-dollar-donors-president-campaign/.

93. Lach, "Presidential Candidates Are Begging for Five Dollars."

94. Donald J. Trump (@realDonaldTrump), "I am pleased to announce the launch of http://tmagac.winred.com. This new platform will allow my campaign and other Republicans to compete with the Democrats money machine. This has been a priority of mine and I'm pleased to share that it is up and running! #KeepAmericaGreat," Twitter post, June 24, 2019, https://twitter.com/realDonaldTrump/status/1143159975277187072.

95. Karl Rove, "The Democrats' Tech Cash Machine," *Wall Street Journal*, June 26, 2019, https://www.wsj.com/articles/the-democrats-tech-cash-machine-11561589350.

96. Carrie Levine and Peter Overby, "Red Shift: How Republicans Plan to Catch Democrats in Online Fundraising," NPR, July 1, 2019, https://www.npr.org/2019/07/01/736990455/red-shift-how-republicans-plan-to-catch-

democrats-in-online-fundraising?utm_campaign=politics&utm_source=twitter. com&utm_medium=social&utm_term=nprnews.

97. Levine and Overby, "Red Shift."

98. Adam Hughes, "5 Facts about U.S. Political Donations," *Pew Research Center*, May 17, 2017, https://www.pewresearch.org/fact-tank/2017/05/17/5-facts-about-u-s-political-donations/.

99. Steve Peoples and Brian Slodysko (Associated Press), "2020 Presidential Candidates at Risk of Being Cut from Debates," *PBS NewsHour*, July 1, 2019, https:// www.pbs.org/newshour/politics/2020-presidential-candidates-at-risk-of-being-cut-from-debates.

100. Kirsten Gillibrand, "Contest: Join Kirsten for a Drink," *Facebook*, July 2, 2019, https://www.facebook.com.

101. Gillibrand, "Contest."

102. Joe Andrews, "Majority of Americans Say They Won't Donate to 2020 Presidential Campaigns," CNBC, July 1, 2019, https://www.cnbc.com/2019/06/28/ majority-of-americans-wont-donate-to-2020-presidential-campaigns.html.

103. Wendy L. Hansen, Michael S. Rocca, and Brittany Leigh Ortiz, "The Effects of Citizens United on Corporate Spending in the 2012 Presidential Election," *The Journal of Politics* 77, no. 2 (April 2015): 535.

CHAPTER 5: NEW TRENDS IN CONGRESSIONAL CAMPAIGNS

1. Paul S. Herrnson, *Congressional Elections: Campaigning at Home and in Washington*, 6th ed. (Washington, DC: CQ Press, 2015).

2. Paul S. Herrnson, Jennifer A. Heerwig, and Douglas M. Spencer, "The Impact of Organizational Characteristics on Super PAC Financing," in *The State of the Parties: The Changing Role of Contemporary American Political Parties*, ed. John C. Green, Daniel J. Coffey, and David B. Cohen (New York: Rowman & Littlefield, 2018), 260–61.

3. Diana Dwyre and Evelyn Braz, "Super PAC Spending Strategies and Goals," *The Forum* 13, no. 2 (2015): 245–67, doi:10.1515/for-2015–0020.

4. "Most Expensive Midterm Ever: Cost of 2018 Election Surpasses $5.7 Billion," Center for Responsive Politics, February 6, 2019, https://www.opensecrets. org/news/2019/02/cost-of-2018-election-5pnt7bil/.

5. Center for Responsive Politics, "Most Expensive Midterm Ever."

6. Michael J. Malbin, "Campaign Finance Institute: Massive Amounts Were Spent by the Candidates and Independent Spenders in the Races That Decided the 2018 Midterms," Campaign Finance Institute, November 13, 2018, http://www.cfinst.org/ pdf/Federal/PostElec_2018_Table1.pdf.

7. Malbin, "Campaign Finance Institute."

8. Center for Responsive Politics, "Most Expensive Midterm Ever."

9. Center for Responsive Politics, "Most Expensive Midterm Ever."

10. Brendan Glavin, "Democrats Outspending Republicans Two-to-One in Final Independent Spending Push," Campaign Finance Institute, November 5, 2018, https://www.followthemoney.org/research/blog/cfi-democrats-outspending-republi cans-two-to-one-in-final-independent-spending-push.

11. "Most Expensive Races," Center for Responsive Politics, accessed September 1, 2019, https://www.opensecrets.org/overview/topraces.php?cycle=2018& display=currcandsout.

12. Michael S. Lewis-Beck and Charles Tien, "Election Forecasting: The Long-View," in *Oxford Handbooks Online*, ed. David Pervin (Oxford: Oxford University Press, 2016), 1–18, 10.1093/oxfordhb/9780199935307.013.92.

13. Alex Cukierman, "Asymmetric Information and the Electoral Momentum of Public Opinion Polls," *Public Choice* 70, no. 2 (1991): 181–213, http://www.jstor.org/stable/30025460.

14. Gary C. Jacobson, "Measuring Campaign Spending Effects in U.S. House Elections," in *Capturing Campaign Effects*, ed. Henry E. Brady and Richard Johnston (Ann Arbor: University of Michigan Press, 2006), 199–220.

15. Stephen Ansolabehere and James M. Snyder, Jr., "The Incumbency Advantage in U.S. Elections: An Analysis of State and Federal Offices, 1942–2000," *Election Law Journal* 1, no. 3 (September 2002): 315–38.

16. Gary C. Jacobson, "It's Nothing Personal: The Decline of the Incumbency Advantage in US House Elections," *The Journal of Politics* 77, no. 3 (July 2015): 861.

17. Gary C. Jacobson, "How Do Campaigns Matter?," *Annual Review of Political Science* 18, no. 1 (May 2015): 42–44.

18. Jeff Milyo, "Campaign Spending and Electoral Competition: Towards More Policy Relevant Research," final draft of article to be published in *The Forum* 11, no. 3 (October 2013): 437–54, http://www.cfinst.org/pdf/papers/04_Milyo_Competition.pdf.

19. Gary C. Jacobson and Jamie L. Carson, *The Politics of Congressional Elections* (Lanham, MD: Rowman & Littlefield, 2015).

20. Brandon Barutt and Norman Schofield, "Measuring Campaign Spending Effects in Post-Citizens United Congressional Elections," in *The Political Economy of Social Choices*, ed. Maria Gallego and Norman Schofield (Basel, Switzerland: Springer International Publishing, 2016), ch. 9, https://link.springer.com/book/10.1007 percent2F978-3-319-40118-8.

21. Gary C. Jacobson, "The Effects of Campaign Spending in Congressional Elections," *American Political Science Review* 72, no. 2 (1978): 469–91.

22. Jacobson, "The Effects of Campaign Spending."

23. Steven D. Levitt, "Using Repeat Challengers to Estimate the Effect of Campaign Spending on Election Outcomes in the U.S. House," *Journal of Political Economy* 102, no. 4 (August 1994): 795, http://www.jstor.org/stable/2138764.

24. Thomas Stratmann, "Some Talk: Money in Politics. A (Partial) Review of the Literature," *Public Choice* 124, no. 1/2 (2005): 135–56, http://www.jstor.org/stable/30026707.

25. Ciara Torres-Spelliscy, "The Incumbency Problem Has Everything to Do with Money," *Hill*, May 19, 2009, https://thehill.com/blogs/congress-blog/politics/25496-the-incumbency-problem-has-everything-to-do-with-money.

26. Alexander Fouirnaies, "How Do Campaign Spending Limits Affect Electoral Competition? Evidence from Great Britain 1885–2010" (working paper, Harris School, University of Chicago, 2018), https://projects.iq.harvard.edu/files/pegroup/files/fouirnaies2018.pdf.

27. Thomas Ferguson, Paul Jorgensen, and Jie Chen, "How Money Drives US Congressional Elections" (Institute for New Economic Thinking Working Paper Series No. 48, August 1, 2016), http://dx.doi.org/10.2139/ssrn.2817705.

28. Ferguson, Jorgensen, and Chen, "Money Drives Elections."

29. Aaron Dusso, Thomas T. Holyoke, and Henrik Schatzinger, "The Influence of Corporate Lobbying on Federal Contracting," *Social Science Quarterly* (2019): 13, doi:10.1111/ssqu.12665.

30. Malbin, "Campaign Finance Institute."

31. Bruce I. Newman, Wojciech Cwalina, and Andrzej Falkowski, "Political Marketing and Public Affairs," in *The SAGE Handbook of International Corporate and Public Affairs*, ed. Phil Harris and Craig S. Fleisher (Thousand Oaks, CA: SAGE, 2017), 204.

32. Diana Dwyre and Evelyn Braz, "Super PAC Spending Strategies and Goals," *The Forum* 13, no. 2 (2015): 245–67, doi:10.1515/for-2015–0020.

33. Matea Gold and Anu Narayanswamy, "The New Gilded Age: Close to Half of All Super-PAC Money Comes from 50 Donors," *Washington Post*, April 15, 2016, https://www.washingtonpost.com/politics/the-new-gilded-age-close-to-half-of-all-super-pac-money-comes-from-50-donors/2016/04/15/63dc363c-01b4-11e6-9d36-33d198ea26c5_story.html.

34. John W. Schoen, "It's Still Early in the Midterm Cycle, but Long-Distance Donors Are Already Flooding Tight House Races with Cash," CNBC, April 24, 2018, https://www.cnbc.com/2018/04/24/long-distance-donors-are-already-flooding-tight-house-races-with-cash.html.

35. J. T. Stepleton, "Independent Spending Overview, 2015 and 2016," National Institute on Money in Politics, February 14, 2018, https://www.followthemoney.org/research/institute-reports/independent-spending-overview-2015-and-2016.

36. Jesse H. Rhodes, Brian F. Schaffner, and Raymond J. La Raja, "Detecting and Understanding Donor Strategies in Midterm Elections," *Political Research Quarterly* 71, no. 3 (September 2018): 503–16, doi:10.1177/1065912917749323.

37. Peter L. Francia, John C. Green, Paul S. Herrnson, Lynda W. Powell, and Clyde Wilcox, *The Financiers of Congressional Elections: Investors, Ideologues, and Intimates* (New York: Columbia University Press, 2016).

38. Damon M. Cann, *Sharing the Wealth. Member Contributions and the Exchange Theory of Party Influence in the U.S. House of Representatives* (Albany: State University of New York Press, 2008).

39. Michael Rocca and Jared Clay, "Allocating Unlimited Money: Which Congressional Elections Attract Super PAC Expenditures?" (paper presented at the annual meeting of the Midwest Political Science Association, Chicago, IL, April 3–7, 2019).

40. Elizabeth A. Bennion, "Caught in the Ground Wars: Mobilizing Voters during a Competitive Congressional Campaign," *The Annals of the American Academy of Political and Social Science* 601, no. 1 (September 2005): 123–41, doi:10.1177/0002716205277863.

41. Dwyre and Braz, "Super PAC Spending Goals," 258–260.

42. Herrnson, Heerwig, and Spencer, "Organizational Characteristics," 253.

43. Herrnson, Heerwig, and Spencer, "Organizational Characteristics," 248–262.

44. Herrnson, Heerwig, and Spencer, "Organizational Characteristics," 248–262.

45. Herrnson, Heerwig, and Spencer, "Organizational Characteristics," 248–262.

46. Herrnson, Heerwig, and Spencer, "Organizational Characteristics," 248–262.

47. Jessica Guynn, John Fritze, and Christopher Schnaars, "Midterms: 'Furious' Democrats Purchase Blitz of Facebook Ads on Kavanaugh, Far Outpacing GOP Spending," *USA Today*, October 11, 2019, https://www.usatoday.com/story/news/politics/elections/2018/10/11/democrats-blitz-facebook-anti-kavanaugh-ads-before-midterms/1579577002/.

48. Guynn, Fritze, and Schnaars, "Midterms."

49. Guynn, Fritze, and Schnaars, "Midterms."

50. Guynn, Fritze, and Schnaars, "Midterms."

51. Katie Notopoulos, "Facebook Will Now Show You How to Opt Out of Targeted Ads," *Buzzfeed*, July 11, 2019, https://www.buzzfeednews.com/article/katienotopoulos/facebook-data-broker-why-i-see-ad.

52. "Your Ad Preferences," Facebook, accessed July 13, 2019, https://www.facebook.com/ads/preferences/.

53. Lawrence Lessig, "What's So Bad about a Super PAC?," *Medium*, June 4, 2014, https://medium.com/@lessig/whats-so-bad-about-a-superpac-c7cbcf617b58.

54. Brian Schwartz, "Conservative Dark Money Group American Action Network Reveals Spending Blitz to Support Trump's Tax Cut Law," CNBC, May 23, 2019, https://www.cnbc.com/2019/05/23/conservative-dark-money-group-american-action-network-reveals-spending-blitz-to-push-trump-tax-cut.html.

55. Schwartz, "Conservative Dark Money Group."

56. *Citizens United v. Federal Election Commission*, 558 U.S. 310 (2010).

57. *Citizens United v. Federal Election Commission*.

58. Anthony Kennedy, "Supreme Court Associate Justice Anthony Kennedy Visits HLS," interview by Martha Minow, October 26, 2015, video, 59:57, https://www.youtube.com/watch?time_continue=4&v=ZHbMPnA5n0Q.

59. Maggie Severns and Derek Willis, "The Hidden Money: Funding the Midterms," *Politico*, December 21, 2018, https://www.politico.com/interactives/2018/hidden-money-funding-midterms-superpacs/.

60. Severns and Willis, "The Hidden Money."

61. Severns and Willis, "The Hidden Money."

62. Maggie Severns, "'Oh That's Cool—Do That!': Super PACs Use New Trick to Hide Donors," *Politico*, August 17, 2018, https://www.politico.com/story/2018/08/17/super-pacs-hidden-donors-disclosures-741795.

63. "Enforcement Down at the Four-Member FEC, but Risks Remain for the Unwary," *Covington*, July 11, 2018, https://www.cov.com/-/media/files/corporate/publications/2018/07/enforcement_down_at_the_four_member_fec_but_risks_remain_for_the_unwary.pdf.

64. Citizens for Responsibility and Ethics in Washington, "Crew Complaint Results in Record Post-*Citizens United* Penalty," November 20, 2017, https://www.citizensforethics.org/press-release/crew-complaint-results-record-post-citizens-united-penalty/

65. Marc Caputo, "Democrats Roll Out $90 Million Super PAC Aimed at Swing States," *Politico*, May 31, 2019, https://www.politico.com/story/2019/05/31/democrats-super-pac-swing-states-1348502.

66. Jonathan Easley, "Exclusive: Top Trump Super PACs Join Forces on Voter Mobilization Effort," *The Hill*, June 4, 2019, https://thehill.com/homenews/

campaign/446980-exclusive-top-trump-super-pacs-join-forces-on-voter-mobiliza
tion-effort#.XPhBNACQPaQ.twitter.

67. Anne Baker, "The Fundraising Disadvantages Confronting American Political
Parties," *The Forum* 13, no. 2 (September 2015): 236–40.

68. Cory Manento, "Party Crashers: Interest Groups as a Latent Threat to Party
Networks in Congressional Primaries," *Party Politics* (March 2019), doi:10.
1177/1354068819834528.

69. Manento, "Party Crashers," 9–10.

70. Keith E. Hamm, Michael J. Malbin, Jaclyn J. Kettler, and Brendan Glavin,
"Independent Spending in State Elections, 2006–2010: Vertically Networked Political Parties Were the Real Story, Not Business," *The Forum* 12, no. 2 (2014): 305–28,
doi:10.1515/for-2014–5003.

71. "Making Independent Expenditures," Federal Election Commission, accessed
June 13, 2019, https://www.fec.gov/help-candidates-and-committees/making-
independent-expenditures/.

72. The terms "party leadership Super PAC" and "party leadership-aligned Super
PAC" have been used by other scholars. We did not create these terms.

73. Ken Vogel, "Get to Know a Super PAC: Congressional Leadership Fund,"
Politico, July 23, 2012, https://www.politico.com/video/2012/07/get-to-know-a-
Super-pac-congressional-leadership-fund-011611.

74. David M. Drucker, "Paul Ryan-Aligned Super PAC Moves to Save GOP House
Seat," *Washington Examiner*, March 31, 2017, https://www.washingtonexaminer.
com/paul-ryan-aligned-Super-pac-moves-to-save-gop-house-seat.

75. "About CLF," Congressional Leadership Fund, accessed June 13, 2019, https://
www.congressionalleadershipfund.org/about/.

76. "Senate Leadership Fund," Ballotpedia, accessed June 13, 2019, https://ballot
pedia.org/Senate_Leadership_Fund.

77. "Leadership Team," Senate Leadership Fund, accessed June 13, 2019, "https://
www.senateleadershipfund.org/leadership-team/.

78. "Congressional Leadership Fund: Contributors, 2012 Cycle," Center for
Responsive Politics, accessed June 13, 2019, https://www.opensecrets.org/pacs/
pacgave2.php?cmte=C00504530&cycle=2012.

79. "Senate Leadership Fund: Spending by Cycle," Center for Responsive Politics, accessed June 13, 2019, https://www.opensecrets.org/pacs/lookup2.php?
strID=C00571703.

80. "Senate Majority PAC: Spending by Cycle," Center for Responsive Politics,
accessed June 13, 2019, https://www.opensecrets.org/pacs/lookup2.php?strID=
C00484642&cycle=2018.

81. "New Republican PAC: Spending by Cycle," Center for Responsive Politics,
accessed June 13, 2019, https://www.opensecrets.org/pacs/lookup2.php?cycle=
2018&strID=C00544544.

82. The analysis is based on various data collected by the Center for Responsive
Politics.

83. Richard N. Engstrom and Christopher Kenny, "The Effects of Independent
Expenditures in Senate Elections," *Political Research Quarterly* 55, no. 4 (December 2002): 885–905.

84. Victoria Farrar-Myers, Jeff J. Gulati, and Richard Skinner, "The Impact of Super PACs on the 2010 and 2012 Congressional Elections" (paper presented at Annual Meeting of the American Political Science Association, Chicago, IL, August 29–September 1, 2013).

85. Farrar-Myrers, Gulati, and Skinner, "The Impact of Super PACs."

86. Victoria Farrar-Myers and Richard Skinner, "Super PACs and the 2012 Elections, " *The Forum* 10, no. 4 (December 2012): 105–18.

87. Victoria Farrar-Myers and Richard Skinner, "Super PACs and the 2012 Elections" (paper presented at the 2012 Annual Meeting of the American Political Science Association, New Orleans, LA, August 30–September 2, 2012), 10–11.

88. Robert G. Boatright, Michael J. Malbin, and Brendan Glavin, "Independent Expenditures in Congressional Primaries after *Citizens United*: Implications for Interest Groups, Incumbents and Political Parties," *Interest Groups & Advocacy* 5, no. 2 (May 2016): 119–40.

89. Reid J. Epstein, "Amazon Founder Jeff Bezos Gives $10 Million to Super PAC in First Major Political Contribution," Foxnews.com, September 5, 2018, https://www.foxnews.com/politics/amazon-founder-jeff-bezos-gives-10-million-to-super-pac-in-first-major-political-contribution.

90. Boatright, Malbin, and Glavin, "Independent Expenditures."

91. Boatright, Malbin, and Glavin, "Independent Expenditures."

92. Patricia Murphy, "Donald Trump Is Right about One Thing," *Roll Call*, January 11, 2016, https://www.rollcall.com/news/donald-trump-is-right-about-one-thing.

93. Murphy, "Donald Trump Is Right."

94. Andrew Prokop, "Political Scientists Think 'The Party' Will Stop Trump. They Shouldn't Be So Sure," Vox.com, September 23, 2015, https://www.vox.com/2015/9/23/9352273/party-decides-trump-sanders.

CHAPTER 6: POLITICAL ADVERTISING IN
THE POST-*CITIZENS UNITED* ERA

1. Maggie Severns, "Mystery Super PAC That Attacked McSally Was Funded by Senate Democrats," *Politico*, September 20, 2018, https://www.politico.com/story/2018/09/20/super-pac-martha-mcsally-secretly-funded-833600.

2. We had difficulty tracking down these ads because Red and Gold no longer has any online presence, but with the help of *Arizona Republic* journalist Yvonne Wingett Sanchez, we were able to find links from Kantar Media of the video and audio of the ad, last accessed July 19, 2019, http://mycmag.kantarmediana.com/KMIcmagvidbin2/USSEN_AZ_REDANDGOLD_IT_HURTS.html and http://mycmag.kantarmediana.com/KMIcmagvidbin2/USSEN_AZ_REDANDGOLD_AGE_TAX.html.

3. Severns, "Mystery Super PAC."

4. Ronald J. Hansen, "George Soros, Son Funded August Attacks on Martha McSally," *AZCentral*, September 20, 2018, https://www.azcentral.com/story/news/politics/arizona/2018/09/20/george-soros-son-funded-pac-attacks-martha-mcsally-kyrsten-sinema-Senate-election/1375834002/.

5. "Red and Gold, Outside Spending Summary 2018," Center for Responsive Politics, accessed July 17, 2019, https://www.opensecrets.org/outsidespending/detail.php?cmte=C00684209&cycle=2018

6. Yvonne Wingett Sanchez, "Why a Democrat Group Is 'Meddling' in Arizona's GOP Senate Primary," *AZCentral*, August 19, 2018, https://www.azcentral.com/story/news/politics/elections/2018/08/19/arizona-elections-democrat-group-red-and-gold-meddling-gop-Senate-primary/1009619002/.

7. Hansen, "George Soros, Son Funded."

8. Erika Franklin Fowler and Travis N. Ridout, "Political Advertising in 2016: The Presidential Election as Outlier?," *The Forum* 14, no. 4 (2016): 462–63.

9. Erika Franklin Fowler and Travis N. Ridout, "Advertising Trends in 2010," *The Forum* 8, no. 4 (2010): 2–5.

10. Erika Franklin Fowler and Travis Ridout, "Negative, Angry, and Ubiquitous: Political Advertising in 2012," *The Forum* 10, no. 4 (2012): 52.

11. Erika Franklin Fowler, "Outside Group Involvement in GOP Contest Skyrockets Compared to 2008," accessed June 4, 2019, http://mediaproject.wesleyan.edu/releases/group-involvement-skyrockets/.

12. Kenneth M. Winneg, Bruce W. Hardy, Jeffrey A. Gottfried, and Kathleen Hall Jamieson, "Deception in Third Party Advertising in the 2012 Presidential Campaign," *American Behavioral Scientist* 58, no. 4 (April 2014): 524.

13. Dan Eggen, "Super PACs: GOP Rivals Reap Benefits of Groups They Claim to Disdain," *Washington Post*, January 17, 2012, https://www.washingtonpost.com/politics/super-pacs-gop-rivals-reap-benefits-of-groups-they-claim-to-disdain/2012/01/17/gIQAEuil6P_story.html.

14. Erika Franklin Fowler and Travis N. Ridout, "Political Advertising in 2014: The Year of the Outside Group," Wesleyan Media Project, February 6, 2015, http://mediaproject.wesleyan.edu/wp-content/uploads/2015/04/2014-Forum-Fowler Ridout_FINAL2.pdf.

15. "Races in Which Outside Spending Exceeds Candidate Spending, 2014 Election Cycle," Center for Responsive Politics, accessed July 16, 2019, https://www.opensecrets.org/outsidespending/outvscand.php?cycle=2014.

16. Fowler and Ridout, "Political Advertising in 2014," 15.

17. Fowler and Ridout, "Political Advertising in 2014," 18. These numbers include gubernatorial races.

18. Fowler and Ridout, "Political Advertising in 2014," 16.

19. Fowler, Franz, and Ridout, "Political Advertising in 2016," 460.

20. Fowler, Franz, and Ridout, "Political Advertising in 2016," 446.

21. Fowler, Franz, and Ridout, "Political Advertising in 2016," 461.

22. Fowler, Franz, and Ridout, "Political Advertising in 2016," 448.

23. Fowler, Franz, and Ridout, "Political Advertising in 2016," 452–54. Trump won Michigan by a small margin of 10,704 votes out of more than 4.5 million votes cast. This was a margin of victory of 0.3 percent of the vote.

24. Fowler, Franz, and Ridout, "Political Advertising in 2016," 451.

25. The Associated Press, "Here's How Much Less than Hillary Clinton Donald Trump Spent on the Election," *Fortune*, December 9, 2016, https://fortune.com/2016/12/09/hillary-clinton-donald-trump-campaign-spending/.

26. "More Dark Money Ads than Any of the Past Four Cycles," Wesleyan Media Project, November 1, 2018, accessed June 2, 2019, http://mediaproject.wesleyan.edu/releases/110118-tv/.

27. Erika Franklin Fowler, Michael Franz, and Travis Ridout, "The Big Lessons of Political Advertising in 2018," *The Conversation*, December 3, 2018, http://thecon versation.com/the-big-lessons-of-political-advertising-in-2018-107673.

28. Darrell M. West, *How Issue Ads Have Reshaped American Politics* (Washington, DC: The Center for Congressional and Presidential Studies, School of Public Affairs, American University, 1989), 8.

29. M. Asif Ismail, "A Most Favored Corporation: Enron Prevailed in Federal, State Lobbying Efforts 49 Times," The Center for Public Integrity, last updated May 19, 2014, https://publicintegrity.org/federal-politics/a-most-favored-corporation-enron-prevailed-in-federal-state-lobbying-efforts-49-times/.

30. Viveca Novak, "Americans for Responsible Leadership Wholly Funded by Koch-Linked Group," Center for Responsible Politics, December 13, 2013, https://www.opensecrets.org/news/2013/12/americans-for-responsible-leadership-wholly-funded-by-koch-linked-group/.

31. "Political Nonprofits: Top Donors," Center for Responsive Politics, accessed July 15, 2019, https://www.opensecrets.org/outsidespending/nonprof_donors.php.

32. Viveca Novak, "Exclusive: Center to Protect Patient Rights Gave Millions in 2011 to Outside Spenders in Election," Center for Responsible Politics, December 17, 2012, https://www.opensecrets.org/news/2012/12/center-to-protect-patient-rights-ga/. The group gave "grants" to nineteen other outside groups.

33. Robert Maquire, "An Encore for the Center to Protect Patient Rights," Center for Responsive Politics, March 5, 2014, https://www.opensecrets.org/news/2014/03/an-encore-for-the-center-to-protect-patient-rightstect-patient-right/.

34. "AstroTurf" was a brand of artificial grass used primarily for athletic venues; hence, the play on words here refers to a fake grass(roots) organization meant to deceive others.

35. Libby Watson, "The Deceptive Campaign to Keep D.C. Service Workers Underpaid," *Splinter News*, June 18, 2018, https://splinternews.com/the-deceptive-campaign-to-keep-d-c-service-workers-und-1826924316.

36. Patricia Callahan and Sam Roe, "Fear Fans Flames for Chemical Makers," May 6, 2012, *Chicago Tribune*, https://www.chicagotribune.com/investigations/ct-met-flame-retardants-20120506-story.html.

37. Marko Kovic, Adrian Rauchfleisch, Marc Sele, and Christian Caspar, "Digital Astroturfing in Politics: Definition, Typology, and Countermeasures," *Studies in Communication Science* 18, no. 1 (December 2018): 71.

38. Kovich et al., "Digital Astroturfing," 73.

39. Brendan Fischer and Maggie Christ, "Digital Deception: How a Major Democratic Dark Money Group Exploited Digital Ad Loopholes in the 2018 Election," Campaign Legal Center, March 12, 2019, https://campaignlegal.org/document/digital-deception-how-major-democratic-dark-money-group-exploited-digital-ad-loopholes.

40. Search results for "the tax scam," Facebook Political Ad Archive, accessed July 17, 2019, https://www.facebook.com/ads/library/?active_status=all&ad_type=political_and_issue_ads&country=US&impression_search_field=has_impress ions_lifetime&q=the percent20tax percent20scam.

41. Winneg et al., "Deception in Third Party Advertising," 2.

42. Winneg et al., "Deception in Third Party Advertising," 9.

43. Winneg et al., "Deception in Third Party Advertising," 10.

44. Winneg et al., "Deception in Third Party Advertising," 10.

45. Amy Jasperson and David P. Fan, "An Aggregate Examination of the Backlash Effect in Political Advertising: The Case of the 1996 U.S. Senate Race in Minnesota," *Journal of Advertising* 31, no. 1 (2002): 1–12. See also Bruce Pinkleton, "The Effects of Negative Advertising on Candidate Evaluations and Advertising Evaluations: An Exploration," *Journal of Advertising* 26, no. 1 (1997): 19–29.

46. For example, the organization Issue One reports that they were able to identify only a meager 2 percent of the money raised by "two dark money giants," 45Committee and Crossroads GPS. See "Dark Money Illuminated," Issue One, 9, https://www.issueone.org/wp-content/uploads/2018/09/Dark-Money-Illuminated-Report.pdf.

47. Deborah Jordan Brooks and Michael Murov, "Assessing Accountability in a Post-*Citizens United* Era: The Effects of Attack Ad Sponsorship by Unknown Independent Groups," *American Politics Research* 40, no. 3 (2012): 383–418; Tyler Johnson, Johanna Dunaway, and Christopher R. Weber, "Consider the Source: Variation in the Effects of Negative Campaign Messages," *Journal of Integrated Social Sciences* 2, no. 1 (2011): 98–127; Travis N. Ridout, Michael M. Franz, and Erika Franklin Fowler, "Sponsorship, Disclosure, and Donors: Limiting the Impact of Outside Group Ads," *Political Research Quarterly* 68, no. 1 (March 2015): 154–66.

48. "Outside Group Activity, 2000–2016" (special report from the Center for Responsive Politics and the Wesleyan Media Project, August 2016), http://media project.wesleyan.edu/blog/disclosure-report/.

49. "Outside Group Activity, 2000–2016."

50. Sean J. Miller, "Digital Ad Spending Tops Estimates," Campaigns and Elections, January 4, 2017, https://www.campaignandelections.com/campaign-insider/digital-ad-spending-tops-estimates.

51. Sara Fischer, "Political Ad Spending Hits New Record for 2018 Midterm Election," *Axios*, November 6, 2018, https://www.axios.com/record-midterm-ad-spend-explodes-money-was-no-object-1541450836-f92d1767-ad5f-4d85-99ee-96d9847e7691.html.

52. Ads archive for political ad spending, Facebook, accessed June 1, 2019, https://www.facebook.com/ads/archive/report/.

53. On June 2, 2019, when we accessed the page, Google was reporting that $84,549,400 had been spent on political advertising since May 31, 2018. Google Transparency Report, https://transparencyreport.google.com/political-ads/region/US?hl=en.

54. Jennifer Valentino-DeVries, "Facebook's Experiment in Ad Transparency Is Like Playing Hide and Seek," *ProPublica*, January 31, 2018, https://www.propublica.org/article/facebook-experiment-ad-transparency-toronto-canada.

55. "AO 2017–12: Nonprofit Must Include Disclaimers on Its Facebook Ads," Federal Election Commission, December 18, 2017, https://www.fec.gov/updates/ao-2017-12-nonprofit-must-include-disclaimers-its-facebook-ads/.

56. Valentino-DeVries, "Facebook's Experiment."

57. "15 Reasons Bernie Sanders Is the Candidate We've Been Waiting For," *Buzz-Feed*, January 8, 2016, https://www.buzzfeed.com/berniesanders/times-bernie-sanders-gave-us-all-hope.

58. "What Mitt Romney's 'Binders Full of Women' Says about His Views," *Buzz-feed* (paid post by Obama for America), October 18, 2012, https://www.buzzfeed.com/obamaforamerica/what-mitt-romneys-binders-full-of-women-s-7i6v?b=1.

59. Erik Sass, "Consumers Can't Tell Native Ads from Editorial Content," *Media-Post*, December 31, 2015, https://www.mediapost.com/publications/article/265789/consumers-cant-tell-native-ads-from-editorial-cont.html.

60. "Getting In-Feed Sponsored Content Right: The Consumer View," Interactive Advertising Bureau, 2014, https://www.iab.com/wp-content/uploads/2015/07/IAB_Edelman_Berland_Study.pdf.

61. "Truth in Advertising," Federal Trade Commission, accessed July 2, 2019, https://www.ftc.gov/news-events/media-resources/truth-advertising.

62. "Section 4: Demographics and Political Views of News Audiences," Pew Research Center, September 27, 2012, https://www.people-press.org/2012/09/27/section-4-demographics-and-political-views-of-news-audiences/.

63. Priyanka Boghani, "Brad Parscale, Trump's 2020 Campaign Manager, Calls Facebook Ad Policy 'A Gift,'" *PBS: Frontline*, November 28, 2018, https://www.pbs.org/wgbh/frontline/article/brad-parscale-trumps-2020-campaign-manager-calls-facebook-ad-policy-a-gift/.

64. Boghani, "Brad Parscale."

65. Boghani, "Brad Parscale."

66. Joshua Green and Sasha Issenberg, "Inside the Trump Bunker, with Days to Go," *Bloomberg*, October 27, 2016, https://www.bloomberg.com/news/articles/2016-10-27/inside-the-trump-bunker-with-12-days-to-go.

67. Joshua Green, "Russia's Voter Suppression Operation Echoed Trump Campaign Tactics, *Bloomberg Businessweek*, December 17, 2018, https://www.bloomberg.com/news/articles/2018-12-18/russia-s-voter-suppression-operation-echoed-trump-campaign-tactics.

68. *Bluman v. Federal Election Commission*, 132 S. Ct. 1087 (2012).

69. U.S. Congress, Senate, Select Committee on Intelligence, Open Hearing: Social Media Influence in the 2016 U.S. Election, "Testimony of Colin Stretch, General Counsel of Facebook," 115th Congress, First Session, 2017, https://www.intelligence.Senate.gov/hearings/open-hearing-social-media-influence-2016-us-elections#.

70. Kovic et al., "Digital Astroturfing," 70.

71. Kovic et al., "Digital Astroturfing," 74.

72. Kovic et al., "Digital Astroturfing," 74.

73. "House Democrats Release More than 3,500 Facebook Ads Created by Russians," *PBS NewsHour*, May 10, 2018, https://www.pbs.org/newshour/politics/house-democrats-release-more-than-3500-facebook-ads-created-by-russians.

74. Cristiano Lima, "A Caged Clinton and Fake 'Woke Blacks': 9 Striking Findings from the Mueller Indictment," *Politico*, February 16, 2018, https://www.politico.com/story/2018/02/16/mueller-indictment-hillary-clinton-key-findings-415692.

75. Lima, "A Caged Clinton."

76. Scott Shane, "These Are the Ads Russia Bought on Facebook in 2016," *The New York Times*, November 1, 2017, https://www.nytimes.com/2017/11/01/us/politics/russia-2016-election-facebook.html.

77. "House Democrats Release More than 3,500 Facebook Ads Created by Russians," *PBS NewsHour*, May 10, 2018, https://www.pbs.org/newshour/politics/house-democrats-release-more-than-3500-facebook-ads-created-by-russians.

78. Lima, "A Caged Clinton."

79. Cecilia Kang, Nicholas Fandos, and Mike Isaac, "Russia-Financed Ad Linked Clinton and Satan," *The New York Times*, November 1, 2017, https://www.nytimes.com/2017/11/01/us/politics/facebook-google-twitter-russian-interference-hearings.html.

80. A repository containing text descriptions of all the known ads the Russian agency put on Facebook has been released by the U.S. House of Representatives Permanent Select Committee on Intelligence, https://intelligence.house.gov/social-media-content/social-media-advertisements.htm.

81. Although much of the literature on political advertising uses "negative ad" and "attack ad" synonymously, we believe there is an important distinction between, for example, saying, "Don't support candidate X because she voted in favor of law Y," versus "Candidate Z is an empty suit and a liar." The former has at least potential merit, whereas the latter is ad hominem.

82. See, for example, Deborah Jordan Brooks and Michael Murov, "Assessing Accountability in a Post-*Citizens United* Era: The Effects of Attack Ad Sponsorship by Unknown Independent Groups," *American Politics Research* 40, no. 3 (April 2012): 385.

83. John G. Geer, *In Defense of Negativity: Attack Ads in Presidential Campaigns* (Chicago: University of Chicago Press, 2006).

84. Deborah Jordan Brooks, "Negative Campaigning Disliked by Most Americans," Gallup, July 17, 2000, https://news.gallup.com/poll/2731/negative-campaigning-disliked-most-americans.aspx.

85. Ruthann Lariscy, "Why Negative Political Ads Work," CNN, January 2, 2012, https://www.cnn.com/2012/01/02/opinion/lariscy-negative-ads/index.html.

86. Richard R. Lau, Lee Sigelman, and Ivy Brown Rovner, "The Effects of Negative Political Campaigns: A Meta-Analytic Reassessment," *The Journal of Politics* 69, no. 4 (November 2007): 1176–209; Michael A. Shapiro and Robert H. Rieger, "Comparing Positive and Negative Political Advertising on Radio," *Journalism and Mass Communication* 69, no. 1 (1992): 135–45.

87. Stephen Ansolabehere, Shanto Iyengar, Adam Simon, and Nicholas Valentino, "Does Attack Advertising Demobilize the Electorate?" *American Political Science Review* 88, no. 4 (December 1994): 829.

88. Richard R. Lau and Ivy Brown Rovner, "Negative Campaigning," *Annual Review of Political Science* 12 (2009): 298. See also Steven E. Finkel and John G. Geer, "A Spot Check: Casting Doubt on the Demobilizing Effect of Attack Advertising," *American Journal of Political Science* 42, no. 2 (April 1998): 573–95.

89. Stephen Ansolabehere and Shanto Iyengar, *Going Negative: How Political Advertisements Shrink and Polarize the Electorate* (New York: Free Press, 1995). 129–30.

90. Conor M. Dowling and Michael G. Miller, *Super PAC! Money, Elections and Voters after Citizens United* (New York: Routledge, 2014), 68.

91. Fowler and Ridout, "Advertising Trends in 2010," 11.

92. Fowler and Ridout, "Negative, Angry, and Ubiquitous," 51–61.

93. Brooks and Murov, "Assessing Accountability," 403–04.

94. Richard Kang, "The Year of the Super PAC." *George Washington Law Review* 81 (2013): 1919.

95. Michael Franz, Erika Franklin Fowler, and Travis N. Ridout, "Loose Cannons or Loyal Foot Soldiers? Towards a More Complex Theory of Interest Group Advertising Strategies, *American Journal of Political Science* 60, no. 3 (July 2016): 738.

96. Brooks and Murov, "Assessing Accountability," 403.

97. Connor M. Dowling and Amber Wichowsky, "Attacks without Consequence? Candidates, Parties, Groups, and the Changing Face of Negative Advertising," *American Journal of Political Science* 59, no. 1 (2015): 19.

98. "Forecasting the Race for the House," *FiveThirtyEight.com*, last updated November 6, 2018, https://projects.fivethirtyeight.com/2018-midterm-election-forecast/house/.

99. Will Lennon, "Florida Senate Race the Most Expensive Ever, Surpassing $200 Million," Center for Responsive Politics, December 7, 2018, https://www.open secrets.org/news/2018/12/florida-Senate-race-most-expensive/.

100. Scott Powers, "Outside Groups Spent $87 Million on Florida's U.S. Senate Race," *Florida Politics*, November 26, 2018, https://floridapolitics.com/archives/281923-outside-groups-spent-87-million-on-floridas-u-s-Senate-race.

101. Anna Massoglia, "Rick Scott Super PAC Learns to Love Rick Scott," Center for Responsive Politics, August 28, 2018, https://www.opensecrets.org/news/2018/08/rick-scott-new-gop-super-pac/.

102. New Republican PAC, "Generations," uploaded October 30, 2018, YouTube video, 0:30, https://www.youtube.com/watch?v=7jMi_Ak6Gu8. There was also a fifteen-second version of "Generations," uploaded October 30, 2018, YouTube video, 0:15, https://www.youtube.com/watch?v=oox3wRxBQj8

103. New Republican PAC, "Lining," uploaded October 26, 2018, YouTube video, 0:15, https://www.youtube.com/watch?v=ZM2SrJ8DY4M.

104. New Republican PAC, "Puppet," uploaded October 26, 2018, YouTube video, 0:15, https://www.youtube.com/watch?v=MOd3XpVW6eY.

105. These ads can be viewed on YouTube by accessing the channel of the New Republican PAC at https://www.youtube.com/channel/UCJv3k7hzx1nwt-rfMZdnIfw.

106. Patricia Mazzei, Frances Robles, and Maggie Astor, "Rick Scott Wins Florida Senate Recount as Bill Nelson Concedes," *The New York Times*, November 18, 2018, https://www.nytimes.com/2018/11/18/us/florida-recount-Senate-rick-scott-bill-nelson.html.

107. Jonathan Easley, "Top Dem Super PAC Launches Ad Campaign in Florida Ahead of Trump Reelection Launch," *Hill*, June 16, 2019, https://thehill.com/home-news/campaign/448865-top-dem-super-pac-launches-ad-campaign-in-florida-ahead-of-trump-reelection.

108. More than half of the ads aired by or on behalf of Democrats mentioned health care. See "2018: The Health Care Election," Wesleyan Media Project, October 18, 2018, http://mediaproject.wesleyan.edu/releases/101818-tv/.

109. Priorities USA, "John and Deborah," uploaded June 17, 2019, YouTube video 0:30, https://www.youtube.com/watch?v=IxUEHvXEUp4.

110. Priorities USA, "Chuck," uploaded April 16, 2019, YouTube video, 0:30, https://www.youtube.com/watch?v=UeGT9hKIBhw.

111. Priorities USA, "Trump," uploaded April 16, 2019, YouTube video, 0:30, https://www.youtube.com/watch?v=NMqxedB384E.

112. Gregory A. Huber and Kevin Arceneaux, "Identifying Persuasive Effects of Political Advertising," *American Journal of Political Science* 51, no. 4 (October 2007): 974.

113. Henry E. Brady, Richard Johnston, and John Sides, "The Study of Political Campaigns," in *Capturing Campaign Effects*, ed. Henry E. Brady and Richard Johnston (Ann Arbor: University of Michigan Press, 2006), 4.

114. "Presidential Election Results: Donald J. Trump Wins," *The New York Times*, last updated August 9, 2017, https://www.nytimes.com/elections/2016/results/president.

115. Jorg L. Spenkuch and David Toniatti, "Political Advertising and Election Results, *Quarterly Journal of Economics* 133, no. 4 (November 2018): 2031.

116. Joshua K. Kalla and David E. Broockman, "The Minimal Persuasive Effects of Campaign Contact in General Elections: Evidence from 49 Field Experiments," *American Political Science Review* 112, no. 1 (February 2018): 149.

117. Kalla and Broockman, "Minimal Persuasive Effects," 149.

118. "Outside Group Activity, 2000–2016."

119. David Lynn Painter, "Collateral Damage: Involvement and the Effects of Negative Super PAC Advertising," *American Behavioral Scientist* 58, no. 4 (April 2014): 510–23.

120. Fowler, Ridout, and Franz, "Political Advertising in 2016," 467.

121. Larry M. Bartels, "Remember to Forget: A Note on the Duration of Campaign Advertising Effects," *Political Communication* 31, no. 4 (2014): 532–44. See also Seth J. Hill, James Lo, Lynn Vavreck, and John Zaller, "How Quickly We Forget: The Duration of Persuasion Effects from Mass Communication," *Political Communication* 30, no. 4 (2013): 521–47.

122. Alan S. Gerber, James G. Gimpel, Donald P. Green, and Daron Shaw, "How Large and Long-Lasting Are the Persuasive Effects of Televised Campaign Ads? Results from a Randomized Field Experiment," *The American Political Science Review* 105, no. 1 (February 2011): 135–50.

123. Gary C. Jacobson and Jamie L. Carson, *The Politics of Congressional Elections* (Lanham, MD: Rowman & Littlefield, 2015), 65.

124. Larry M. Bartels, "Instrumental and 'Quasi-Instrumental' Variables," *American Journal of Political Science* 35, no. 3 (August 1991): 777–800; Robert K. Goidel and Donald A. Gross, "A Systems Approach to Campaign Finance in U.S. House Elections," *American Politics Quarterly* 22, no. 2 (April 1994), 125–53; Christopher Kenny and Michael McBurnett, "An Individual-Level Multiequation Model of Expenditure Effects in Contested House Elections," *American Political Science Review* 88, no. 3 (September 1994): 699–707.

125. Peter L. Francia, "Free Media and Twitter in the 2016 Presidential Election: The Unconventional Campaign of Donald Trump," *Social Science Computer Review* 36, no. 4 (August 2018): 440–55, doi:10.1177/0894439317730302.

126. Francia, "Free Media and Twitter."

127. However, we do not necessarily know how many of these Twitter accounts are real people. See Ryan Bort, "Nearly Half of Donald Trump's Twitter Followers Are Fake Accounts and Bots," *Newsweek*, May 30, 2017, https://www.newsweek.com/donald-trump-twitter-followers-fake-617873.

128. Francia, "Free Media and Twitter," 449.

129. Laeeq Khan, "Trump Won Thanks to Social Media," *The Hill*, November 15, 2016, https://thehill.com/blogs/pundits-blog/technology/306175-trump-won-thanks-to-social-media.

130. Francia, "Free Media and Twitter," 449.

131. Gunn Enli, "Twitter as Arena for the Authentic Outsider: Exploring the Social Media Campaigns of Trump and Clinton in the 2016 US Presidential Election," *European Journal of Communication* 32, no. 1 (February 2017): 50, doi:10.1177/0267323116682802.

132. Simon Romero, "Kyrsten Sinema Declared Winner in Arizona Senate Race," *The New York Times*, November 12, 2018, https://www.nytimes.com/2018/11/12/us/kyrsten-sinema-arizona-senator.html.

CHAPTER 7: REFORM IDEAS

1. Jill Ornitz and Ryan Struyk, "Donald Trump's Surprisingly Honest Lessons about Big Money in Politics," ABCNews.com, August 11, 2015, https://abcnews.go.com/Politics/donald-trumps-surprisingly-honest-lessons-big-money-politics/story?id=32993736.

2. Ornitz and Struyk, "Donald Trump's Surprisingly Honest Lessons."

3. Trevor Burrus and Patrick Moran, "Why Alexandria Ocasio-Cortez Should Support Eliminating Limits on Campaign Contributions," *USA Today*, March 7, 2019, https://www.usatoday.com/story/opinion/2019/03/07/limits-campaign-contributions-hurt-newcomers-like-aoc-column/3083429002/.

4. Philip M. Nichols, "The Perverse Effect of Campaign Contribution Limits: Reducing the Allowable Amount Increases the Likelihood of Corruption in the Federal Legislature," *American Business Law Journal* 48, no. 1 (2011): 3.

5. Nichols, "Perverse Effect," 3. See also Bradley A. Smith, "No Compelling Government Interest in Limiting the Size of Contributions," *The New York Times*, February 24, 2016, https://www.nytimes.com/roomfordebate/2013/10/06/why-limit-political-donations/no-compelling-government-interest-in-limiting-the-size-of-contributions.

6. Nichols, "Perverse Effect," 17.

7. "Good Things Come in Big Bundles," Center for Responsive Politics, accessed July 12, 2019, https://www.opensecrets.org/resources/10things/02.php.

8. "Obama Administration: Ambassadors," Center for Responsive Politics, accessed July 20, 2019, https://www.opensecrets.org/obama/ambassadors.php. The Center for Responsive Politics points out that the George W. Bush and Bill Clinton administrations had similar practices.

9. Joseph Bafumi and Michael C. Herron, "Leapfrog Representation and Extremism: A Study of American Voters and Their Members in Congress," *American Political Science Review* 104, no. 3 (August 2010): 519–42.

10. Nicholas Stephanopoulos, "Aligning Campaign Finance Law," in *Democracy by the People: Reforming Campaign Finance in America*, ed. Eugene D. Mazo and Timothy H. Kuhner (Cambridge: Cambridge University Press, 2018), 77.

11. Ilya Shapiro, "The Supreme Court Should Strike Down All Contribution Limits, *The New York Times*, October 30, 2014, https://www.nytimes.com/

roomfordebate/2013/10/06/why-limit-political-donations/the-supreme-court-should-strike-down-all-contribution-limits.

12. Bruce Mentzer, "Super PACs and Issue Advertisers Pay More than Candidates. How Much More?" Mentzer Media, September 21, 2015, http://www.mentzer media.com/issue-advertisers-pay-candidates-much-lot/.

13. Richard Briffault, "The Future of Public Financing," in *Democracy by the People: Reforming Campaign Finance in America*, ed. Eugene D. Mazo and Timothy H. Kuhner (Cambridge: Cambridge University Press, 2018), 107.

14. Libby Watson, "Why Did Only 1 Presidential Candidate Take Public Funding?" Sunlight Foundation, January 27, 2016, https://sunlightfoundation.com/2016/01/27/why-did-only-1-presidential-candidate-take-public-financing/.

15. "§3–705: Optional Public Financing," New York City Campaign Finance Board, accessed July 20, 2019, https://www.nyccfb.info/law/act/optional-public-financing/.

16. "§3–703: Eligibility and Other Requirements," New York City Campaign Finance Board, accessed July 23, 2019, https://www.nyccfb.info/law/act/eligibility-and-other-requirements/.

17. New York City Campaign Finance Board; see "§3–706: Expenditures Limitations" and "§3–716: Application of the Contribution and Expenditure Limitations to Certain Activities," accessed July 21, 2019, https://www.nyccfb.info/law/act/?.

18. "§3–709.5: Mandatory Debates," New York City Campaign Finance Board, accessed July 23, 2019, https://www.nyccfb.info/law/act/mandatory-debates/.

19. Empowering Citizens Act, H.R. 3955, 115th Congress (2017), https://www.congress.gov/bill/115th-congress/house-bill/3955/text#toc-H7F6C596A537B47C2B4A15AA238933890. The ratio and the dollar amounts have changed in different versions of this bill, but the idea remains the same.

20. "Empowering Citizens Act," Brennan Center for Justice, January 15, 2013, https://www.brennancenter.org/legislation/empowering-citizens-act. This particular website is reporting on an earlier version of the act, which is why the dollar figures and ratios are different from the more recently introduced act.

21. For more detailed information on the various public funding programs of states, counties, and municipalities, see "Public Funding for Electoral Campaigns," Demos, accessed June 14, 2019, https://www.demos.org/sites/default/files/publications/Public_Financing_Factsheet_FA percent5B5 percent5D.pdf; see also Michael J. Malbin, "Citizen Funding for Elections," The Campaign Finance Institute (2015), 5–6, http://www.cfinst.org/pdf/books-reports/CFI_CitizenFundingforElections.pdf.

22. Lawrence Norden and Douglas Keith, *Small Donor Tax Credits: A New Model* (Brennan Center for Justice, 2017), 5, https://www.brennancenter.org/sites/default/files/publications/Small percent20Donor percent20Tax percent20Credit.pdf.

23. Renu Zaretsky, "Political Campaigns and Tax Incentives: Do We Give What We Get?," *Tax Policy Center*, Jan. 2, 2019, https://www.taxpolicycenter.org/taxvox/political-campaigns-and-tax-incentives-do-we-give-get.

24. Norden and Keith, 2.

25. Richard Hasen, *Plutocrats United: Campaign Money, the Supreme Court, and the Distortion of American Elections* (New Haven, CT: Yale University Press, 2016), 9–10, 89–90.

26. "Democracy Voucher Program," Seattle.gov, accessed July 21, 2019, https://www.seattle.gov/democracyvoucher/about-the-program.

27. Hasen, *Plutocrats United*, 152–59.

28. "Overview of State Laws on Public Financing," National Conference of State Legislatures, accessed July 13, 2019, http://www.ncsl.org/research/elections-and-cam paigns/public-financing-of-campaigns-overview.aspx.

29. Michael J. Malbin, Peter W. Brusoe, and Brendan Glavin, "Small Donors, Big Democracy: New York City's Matching Funds as a Model for the Nation and States," *Election Law Journal* 11, no. 1 (2012): 3–20.

30. Malbin, "Citizen Funding," 15.

31. "Letter from Common Cause to the Government Accountability Office," June 4, 2010, https://www.mainecleanelections.org/sites/default/files/research/ Response_to_2010_GAO_report_on_Clean_Elections.pdf.

32. Malbin, "Citizen Funding," 17.

33. Malbin, "Citizen Funding," 2.

34. We use the shorthand label "Super PAC insurance" for the sake of convenience, but the concept could also cover expenditures from 527s and 501(c)s as well.

35. Nick Warshaw, "Super PAC Insurance: A Private Sector Solution to Reform Campaign Finance," in *Democracy by the People: Reforming Campaign Finance in America*, ed. Eugene D. Mazo and Timothy H. Kuhner (Cambridge: Cambridge University Press, 2018), 220–239.

36. Warshaw, "Super PAC Insurance," 221.

37. Warshaw, "Super PAC Insurance," 223–24.

38. Warshaw, "Super PAC Insurance," 235–37.

39. Dale Eisman, "Why We Need the People's Pledge," Common Cause, August 20, 2015, https://www.commoncause.org/democracy-wire/why-we-need-the-peoples-pledge/.

40. Judiciary and Judicial Procedure, U.S. Code 28 §455(b)(4).

41. "50 State Table: Voting Recusal Provisions," National Council of State Legislatures, last updated May 8, 2019, http://www.ncsl.org/research/ethics/50-state-table-voting-recusal-provisions.aspx.

42. Louis J. Virelli III, "Congress, the Constitution, and Supreme Court Recusal," *Washington and Lee Law Journal* 69, no. 3 (Summer 2012): 1535–606.

43. Eugene D. Mazo, "Regulating Campaign Finance through Legislative Recusal Rules," in *Democracy by the People: Reforming Campaign Finance in America*, ed. Eugene D. Mazo and Timothy H. Kuhner (Cambridge: Cambridge University Press, 2018), 321.

44. Rodrigo Praino, Daniel Stockmeyer, and Vincent G. Moscardelli, "The Lingering Effect of Scandals in Congressional Elections: Incumbents, Challengers, and Voters," *Social Science Quarterly* 94, no. 4 (December 2013): 1045–61.

45. Nicholas Chad Long, "The Impact of Incumbent Scandals on Senate Elections, 1972–2016," *Social Sciences* 8, no. 4 (April 2019), https://doi.org/10.3390/ socsci8040114.

46. Michael J. Malbin and Thomas Gais, *The Day after Reform: Sobering Campaign Finance Lessons from the American States*, (Albany, NY: Rockefeller Institute Press, 1998), 36.

47. Katherine Shaw, "Reorienting Disclosure Debates in a Post-*Citizens United* World," in *Democracy by the People: Reforming Campaign Finance in America*, ed. Eugene D. Mazo and Timothy H. Kuhner (Cambridge: Cambridge University Press, 2018), 154.

48. Shaw, "Reorienting Disclosure Debates," 167.

49. Chisun Lee, Katherine Valde, Benjamin T. Brickner, and Douglas Keith, "Secret Spending in the States," Brennan Center for Justice, June 26, 2016, https://www.brennancenter.org/publication/secret-spending-states.

50. Shaw, "Reorienting Disclosure Debates," 159.

51. Lili Levi, "Plan B for Campaign-Finance Reform: Can the FCC Help Save American Politics after *Citizens United?*" *Catholic University Law Review* 61, no. 1 (Winter 2011): 101.

52. Jennifer A. Heerwig, "Diagnosing Disclosure: A Social Scientific Perspective on Campaign Finance Disclosure," *Yale Law & Policy Review Inter Alia* 34, no. 8 (Spring 2016): 9.

53. Heerwig, "Diagnosing Disclosure," 15.

54. Heerwig, "Diagnosing Disclosure," 16–17.

55. Shaw, "Reorienting Disclosure Debates," 169.

56. Justin Levitt, "Confronting the Impact of Citizens United," *Yale Law & Policy Review* 29 (2010): 227.

57. "AO 2017–12: Nonprofit Must Include Disclaimers on Its Facebook Ads," Federal Election Commission, December 18, 2017, https://www.fec.gov/updates/ao-2017-12-nonprofit-must-include-disclaimers-its-facebook-ads/.

58. Jennifer Valentino-DeVries, "I Approved This Facebook Message—but You Don't Know That," *ProPublica*, February 13, 2018, https://www.propublica.org/article/i-approved-this-facebook-message-but-you-dont-know-that.

59. For a discussion of how the FEC ruled in 2002 and 2010 on digital disclaimers, see Valentino-DeVries, "I Approved This Facebook Message."

60. "Advertising and Disclaimers," Federal Election Commission, accessed July 20, 2019, https://www.fec.gov/help-candidates-and-committees/making-disbursements/advertising/.

61. The Campaign Legal Center has been advocating updated digital ad disclaimer rules to the FEC for several years. To read several of its letters to the FEC, see "Comments on Notice 2018–06: Internet Communication Disclaimers and Definition of 'Public Communication," Campaign Legal Center, May 24, 2018, https://campaignlegal.org/sites/default/files/05-24-18 percent20CLC percent20comments percent20internet percent20NPRM percent20 percent28REG percent202011–02 percent29.pdf, and July 18, 2018, https://campaignlegal.org/sites/default/files/2018-11/CLC percent20Comments.pdf.

62. Luke Wachob, Bradley Smith, and Scott Blackburn, "Compulsory Donor Disclosure: When Government Monitors Its Citizens," The Heritage Foundation, November 3, 2015, https://www.heritage.org/report/compulsory-donor-disclosure-when-government-monitors-its-citizens; Eric Wang, "Staring at the Sun: An Inquiry into Compulsory Campaign Finance Donor Disclosure Laws," Cato Institute, December 14, 2017, https://www.cato.org/publications/policy-analysis/staring-sun-inquiry-compulsory-campaign-finance-donor-disclosure-laws.

63. Wachob, Smith, and Blackburn, "Compulsory Donor Disclosure."

64. Michael W. Sances, "Is Money in Politics Harming Trust in Government? Evidence from Two Survey Experiments," *Election Law Journal* 12, no. 1 (March 2013): 53–73.

65. Fred Wertheimer and Don Simon, "The FEC: The Failure to Enforce Commission," American Constitution Society, January 2013, https://www.acslaw.org/

wp-content/uploads/2013/02/Wertheimer_and_Simon_-_The_Failure_to_Enforce_
Commission.pdf.

66. "Kilmer, Buck Lead Bipartisan Call to President Trump: Fill Vacant Seats on
Federal Election Commission Immediately," press release, including original letter,
from Derek Kilmer, February 14, 2018, https://kilmer.house.gov/news/press-releases/
kilmer-buck-lead-bipartisan-call-to-president-trump-fill-vacant-seats-on-federal-
election-commission-immediately.

67. Caitlin Cruz, "FEC Chair to 'Daily Show:' Agency Is 'Enormously Dysfunctional,'" talking points memo, November 13, 2015, https://talkingpointsmemo.com/
livewire/daily-show-federal-election-commission-chair-enormously-dysfunctional-
male-nipples.

68. As of July 24, 2019, there are only four commissioners. This means, at the
time of this writing, a unanimous vote is needed for any action to take place. This
is even less likely than getting four out of six to vote affirmatively. Every current
commissioner is serving as a "holdover," well past their original terms. See "Commissioners," Federal Election Commission, accessed July 24, 2019, https://www.
fec.gov/press/resources-journalists/commissioners/. See also Dave Levinthal, "FEC's
Commissioners' Terms Expired Long Ago, but Trump, Congress Won't Replace
Them," NBC News, April 30, 2018, https://www.nbcnews.com/politics/elections/
fec-commissioners-terms-expired-long-ago-trump-congress-won-t-n870071.

69. Wertheimer and Simon, "The FEC," 5.

70. Daniel Weiner, "Fixing the FEC: An Agenda for Reform," Brennan Center
for Justice, April 2019, https://www.brennancenter.org/sites/default/files/publica
tions/2019_04_FECV_Final.pdf.

71. Wertheimer and Simon, "The FEC," 11.

72. "Why our Democracy Needs Disclosure," Campaign Legal Center, August 17,
2011, https://campaignlegal.org/update/why-our-democracy-needs-disclosure.

73. Wertheimer and Simon, "The FEC," 13.

74. Weiner, "Fixing the FEC," 5.

75. "Fix the FEC: Background Memorandum on New Bipartisan Legislation to
Address Dysfunctional Agency," Campaign Legal Center, September 17, 2015,
https://campaignlegal.org/media-mentions/fix-fec-background-memorandum-
new-bipartisan-legislation-address-dysfunctional.

76. Daniel P. Tokaji, "Beyond Repair: FEC Reform and Deadlock Deference," in
Democracy by the People: Reforming Campaign Finance in America, ed. Eugene D.
Mazo and Timothy H. Kuhner (Cambridge: Cambridge University Press, 2018), 186.

77. Weiner, "Fixing the FEC," 9.

78. Ellen Weintraub, "Statement of Vice Chair Ellen L. Weintraub on the D.C.
Circuit's Decision in *CREW v. FEC*," June 22, 2018, https://www.fec.gov/resources/
cms-content/documents/2018-06-22_ELW_statement_re_CREWvFEC-CHGO.pdf.

79. Tokaji, "Beyond Repair," 189–90.

80. Tokaji, "Beyond Repair," 184, 195–99.

Index

★ ★ ★

Note: Page references for figures are *italicized* and tables are **bold**.

Credits

★ ★ ★

Figure 1.1	Data compiled from Center for Responsive Politics
Figure 1.2	Campaign Finance Institute, Sources of Funds for Presidential Super PACs, http://www.cfinst.org/data.aspx.
Figure 1.3	Data compiled from Center for Responsive Politics
Figure 3.1	Center for Responsive Politics, https://www.opensecrets.org/news/2019/01/citizens-united
Figure 3.2	Data from Center for Responsive Politics with analysis by Issue One, https://www.issueone.org/in-2018-mid terms-liberal-dark-money-groups-outspent-conservative -counterparts-for-first-time-since-citizens-united
Figure 4.1	Data compiled from Center for Responsive Politics
Figure 5.1	Center for Responsive Politics, https://www.opensecrets.org/news/2019/01/citizens-united
Figure 5.2	Center for Responsive Politics, https://www.opensecrets.org/news/2019/01/citizens-united
Figure 5.3	Campaign Finance Institute, http://www.cfinst.org/pdf/Federal/PostElec_2018_Table6.pdf
Figure 5.4	Campaign Finance Institute, http://www.cfinst.org/pdf/Federal/PostElec_2018_Table5.pdf
Figure 5.5	Campaign Finance Institute, http://www.cfinst.org/pdf/Federal/IEs/2018_Primary_Table4.pdf
Figure 5.6	Data compiled from Center for Responsive Politics
Figure 6.1	Kantar Media/CMAG, with analysis by Wesleyan Media Project (data for 2016 was through August 1, 2016)
Figure 6.2	Campaign Finance Institute, Non-Party Independent Expenditures, http://cfinst.org/data.aspx